W9-CRN-805

# FILTERWORLD

**ALSO BY KYLE CHAYKA**

*The Longing for Less*

# FILTERWORLD

## HOW ALGORITHMS FLATTENED CULTURE

# Kyle Chayka

Doubleday · New York

Copyright © 2024 by Kyle Chayka

All rights reserved. Published in the United States by Doubleday,
a division of Penguin Random House LLC, New York, and distributed
in Canada by Penguin Random House Canada Limited, Toronto.

www.doubleday.com

DOUBLEDAY and the portrayal of an anchor with a dolphin are registered
trademarks of Penguin Random House LLC.

Jacket design by Oliver Munday
Book design by Betty Lew

Library of Congress Cataloging-in-Publication Data
Names: Chayka, Kyle, author.
Title: Filterworld : how algorithms flattened culture / Kyle Chayka.
Description: First edition. | New York : Doubleday, [2024] |
Identifiers: LCCN 2023020397 (print) | LCCN 2023020398 (ebook) |
ISBN 9780385548281 (hardcover) | ISBN 9780385548298 (ebook)
Subjects: LCSH: Culture. | Culture—Mathematical models.
Classification: LCC HM621 .C488 2024 (print) |
LCC HM621 (ebook) | DDC 306—dc23/eng/20231011
LC record available at https://lccn.loc.gov/2023020397
LC ebook record available at https://lccn.loc.gov/2023020398

MANUFACTURED IN THE UNITED STATES OF AMERICA

10 9 8 7 6 5 4 3 2 1

First Edition

**For Jess**

You may not use social media, but it's using you.

—EILEEN MYLES

■  ■  ■

The message of many things in America is
"Like this or die."

—GEORGE W. S. TROW

# Contents

INTRODUCTION: Welcome to Filterworld     1

CHAPTER 1: The Rise of Algorithmic Recommendations     11

CHAPTER 2: The Disruption of Personal Taste     43

CHAPTER 3: Algorithmic Globalization     88

CHAPTER 4: The Influencer Economy     130

CHAPTER 5: Regulating Filterworld     183

CHAPTER 6: In Search of Human Curation     223

Conclusion     275

Acknowledgments     283

# FILTERWORLD

JOSEPH RACKNITZ'S 1789
SPECULATIVE DIAGRAM OF
THE MECHANICAL TURK

# Welcome to Filterworld

## THE MECHANICAL TURK

In 1769, a civil servant in the Habsburg Empire named Johann Wolfgang Ritter von Kempelen built a device nicknamed "the Mechanical Turk." It was a gift created to impress the Habsburg empress, Maria Theresa of Austria. Von Kempelen's nigh magical machine could play and win a game of chess against a human opponent simply by means of internal clockwork gears and belts. As seen in historical etchings, the Mechanical Turk was a large wooden cabinet, about four feet wide, two and a half feet deep, and three feet tall, with doors exposing the elaborate machinery inside. On top sat a humanoid automaton the size of a child, dressed in a robe and turban and sporting a dramatic mustache, leaning over a chessboard. (The Orientalist archetype seen from the European perspective conflated the foreign-human and the foreign-machine.) The Turk's left arm hovered over the chessboard, grasped pieces, and moved them. The machine chimed when a move was made, detected when the other player cheated, and made various facial expressions. So befuddling was von Kempelen's Mechanical Turk that it traveled internationally, matching up with the likes of Benjamin Franklin in 1783 and Napoleon Bonaparte in 1809. Both men lost.

What the Mechanical Turk could not actually do, however, was play chess. There was no artificial intelligence driving the machine, no set of gears that mechanically determined its next move. Instead, a short-statured human pilot curled himself inside the cabinet. He was a chess expert who could observe the game by means of magnet-connected markers underneath the board that corresponded to the pieces on top—marking the locations of the pawns, the knights, the king as the game was played. The pilot maneuvered the automaton's hand by means of levers and strings to grab the pieces and move them, moving the magnets in turn. Smoke from a candle lamp, which the pilot used for illumination to work the machine, leaked out of hidden holes in the back. All the internal clockwork was just for show; it didn't do anything. If the audience wanted to peek inside, the pilot could slide back and forth on a mobile seat to hide as the cabinet's doors were opened in a faked demonstration of transparency, something like a false bottom in a magic-show prop.

The Mechanical Turk offered the impressive illusion of a machine that could make decisions for itself, that seemed to be smarter than a human, though a human ultimately controlled it. Some viewers suspected that it was fake. "To call it an automaton is an imposition, and merits a public detection," wrote the skeptical British eccentric Philip Thicknesse in a 1784 book, arguing that the machine was controlled "by invisible confederates." Thicknesse continued, "The Automaton Chess-Player is a man within a man; for whatever his outward form be composed of, he bears a living soul within." Thicknesse was correct, of course, but the secret was not fully revealed until 1860, at which point the machine had toured the United States and landed in the collection of Edgar Allan Poe's personal physician, John Kearsley Mitchell. The original artifact was destroyed in a fire, and Mitchell's son wrote a tell-all for the *Chess Monthly*. That the machine was a blatant illusion only increased the Mechanical Turk's significance, however.

Over the two centuries since its invention, the device has become a prevalent metaphor for technological manipulation. It represents the human lurking behind the facade of seemingly advanced technology as well as the ability of such devices to deceive us about the way they work. (In 2005, Amazon named its service for accomplishing digital tasks, like tagging photos or cleaning data, using an invisible marketplace of outsourced human labor "Mechanical Turk.") The Mechanical Turk is like *The Wizard of Oz*'s man behind the curtain—an all-knowing, uncanny entity that is ultimately revealed as something much more mundane and comprehensible. The machine and the trick reinforce each other. With its doubled deceptions, the Turk is able, as Walter Benjamin wrote reflecting on the device in a 1940 essay, to "win all the time."

I think about the Mechanical Turk quite often lately because it reminds me of the technological specter haunting our own era of the early twenty-first century. That specter goes by the name of "the algorithm." *Algorithm* is usually shorthand for "algorithmic recommendations," the digital mechanisms that absorb piles of user data, push it through a set of equations, and spit out a result deemed most relevant to preset goals. Algorithms dictate the websites we find in Google Search results; the stories we see on our Facebook feeds; the songs that Spotify plays in never-ending streams; the people we see as potential matches on dating apps; the movies recommended by the Netflix home page; the personalized feed of videos presented by TikTok; the order of posts on Twitter and Instagram; the folders our emails are automatically sorted into; and the ads that follow us around the Internet. Algorithmic recommendations shape the vast majority of our experiences in digital spaces by considering our previous actions and selecting the pieces of content that will most suit our patterns of behavior. They are supposed to interpret and then show us what we want to see.

Today, we are constantly contending with algorithms of all kinds, each one attempting to guess what we are thinking of, seeking, and desiring before we may even be aware of the answers. When I write an email, my Gmail app predicts which words and phrases I am trying to type and fills them in for me, as if reading my mind. Spotify stocks its screen with the musicians and albums it predicts that I am likely to listen to, which I often end up selecting simply out of habit. When I unlock my phone, photos from the past I may want to see—labeled "memories," as if they existed in my subconscious—are preloaded, as are suggestions for apps I may want to open and friends I may want to text. Instagram offers a mood board of what its algorithm perceives as my interests: top-down photos of food, architecture snapshots, looping clips of prestige television shows. TikTok serves me an inexplicable avalanche of videos of people retiling their showers, and I inexplicably keep watching them, compelled in spite of myself. Surely there is more to my identity as a consumer of culture?

All of these small decisions used to be made one at a time by humans: A newspaper editor decided which stories to put on the front page, and a magazine photo editor selected photographs to publish; a film programmer picked out which films to play in a theater's season; an independent radio station DJ assembled playlists of songs that fit their own mood and the particular vibe of a day or a place. While these decisions were of course subject to various social and economic forces, the person in charge of them ensured a basic level of quality, or even safety, that can be missing from the Internet's accelerated feeds.

Algorithmic recommendations are the latest iteration of the Mechanical Turk: a series of human decisions that have been dressed up and automated as technological ones, at an inhuman scale and speed. Designed and maintained by the engineers of monopolistic tech companies, and running on data that we users continuously provide by logging in each day, the technology is both constructed by us and dominates us, manipulating our perceptions and attention. The algorithm *always* wins.

## DISCOVERING FILTERWORLD

*Filterworld,* the title of this book, is my word for the vast, interlocking, and yet diffuse network of algorithms that influence our lives today, which has had a particularly dramatic impact on culture and the ways it is distributed and consumed. Though Filterworld has also changed politics, education, and interpersonal relationships, among many other facets of society, my focus is on culture. Whether visual art, music, film, literature, or choreography, algorithmic recommendations and the feeds that they populate mediate our relationship to culture, guiding our attention toward the things that fit best within the structures of digital platforms. The automated recommendations are filters that both sift what gets attention from what is ignored and subtly warp the appearance of these things, like a photo filter on Instagram, exaggerating some qualities and downplaying others. The cultural successes of Filterworld are obvious. They include phenomena like the countrified TikTok dance that propelled Lil Nas X's 2018 song "Old Town Road" to global fame; the cliché design trends that plague Instagram, like minimalist interiors and the monotonous sans serif logos that fashion brands have adopted in recent years; and the rage-triggering deluge of meaningless Twitter controversies.

Algorithmic recommendations dictate genres of culture by rewarding particular tropes with promotion in feeds, based on what immediately attracts the most attention. In 2018, the writer Liz Pelly identified "streambait" as one such genre: the "muted, mid-tempo, melancholy pop" characteristic of Spotify. In 2019, the writer Jia Tolentino similarly identified "Instagram face," the "distinctly white but ambiguously ethnic" mix of features made popular on the platform and enabled by plastic surgery: "It has catlike eyes and long, cartoonish lashes; it has a small, neat nose and full, lush lips." "TikTok voice" emerged as a term for the rushed, monotone drawl of so many influencer voice-overs in TikTok videos. Each platform develops its own stylistic archetype, which is informed not just by aesthetic preferences but by biases of race, gender, and politics as well as by the fundamental business model of the corporation that owns it.

The culture that thrives in Filterworld tends to be accessible, replicable, participatory, and ambient. It can be shared across wide audiences and retain its meaning across different groups, who tweak it slightly to their own ends. (In Filterworld, everything must be a meme, like a remixable joke or image optimized to travel across the Internet.) It is also pleasant or average enough that it can be ignored and unobtrusively fade into the background, oftentimes going unnoticed until you look for it. After you notice it, however, you tend to see it everywhere, as in the sudden popularity in winter 2018 of a single "Amazon coat," a lumpy puffer jacket that was recommended to Amazon Prime members on its online marketplace, yet another algorithmic space. In the following years, that original Orolay jacket inspired the manufacturing of dozens of replicas and look-alikes, including one by Amazon itself. Filterworld culture is ultimately homogenous, marked by a pervasive sense of sameness even when its artifacts aren't literally the same. It perpetuates itself to the point of boredom.

I began to observe the effects of Filterworld in coffee shops around 2015. Whenever I traveled to different cities for my work as a freelance journalist over the 2010s—Kyoto, Berlin, Beijing, Reykjavík, Los Angeles—I always found a café that looked like so many others I had seen across the world, giving me a precipitous case of déjà vu. The Generic Coffee Shop, as I came to think of it, had white subway tiles lining the walls, broad industrial tables made of reclaimed wood, mid-century modern chairs with spindly legs, and hanging pendant lamps fitted with Edison bulbs. (An "Instagrammy" aesthetic.) And no matter the city, no matter the time of day, the café was reliably filled with a group of people similar to me: freelancers tapping at their laptops, often surfing social media. Why did the interiors look and function the same across such geographical distances? The strict sameness surpassed the usual indicators of globalization. I wanted to find its root cause.

A well-traveled millennial business consultant from Berlin named Igor Schwarzmann, who also noticed the Generic Coffee Shops, described the phenomenon to me as an international "harmonization of tastes." Through algorithmic digital platforms like Instagram, Yelp, and Foursquare, more people around the world are learning to enjoy and seek out similar products and experiences in their physical lives. Through their feeds, they are consuming similar kinds of digital content, no matter where they live, and so their preferences are shaped in that image. Algorithms are manipulative; the apps guide them through physical space to places that have adopted digitally popular aesthetics, winning attention and ratings from other users. With higher ratings come yet more algorithmic promotion and thus more visitors. Yet as international as these effects are, the platforms that undergird them are Western, largely based in the tiny American locus of Silicon Valley and controlled by a handful of unfathomably wealthy white men—the opposite of diversity.

As the Indian literary theorist Gayatri Spivak wrote in 2012, "Globalization takes place only in capital and data. Everything else is damage control." In the Filterworld era, digital platforms like Facebook, Instagram, and TikTok have accumulated and spread their data, in the form of user activity, and their capital, in the form of server farms and algorithmic technology, around the world, capturing billions of users. The homogenous culture is the inevitable reaction to the damage of that spread, a way of coping with or adapting to it. For a long time, I assumed the Generic Coffee Shop aesthetic would fade, that it might just be an ephemeral trend. But it has only become more entrenched. As digital platforms have expanded, the homogeneity they cause has spread, too.

Filterworld and its slick sameness can induce a breathtaking, near-debilitating sense of anxiety. The sameness feels inescapable, alienating even as it is marketed as desirable. "Surveillance capitalism," as the scholar Shoshana Zuboff has labeled it, is how tech companies monetize the constant absorption of our personal data, an intensification of the attention economy. And yet for all that data, algorithmic feeds oftentimes misunderstand us, connecting us to the wrong people or recommending the wrong kinds of content, encouraging habits that we don't want. The network of algorithms makes so many decisions for us, and yet we have little way of talking back to it or changing how it works. This imbalance induces a state of passivity: We consume what the feeds recommend to us without engaging too deeply with the material. We also adapt the way we present ourselves online to its incentives. We write tweets, post on Facebook, and take Instagram photos in forms we know will grab attention and attract likes or clicks, which drive revenue for the tech companies. Scientific studies have shown that those likes trigger rushes of dopamine in our brains, meaning that chasing them, and complying with the feed, is addictive.

On the other side of our algorithmic anxiety is a state of numbness. The dopamine rushes become inadequate, and the noise and speed of the feeds overwhelming. Our natural reaction is to seek out culture that embraces nothingness, that blankets and soothes rather than challenges or surprises, as powerful artwork is meant to do. Our capacity to be moved, or even to be interested and curious, is depleted.

## THE FLATTENING OF CULTURE

In order to understand how Filterworld shapes our experiences, we have to understand how it came to be. The dominance of algorithmic feeds is a relatively recent phenomenon. In the early days of social networks like Twitter, Facebook, Instagram, and Tumblr, the sites' content feeds were more or less chronological. You chose who to friend or follow, and their posts showed up in the order they were published. As the platforms grew to millions and billions of users over the 2010s, and users connected with more people at once, fully chronological feeds became cumbersome and weren't always interesting. You might miss a popular or compelling post just because you weren't scrolling at the right time. So feeds were gradually filled with a higher percentage of recommended posts, out of chronological order. These algorithmically determined posts might even be from accounts you don't follow or subjects you don't care about, interpolated into the feed just so there is something there when you open the app.

The motivation for that switch was less usability than profit. The more time users spend on an app, the more data they produce, the more easily they can be tracked, and the more efficiently their attention can be sold to advertisers. Feeds have become increasingly algorithmic over time, particularly in the watershed moment of the mid-2010s.

TikTok, which launched in the United States in 2018, achieved its major innovation by making its main "For You" feed almost entirely algorithmic. The app experience was less about who the users chose to follow than which content the recommendation algorithm selected for them (hence my bombardment with shower-tiling videos). TikTok quickly became the fastest-growing social network ever, reaching more than 1.5 billion users in less than five years, and its competitors, struggling to catch up, have followed suit into algorithmification. Instagram added a recommendations-driven "Reels" video feed in 2020, and Twitter, following its takeover by Elon Musk, introduced a "For You" column of recommended tweets in 2022. At least for the major corporations that comprise most of the Internet, the algorithmic tide shows no sign of reversing.

In place of the human gatekeepers and curators of culture, the editors and DJs, we now have a set of algorithmic gatekeepers. While this shift has lowered many cultural barriers to entry, since anyone can make their work public online, it has also resulted in a kind of tyranny of real-time data. Attention becomes the only metric by which culture is judged, and what gets attention is dictated by equations developed by Silicon Valley engineers. The outcome of such algorithmic gatekeeping is the pervasive flattening that has been happening across culture. By *flatness* I mean homogenization but also a reduction into simplicity: the least ambiguous, least disruptive, and perhaps least meaningful pieces of culture are promoted the most. Flatness is the lowest common denominator, an averageness that has never been the marker of humanity's proudest cultural creations.

I came across a metaphor for Filterworld in *Somehow, Crystal*, a 1980 Japanese novel by Yasuo Tanaka. The novel is more a list of fashion labels, product brands, restaurants, and boutiques than it is a dramatic narrative. It captures in perfect detail the consumerist environment surrounding a young woman named Yuri in Tokyo, recounting what she buys as well as the various devices she uses—it is the literary equivalent of an influencer's Instagram account. The novel opens with Yuri waking up and turning on the stereo next to her bed. She pushes a tuner button preset to make the radio jump to FEN, a station that plays American rock music. In a footnote, the book meditates on the technology of that button: It's "a nice feature where you can set the frequency for the station you want in advance," but "a little bit of the maniac fun of manual tuning has been lost."

The author observes the difference between hitting a button to instantly tune into the station and wiggling a knob back and forth, navigating through static, and eventually finding the perfect analog position. The latter might be less precise and less convenient, but it's slightly more magical and humane. There is no preset, no predetermined solution. The culture of Filterworld is the culture of presets, established patterns that get repeated again and again. The technology limits us to certain modes of consumption; you can't stray outside of the lines. "Maniac fun," as Yuri says, is gone—that is to say, a certain degree of originality, unprecedentedness, creativity, and surprise disappears when so much weighs on culture's ability to spread through digital feeds.

The aim of this book is not just to diagram Filterworld and discover its consequences but to deconstruct it. In doing so, we can determine ways to escape it and resolve the omnipresent atmosphere of anxiety and ennui that algorithmic feeds have produced. We can dispel their influence only by understanding them—by opening the cabinet of the Mechanical Turk to reveal the operator inside.

■　■　■

# CHAPTER 1

# The Rise of Algorithmic Recommendations

## EARLY ALGORITHMS

*Algorithm* as a term simply describes an equation: any formula or set of rules that produces a desired result. The earliest examples come from ancient Babylon, in the region that is now Iraq. Cuneiform tablets, dating back to 1800–1600 BCE, record algorithms for purposes like calculating the length and width of a cistern using its depth and the volume of earth excavated for it. According to the mathematician Donald E. Knuth, the Babylonians "represented each formula by a step-by-step list of rules for its evaluation, i.e., by an algorithm for computing that formula." They had a specialized system for recording calculations, using "a 'machine language' representation of formulas instead of a symbolic language," Knuth wrote. The written explanation of each Babylonian algorithm ended with the same phrase: "This is the procedure." That line emphasizes an inherent quality of algorithms: they can be repeated, equally applicable and effective every time a given situation occurs. An acolyte of Silicon Valley today might describe them as scalable.

Algorithms are key to the history of early mathematics. Around 300 BCE, the Greek philosopher Euclid recorded in his treatise *Elements* what is called the Euclidean algorithm, a way of finding the greatest common divisor of two or more numbers. That formula and the Sieve of Eratosthenes, an algorithm from the third century BCE that identifies prime numbers within a set of numbers, are still used today, particularly in the realm of cryptography. But the actual word *algorithm* comes from a single person—or at least his birthplace.

Muhammad ibn Musa al-Khwarizmi was a Persian scholar born around 780 CE in Khwarazm, an area around present-day Turkmenistan and Uzbekistan. Though little is known about his life, Al-Khwarizmi made his way to Baghdad, which had become the intellectual center of the region after the Muslim Abassid caliphate conquered Persia in the seventh century. There he worked at the House of Wisdom, also known as the Grand Library of Baghdad, researching astrology, geography, and math. Like its predecessor the Egyptian Library of Alexandria, the House of Wisdom was an interdisciplinary center of learning where scientific study was prized and texts in Greek, Latin, Sanskrit, and Persian were translated into Arabic. Around 820, al-Khwarizmi completed *On the Calculation with Hindu Numerals,* the text that eventually introduced the numeral system we use today to Europe. He also wrote *The Rules of Restoration and Reduction,* a book on strategies for solving equations. Its Arabic name was shortened to *al-jabr* (meaning restoration, or canceling like terms on either side of an equation), which provided the source for the word and the discipline of algebra. *Restoration and Reduction* included solutions for quadratic equations and methods of calculating area and volume, with approximations of pi.

In the mid-twelfth century, an English scholar of Arabic named Robert of Chester was living in Spain, where Muslim, Jewish, and Christian cultures overlapped, at some times peacefully and at others less so. It was another moment when ideas were exchanged and disseminated, crossing between civilizations. In 1145, Robert translated *The Rules of Restoration and Reduction* into Latin. *Al-jabr* became "algeber," and al-Khwarizmi became "Algoritmi." At that time, "algorismus" referred generally to any kind of mathematical procedure using Hindu-Arabic numerals, and those who practiced such an art were called algorists. (That term was adopted by visual artists using algorithmic processes beginning in the 1960s, but it seems apt for anyone working on today's version of algorithms.) The long arc of algorithm's etymology shows that calculations are a product of human art and labor as much as repeatable scientific law.

## THE INVENTION OF COMPUTER PROGRAMMING

All computers are built from series of equations performed repeatedly. Results are encoded in zeros and ones and then passed on through yet more equations to achieve an outcome. In 1822, the British inventor Charles Babbage outlined his concept for the "application of machinery to the computation of astronomical and mathematical tables"—a way to automate calculations using an assemblage of numbered wheels and gears called the Difference Engine. The machine was never fully built, but later executions look something like the inside of a piano, with wheels in long rows instead of hammers. Babbage's design would have been eight feet high and weighed four tons. His later iteration, the Analytical Engine, could, if built, take commands programmed via punch cards and perform simple programming features like loops and conditions. It was the basis for all the much more complicated modern computing that followed. As Babbage's son Henry wrote in 1888, "It is only a question of cards and time."

Ada Lovelace, the daughter of Lord Byron, is now widely regarded as the first computer programmer; she wrote algorithms for the machine as Babbage designed it, including a process for calculating Bernoulli numbers. Lovelace also realized that the repeating mechanical processes that the machine enabled could be applied to fields beyond mathematics. In 1843, Lovelace wrote that the Analytical Engine "might act upon other things besides number, were objects found whose mutual fundamental relations could be expressed by those of the abstract science of operations, and which should be also susceptible of adaptations to the action of the operating notation and mechanism of the engine." In other words, anything that can be turned into something like data—a series of numbers— could be manipulated in a formulaic way. That might include text, music, art, or even a game like chess. Lovelace imagined one form of such automation: "Supposing, for instance, that the fundamental relations of pitched sounds in the science of harmony and of musical composition were susceptible of such expression and adaptations, the engine might compose elaborate and scientific pieces of music of any degree of complexity or extent." She was envisioning something like what the composer Brian Eno created in 1995 and popularized as "generative music," a series of ambient synth compositions driven by musical software that created different tunes each time the software ran. Lovelace was envisioning how culture could be both molded and perpetuated by the new technology, the way algorithmic feeds do today.

Lovelace was early in discovering that manipulating such mechanical commands could be its own form and self-expression. In the 1990s and 2000s, computer programming began to take its place alongside basic math and science as a skill that was necessary for a child's complete education. I was introduced to it on "computer room" desktops in my high school circa 2002, where we played educational video games that resembled programming languages. But where I really learned was on the chunky plastic TI-83 calculators that we had to acquire for advanced math classes. The calculators came with the ability to code in a language called TI-BASIC, which had simple if-then loops and variable functions. At first, I made modest programs to automate formulas I needed to know for tests, but once I became more fluent in the language, I made my own versions of tic-tac-toe and Connect Four. The machine was a partner in my creativity; it felt like magic.

A century after Lovelace, during World War II, Alan Turing, a British mathematician and computer scientist, was working in code breaking for the government—he helped to decode the German Enigma cipher machine. In 1946, with the war over, Turing wrote a report for the National Physical Library proposing the development of an "Automatic Computing Engine." It was the first description of artificial intelligence as a real possibility instead of a theoretical concept. Calculating and sorting machines designed to perform specific tasks already existed, Turing wrote, but his proposal went beyond that: "Instead of repeatedly using human labor for taking material out of the machine and putting it back at the appropriate moment all this will be looked after by the machine itself."

According to Turing, the device would be able to perform any kind of calculation and at any scale without needing to be reconfigured. It had its own internal logical language that could be adapted to different ends, to solve any type of problem. "How can one expect a machine to do all this multitudinous variety of things?" Turing wrote. "The answer is that we should consider the machine to be doing something quite simple, namely carrying out orders given to it in a standard form which it is able to understand." It would execute algorithms. He hinted at the way that machine learning algorithms today evolve over time, incorporating adjustments without human decision-making.

Such a system would perform calculations much faster and at higher levels of complexity, exceeding humans. Turing wrote: "The speed of the machine is no longer limited by the speed of the human operator." He did not see such machines as utopian tools, however. Just because they would be automatic didn't mean they would always be right. "The human element of fallibility is eliminated, although it may to an extent be replaced by mechanical fallibility," Turing continued. His report predicted many now-familiar elements of personal computers, from erasable memory units to input mechanisms, conversion from binary language, and even temperature control so the machine wouldn't overheat. For Turing, however, the word *computer* referred not to the machine but to the person doing the computing, once again emphasizing that organic element.

As early as 1936, Turing conceived of what is now called a "Turing machine," which he sketched in detail in a 1948 essay called "Intelligent Machinery." The Turing machine is "an infinite tape marked out into squares, on each of which a symbol could be printed." The tape moves through a reader that scans one square at a time and performs the operation dictated by the symbol in the square, which can also be erased or overwritten. Any algorithm, in the historical sense of a mathematical process, can be calculated by such a Turing Machine. And any computational system that can compute anything that a Turing Machine can is said to be "Turing-complete." All programming languages, for example, are Turing-complete because they can model any kind of equation. (Even the spreadsheet software Excel became Turing-complete in 2021.) What Turing correctly concluded was that any computing machine would be able to do the work of any other—even Charles Babbage's nineteenth-century Analytical Engine could theoretically perform the complex tasks that our laptops do now, if given infinite scale and time.

There is something of the clash between mechanical rules and human operation within Turing's life, too. In 1952, Turing was charged with gross indecency for "homosexual expression"—the legalistic phrase for having sex with another man—during messy legal proceedings that he initiated after his own house was robbed. Homosexual sex among consenting adults remained illegal in England all the way to 1967—the law is its own kind of algorithm, deciding judgment based on an implacable set of rules. Turing eventually pled guilty to the charges and was convicted. Rather than be imprisoned, he was forced to undergo chemical castration. In June 1954, Turing, forty-one, was found dead by his housekeeper. The cause was cyanide poisoning, and his death has long been considered suicide, the suspected delivery mechanism a half-eaten apple at Turing's bedside.

When we talk about "the algorithm," it often feels like a force that began to exist only recently, in the era of social networks. But we're discussing a technology with a history and legacy that has slowly formed over centuries, long before the Internet existed. Restoring this larger picture can help us better understand the power that algorithms have today. Still, no matter how complex, an algorithm remains in its essence an equation: a method to arrive at a desired conclusion, whether it's a Sumerian diagram to divide an amount of grain equally among several men or the Facebook feed determining which post to show you first when you open the website. All algorithms are engines of automation, and, as Ada Lovelace predicted, automation has now moved into many facets of our lives beyond pure mathematics.

## ALGORITHMIC DECISION-MAKING

In 1971, in Santiago, Chile, a hexagonal room designed as a kind of control room for the entire country was built in a downtown office building. Monitors and backlit displays adorned the room's wood-paneled walls, displaying data readouts with metrics like national raw material supplies and labor participation rates. Seven chairs were arrayed in a circle facing each other in the center of the room, white fiberglass wingback seats that resembled the captain's chair in a science-fictional space cruiser. Each chair had a control panel on the right-hand side to navigate the various screens, as well as an ashtray and a cupholder, perhaps for a tumbler of whiskey. The room, which was named the Operations Room under the aegis of the larger Project Cybersyn, was designed under the socialist Chilean president Salvador Allende and the consultancy of Stafford Beer, a British man who, in his own country, was known for applying the practice of "cybernetics" to business management. Beer described cybernetics as "the science of control." It involves analyzing complex systems, whether corporations or biology, and determining how they work to better model or create such intelligent, self-correcting systems. (In the United States, a similar practice of systems analysis was pioneered by the RAND Corporation in the 1950s.) Project Cybersyn was meant to provide an ideal model, aiding the Chilean government's decision-makers in real time as they sat in the room and smoked their cigarettes and drank their whiskey—another meeting of the coldly technological and the messily human. From the room, the men watched the algorithms that oversaw the nation.

Project Cybersyn's physical design, led by the German consultant Gui Bonsiepe, created an image of mid-century modernist utopianism. The monitors floated on the walls, the underlying wiring connecting them to the chairs hidden from view. The cockpit chairs themselves were sleek and uniform, smoothly curving in one molded form. The room symbolically reduced government down to the manipulation of data, like winning a video game. Project Cybersyn promised to supplant human leadership with technological oversight, the scant few screens encompassing any information that might be needed. You could sit in one of the chairs and observe everything happening in the country.

However, Project Cybersyn's technology was a facade, something akin to "design fiction"—an interactive illusion of what might be possible. What it promised was not yet feasible with computer networks at the time. Its data slideshows were created by hand, not automatically generated. It ran on a single computer, fed by telex machines that Chilean factories could use to send information over telephone lines. And finally, though the room was completed, it was never put into action. On September 11, 1973, with the assistance of the United States CIA, Allende's government was overthrown, and Augusto Pinochet took over.

There remains an undeniable appeal to the photographs of Project Cybersyn. They appear over and over in design mood boards, projecting an aesthetic that still looks like the future many decades later. Perhaps the images are so influential because we retain that dream of the raw data of reality processed and crunched into digital graphs, which are then evaluated and, from there, the correct path of action determined. Project Cybersyn exuded an air of infallibility, even though inventors like Turing knew computers couldn't work so perfectly. As the cybernetics pioneer Stafford Beer argued, we tend to use machines to automate the structures and processes that already exist, which were human creations to begin with. "We enshrine in steel, glass, and semiconductors those very limitations of hand, eye, and brain that the computer was invented precisely to transcend," Beer wrote in his 1968 book *Management Sciences,* pinpointing the paradox. As with the Mechanical Turk, the human persists within the machine.

Today we do have versions of algorithmic government and algorithmic life: banks use machine learning to dictate who receives loans; Spotify uses the data of your past actions to determine songs to recommend, those they deem most aligned with your sensibility. But the technology that accomplishes those feats doesn't look like Project Cybersyn. There are no hexagonal rooms or wingback chairs. Algorithms have become both invisible and omnipresent, contained in the apps we carry around with us on our phones even as their data are hosted physically somewhere distant, within vast air-conditioned server farms set into obscure locations in the natural landscape. Where Project Cybersyn suggested that the world run by data might be coherent and graspable, contained within a room, we now know that it is abstract and diffuse, everywhere and nowhere at once. We're encouraged to forget the presence of algorithms.

New technologies inevitably create new forms of behavior, but the behaviors are rarely those that the inventors expect. The technology has an inherent meaning of its own that eventually comes to the fore. Marshall McLuhan wrote his famous dictum "the medium is the message" in his 1964 book *Understanding Media: The Extensions of Man*. He meant that the structure of a new medium—electric light, the telephone, television—is more important than the content that travels through it. The telephone's ability to connect people exceeds any particular conversation. "The 'message' of any medium or technology is the change of scale or pace or pattern that it introduces into human affairs," McLuhan wrote. In our case, the medium is the algorithmic feed; it has scaled and sped up humanity's interconnection across the world to an unimaginable degree. Its message is that on some level, our collective consumption habits, translated into data, run together into sameness.

## HOW RECOMMENDATION ALGORITHMS WORK

Algorithms are digital machines that turn a series of inputs into a particular output, like a conveyor belt in a factory. What makes one algorithm different from another is less their structure than the ingredients they are built from. All recommendation algorithms work by gathering a set of raw data. The overall term for that dataset is *signal,* the collected inputs that are fed into the machine. The signal data might include a user's past purchases on Amazon or how many other users favorited a particular song on Spotify. The data is quantitative rather than qualitative, since it must be able to be processed by the machine. So even if the data is about something as subjective as music preferences, it is translated into numbers: $x$ number of users rated $y$ band an average of $z$, or $x$ number of users listened to $y$ band $z$ times. The primary signal fed into many social media recommendations is *engagement,* which describes how users are interacting with a piece of content. That might come in the form of likes, retweets, or plays—any kind of button found next to a post. High engagement means the number of likes, views, or shares is higher than the average of other posts.

The signal is fed through a *data transformer* that puts it into usable packages, set to be processed by different kinds of algorithms. Engagement data might need to be separated from ratings data, or data about the subject matter of the content itself. A *social calculator* might be used to add information about how users relate to one another within a single platform—I often engage with Instagram posts from my friend Andrew, for example, which would make a recommender system more likely to rank one of his posts highly in my personal feed.

Then comes the specific equation of an individual algorithm. In today's platforms, there is very rarely only one set algorithm—there are many. What we are experiencing is a series of different equations that consider data variables and process them in a few ways. One equation calculates a result based on engagement alone, perhaps finding the content with the highest average engagement, while another prioritizes the social context of a piece of content for a particular user. Those algorithms are also weighed against each other. *Hybrid filtering* is when multiple techniques are used. Finally, the *output* is the recommendation itself, the next song in the automated playlist or the ordered list of posts. The algorithm decides whether it should put a life update from a friend in your Facebook feed over a politics news story, for example.

An executive at the music cataloging and recommendation service Pandora once described the company's system to me as an "orchestra" of algorithms, complete with a "conductor" algorithm. Each algorithm used different strategies to come up with a recommendation, and then the conductor algorithm dictated which suggestions were used at a given moment. (The only output was the next song to play in a playlist.) Different moments called for different algorithmic recommendation techniques.

There is no single, monolithic "algorithm," because each platform works in its own way, incorporating custom-designed variables and sets of equations. It's important to remember that how the Facebook feed works is a commercial decision, the same as a food manufacturer deciding which ingredients to use. Algorithms also change over time, refining themselves using machine learning. The data they take in is used for gradual self-improvement to encourage even more engagement; the machine adapts to users and users adapt to the machine. The differences between platforms became more prominent and more relevant moving into the mid-2010s, as social media and streaming services doubled down on algorithmic feeds and they began to dominate the user experience.

We users fundamentally do not understand how algorithmic recommendations work on a day-to-day basis. Their equations, variables, and weights are not public because technology companies have little incentive to publicize them. They are closely held trade secrets, almost like nuclear codes for how important they are to the businesses, and are rarely disclosed or hinted at. One reason for that is if the algorithms were public, users could game the system to promote their own content. Another is the fear of competition: other digital platforms could steal the secret sauce and make a better product. Yet these tools, like many digital technologies, started out in a non-commercial context.

Recommendation algorithms as a way of automatically processing and sorting information were put into practice in the 1990s. One of the first examples was a system for sorting email—to this day, an annoying chore. Even in 1992, engineers at Xerox's Palo Alto Research Center (better known as PARC) were already overwhelmed by it. They sought to solve the problem of "the increasing use of electronic mail, which is resulting in users being inundated by a huge stream of Incoming documents," David Goldberg, David Nichols, Brian M. Oki, and Douglas Terry wrote in a 1992 paper. (Little did they know the volume of digital communication we would face in the twenty-first century.) Their email filtering system, called Tapestry, used two kinds of algorithms in tandem: "content-based filtering" and "collaborative filtering." The former, which was already used in several email systems, evaluated the text of emails—say, if you wanted to prioritize everything with the word *algorithm*. But the latter, more innovative technique was based on the actions of other users. Who opened a particular email and how they responded to it would be factored into how much the system prioritized the email. As the paper described it:

> People collaborate to help one another perform filtering by recording their reactions to documents they read. Such reactions may be that a document was particularly interesting (or particularly uninteresting). These reactions, more generally called annotations, can be accessed by others' filters.

Tapestry used a "filterer" to run repeated queries over a set of documents, a "little box" that collected material that might be of interest to the user, and an "appraiser" that could prioritize and categorize documents. Conceptually, it's very similar to the algorithmic feeds we see now: Tapestry's goal was to surface the content that was most likely to be important to the user. But this system required much more up-front action on the part of the user, who had to write queries to determine what they wanted to see, based either on content or on other users' actions. The other users in the system also had to carry out very intentional actions, marking material as compelling or irrelevant in turn. Such a system required a small group of people who already knew one another and understood how their cohort interacted with email—for instance, you may need to be aware in advance that Jeff replies only to particularly important emails, so you want your filter to surface all the emails that Jeff replies to. Tapestry functioned best on a very intimate scale.

In 1995, a paper from Upendra Shardanand and Pattie Maes at the MIT Media Lab described "social information filtering," "a technique for making personalized recommendations from any type of database to a user based on similarities between the interest profile of that user and those of other users." Building on the ideas of Tapestry, it was a response to the overflow of information online: "The volume of things is considerably more than any person can possibly filter through in order to find the ones that he or she will like." Automated filters would be necessary, they concluded: "We need technology to help us wade through all the information to find the items we really want and need, and to rid us of the things we do not want to be bothered with." (Of course, this is still a huge problem online.) Shardanand and Maes argued that content-based filtering had significant drawbacks. It requires the material to be translated into data that the machine can understand, such as text; it lacks serendipity because it can filter only by the terms that the user inputs; and it does not measure inherent quality. It is unable to "distinguish a well written [and] a badly written article if the two articles use the same terms." The inability to evaluate quality brings to mind artificial intelligence: New tools like ChatGPT seem to be able to understand and generate meaningful language, but really, they only repeat patterns inherent in the preexisting data they are trained on. Quality is subjective; data alone, in the absence of human judgment, can go only so far in gauging it.

Social information filtering bypasses those problems because it is instead driven by the actions of human users, who evaluate content on their own—using judgments both quantitative and qualitative. It's more like word of mouth, the way we get advice on what to listen to or watch from friends whose preferences are similar to our own: "Items are recommended to a user based upon values assigned by other people with similar taste," according to the paper. The similarity of one user's taste to another was calculated using statistical correlation. The researchers designed a system called Ringo to make music recommendations using an email list. As a user evaluated music, rating an initial batch of 125 artists on a scale of 1 to 7, a diagram of their preferences was built. Then, by comparing that diagram to other users', the system suggested music that they were likely to enjoy—or hate, which was also an option. Ringo recommendations came with a measure of confidence, signaling how likely a suggestion was to be right and allowing the user to further consider the algorithmic choice. By September 1994, Ringo had twenty-one hundred users and five hundred emails a day evaluating music.

Ringo tested various specific algorithms to make decisions based on the music ratings. The first algorithm measured dissimilarity between users' tastes and based recommendations on the most similar users. The second algorithm measured similarity, then used positive and negative correlations with other users to make decisions. The third algorithm determined the correlation between different artists, recommending artists who were strongly correlated to those a user already liked. The fourth algorithm, and the most effective according to the researchers, matched users based on whether they rated the same things either positive or negatively. In other words, their taste matched. Similarity was the best variable. The more users in the system, and the more input users gave up front, the better Ringo worked—some users even described it as "unnervingly accurate." Ringo's innovation was how it acknowledged that the best recommendations, or the best indications of relevance, were likely to come from other humans rather than analysis of the content itself. It represented a scaling up of human taste.

Early Internet algorithms were designed to sift through a vast body of material for whatever was important to a user, and then present it in a coherent way. Recommendations were the goal: recommending a piece of information, a song, an image, or a social media update. Algorithmic feeds are sometimes more formally and literally labeled "recommender systems," for the simple act of choosing a piece of content.

The first wholly mainstream Internet algorithm, one that almost every Internet user has encountered, was the Google Search algorithm. In 1996, while studying at Stanford University, Sergey Brin and Larry Page, the cofounders of Google, began work on what would become PageRank, a system for crawling the Internet (which at that point amounted to perhaps one hundred million documents in total) and identifying which sites and pages were more useful or informative than others. PageRank worked by measuring how many times a website was linked to by other sites, similar to the way academic papers cite key pieces of past research. The more links, the more important a page was likely to be. The metric of citation "corresponds well with people's subjective idea of importance," Brin and Page wrote in a 1998 paper, "The Anatomy of a Large-Scale Hypertextual Web Search Engine." PageRank mingled a form of collaborative filtering with content filtering. By linking various pages, human users had already formed a subjective map of recommendations that the algorithm could incorporate. It also measured factors like the number of links on a page, the relative quality of the links, and even the size of text—the larger the text, the more relevant it might be for a particular search term. Pages with a higher PageRank were more likely to appear at the top of Google's list of search results.

Page and Brin's prediction that their system would remain functional and scalable as the Internet grew were correct. Decades later, PageRank has become almost tyrannical, a system that dominates how and when websites are seen. It's vital for a business or resource to make it to that first page of Google Search results by adapting to the PageRank algorithm. In the early 2000s, I perused many successive pages of Google results to find exactly what I was looking for. More recently, I hardly ever make it to the second page, in part because Google Search now frontloads text that it gauges will be relevant, pulling it from websites and displaying it directly to the user at the top of the search page, before the actual results. Thus a query like "Can I feed my dog carrots?"—the kind of question I googled incessantly in the early days of puppy ownership—will deliver an answer without a user ever having to load another site, further consolidating Google's authority. "Knowledge itself is power," Francis Bacon wrote in the sixteenth century, but in the Internet era, sorting knowledge might be even more powerful. Information is now easy to find in abundance; making sense of it, knowing which information is useful, is much harder.

Page and Brin wanted their system to be relatively neutral, evaluating each site solely in terms of its relevance. The algorithm's directive was to prioritize the best information for the user. Catering the search to a particular site or business would ruin the results. "We expect that advertising funded search engines will be inherently biased towards the advertisers and away from the needs of the consumers," the entrepreneurs wrote in 1998. Yet, in 2000, they launched Google AdWords as the company's pilot product for advertisers. It is amusing to read their critique today, as advertising now provides the vast majority of Google's revenue—more than 80 percent in 2020. As PageRank attracted billions of users to Google Search, the company could also track what the users were searching for and could thus sell advertisers space on particular search queries. The ads a user sees were just as informed by the algorithm as the search results were. And advertising, built on the search algorithm, turned Google into a behemoth.

By the early 2000s, algorithmic filtering was already dictating our digital experiences. The Amazon website began using collaborative filtering as early as 1998 to recommend products for customers to buy. Rather than attempting to measure similar profiles of users to approximate taste, as Ringo did, the system worked by determining which items were likely to be purchased in tandem—a rattle with a baby bottle, for example. A 2017 paper cowritten by an Amazon employee described the bombardment of such suggestions on the site:

> The homepage prominently featured recommendations based on your past purchases and items browsed in the store. . . . The shopping cart recommended other items to add to your cart, perhaps impulse buys to bundle in at the last minute, or perhaps complements to what you were already considering. At the end of your order, more recommendations appeared, suggesting items to order later.

The algorithmic recommendations resemble the shelves stationed just before the register in a Trader Joe's, one last push of products that you may need. But in this case, what was recommended was tailored to each website user, resulting in "a store for every customer," as the paper described. Amazon found that the personalized product recommendations were much more effective in terms of click-throughs and sales than unpersonalized marketing tactics like banner advertisements and lists of bestselling products, which can't be as tightly targeted. The recommendation algorithm improved business and appeared convenient for the customer, who might find something they didn't know they needed. (Right now, my Amazon home page recommends a cordless power washer and a Japanese omelet pan.)

These early algorithms sorted individual emails, musicians (as opposed to specific songs), web pages, and commercial products. As digital platforms expanded, recommender systems moved into more complex areas of culture and operated at much faster speeds and higher volumes, sorting millions of tweets, films, user-uploaded videos, and even potential romantic partners. Filtering became the default online experience.

This history is also a reminder that recommender systems are not omniscient entities but tools built by groups of tech researchers or workers. They are fallible products. Nick Seaver is a sociologist and a professor at Tufts University who studies recommender systems. His research focuses on the human side of algorithms, how the engineers who make them think about algorithmic recommendations. In my discussions with him, Seaver always made sure to clarify the ambiguous entity of the algorithm, separating the individual equation from the corporate motives behind its design and its eventual impact on the user. "The algorithm is metonymic for companies as a whole," he told me. "The Facebook algorithm doesn't exist; Facebook exists. The algorithm is a way of talking about Facebook's decisions."

The technology is not at issue—one can no more blame an algorithm itself for bad recommendations than blame a bridge for its engineering flaws. And some degree of reordering is necessary to make the vast stores of content on digital platforms comprehensible. The negative aspects of Filterworld might have emerged because the technology has been applied too widely, without enough consideration for the experience of the user, rather than for the advertisers targeting them. The recommendations, such as they are, don't work for us anymore; rather, we are increasingly alienated by them.

## EARLY SOCIAL MEDIA

My first meaningful memories of social media come from Facebook, which I joined after I accepted an admission offer from Tufts University, where I went to college. At that time, in summer 2006, prospective users needed an official .edu email address to access the full college section of the platform. That early iteration of Facebook is nearly unrecognizable when compared to its present-day anatomy. Back then, Facebook's reach was strictly limited; I mainly used it as a means to connect with other incoming Tufts students. If Facebook today is a frenetic highway with exits and on-ramps every few seconds, in the aughts it was more like a high school rec room where only a few people could hang out at a time. You built a profile, updated your status on the profile, and joined groups around common interests—but not much else.

Facebook was hardly the first way to socialize online. Friendster and MySpace were its predecessors. AOL's Instant Messenger and Google's gChat provided engrossing ways to hang out with your friends in real time. By 2006 I had already spent hundreds of hours on older forum websites discussing video games and music. But Zuckerberg's Facebook tied online identity coherently and consistently to the offline world. The platform encouraged users to use their real names rather than arcane aliases and influenced real-life plans in the small world of college: throwing parties, planning academic activities, and conducting relationships. In doing so, it paved the way for the mainstreaming of online social life for millions, and then billions, of users.

In September 2006, not long after I joined the network, Facebook implemented one of its biggest changes, a feature that would set the course for its future as the big-box everything-for-sale store of the Internet. The News Feed, a running list of updates, posts, and alerts, became the primary feature of the platform. It was unignorable, like a newly built highway that cut through a quiet village. "Now, whenever you log in, you'll get the latest headlines generated by the activity of your friends and social groups," Facebook's official update note announced.

The patent for the News Feed, filed that year, though it wasn't granted until 2012, described its purpose: "A system and method provides dynamically selected media content to someone using an electronic device in a social network environment." In other words, the News Feed was a flow of information dictated by an algorithm that determined what to show a user. Another patent claimed the ability to "generate dynamic relationship-based content personalized for the members of the web-based social network." At first the News Feed was just a stream of announcements of changed dating statuses and updated profile pictures. It wasn't particularly threatening.

The News Feed patent application's longer description suggests a system of collaborative filtering, acting on a much larger scale than the email systems of the 1990s. It's worth quoting in full because it predicts what much of life online, from social networks to streaming and e-commerce, became in the decade that followed: so many automated feeds dictated by corporations more so than users, gradually forming a more passive relationship between users and the content feed.

Items of media content are selected for the user based on his or her relationships with one or more other users. The user's relationships with other users are reflected in the selected media content and its format. An order is assigned to the items of media content, for example, based on their anticipated importance to the user, and the items of media content are displayed to the user in the assigned order. The user may change the order of the items of media content. The user's interactions with media content available in the social network environment are monitored, and those interactions are used to select additional items of media content for the user.

All the elements of the algorithmic feed are present in this passage—a system that anticipates a piece of content's relative importance to an individual user, determined by surveillance of content they engaged with in the past, and pushes whichever content is deemed most likely to be equally engaging to the top of the list. The goal was to filter content to select what is most interesting, therefore encouraging a user to consume a higher volume of content and follow more accounts overall. Users being able to use social media more often and stay on the sites longer is what made them viable. (If our friends aren't active on Facebook, which has been the case for me in recent years, then we are likely to tail off our activity, too.)

At first, the News Feed was ordered purely chronologically, with the most recent updates first, but it gradually followed a more algorithmic logic. As Facebook grew and users added more connections, expanding from personal relationships to publications and brands, the volume of individual updates increased. Over time, the updates weren't just mundane notes from friends but messages from groups, links to news stories, and announcements of sales. Casual users couldn't hope to follow a chronological feed with such a volume and variety of posts, and if they tried, they would either be overwhelmed or fail to catch an important post, which might cause dissatisfaction with the platform. Ultimately, the scale and speed of consumption made aggressive algorithmic filtering necessary for Facebook.

Facebook's Like button, with its signature thumbs-up, was introduced in 2009, providing one form of data on how interested a user might be in a particular piece of content. User engagement, measured by likes, comments, and one account's previous interactions with another, factored into the order of the feed. That algorithmic system was called EdgeRank, and Facebook identified its principal variables as affinity score, edge weight, and time decay. "Edge" referred to any action people carry out on Facebook, which is then sent to the News Feed as an update to be listed. Affinity score represented how connected a user was to the poster and the strength of the connection (e.g., consistently commenting on friend's posts). A comment counted more than a like, and recent interactions counted more than older ones. Edge weight evaluated different categories of interactions: an update of a friend posting a new photo might be given more weight by the algorithm than posting a link to a news article or joining a new group. Time decay was the age of the action; recent actions were more likely to be at the top of the News Feed than older ones, if the other factors were equal. The EdgeRank scores were not permanently assigned once, like the outcome of a basketball game in a tournament, but changed instant to instant. And those three categories aren't simply single, neutral data points; they are collections of data packaged and interpreted in specific ways by Facebook.

It's hard to track the evolution of Facebook's algorithmic feed because it is constantly updated, and the company reveals details only intermittently. What we do know about it beyond official announcements comes down to investigative reporting from journalists and the experiences of users, who see the effects of updated algorithms long before they're made public. Familiar websites have a way of feeling different when the feed mechanism changes. On Facebook, for instance, you may notice that you see less of your friends' posts and more from groups or businesses, or that Instagram never shows you posts from a particular friend in your feed and you thus need to hunt them down using the search bar.

The algorithmic feed itself is not consistent or on a linear path toward some ultimate perfection. It changes with a company's priorities. In 2011, Facebook described the News Feed as "your own personal newspaper," suggesting its goal of mingling social updates with news stories from the outside world. In 2013, it said its algorithm worked to "detect content defined as high quality." But chasing whatever the company gauged as "high quality" was something of an absurd game over the course of the 2010s. If you wanted to get attention for your Facebook posts—a big problem for journalism publications and freelance writers—you had to guess at what kind of material was getting prioritized. The relationship was almost oppositional; only if you "gamed" the algorithm would you be heard. You could no longer rely on users who had followed or friended you seeing your posts.

At one point in my freelance journalism career, I recall a rumor going around that links to articles were no longer very highly weighted by the algorithm. So rather than posting our stories directly using a simple link, I and many other journalists added a link to the story only by commenting on the post. The trick was supposed to goose algorithmic promotion, even though it was more confusing for a reader. At another point, it became clear that writing text that resembled a marriage announcement and comments that said "congratulations" pushed posts to the top of the feed. So I began sharing my articles with fake weddings or other life milestones. These phenomena show how algorithms can warp language itself as users attempt to either game them or evade detection. More recently, on TikTok, euphemisms have emerged for terms that trigger the algorithm to block or slow down a video: "unalive" for kill, "SA" for sexual assault, "spicy eggplant" instead of vibrator, as the journalist Taylor Lorenz documented in the *Washington Post*. Such vocabulary was nicknamed "algospeak": speech molded in the image of the algorithm.

It was unclear if the tricks I used on Facebook had much of an impact, but I was willing to try anything to reach potential readers. It was like designing a website for Google search-engine optimization: journalists optimized content for the metrics of the algorithm, or at least what we perceived them to be. The process felt manipulative and at times Kafkaesque; we contended with an unseen, incomprehensible, ever-changing opponent.

Around 2015, Facebook decided to prioritize video content, so the recommendation algorithm promoted videos much more than it did previously. Media companies then "pivoted" to making videos to chase that audience, sometimes with the help of funding from Facebook itself. That effort lasted only a few years, and then Facebook deprioritized videos once more, leading to waves of layoffs at those same media companies, including BuzzFeed, Mashable, and MTV. (After the program ended, it also emerged that Facebook had lied about the traffic the videos were getting, inflating the numbers up to nine times, according to a lawsuit.) The algorithmic feed kept shifting. In 2016, Facebook added "reactions" to posts, so that viewers could respond with a range of emoticons rather than just the Like button. Posts that received many emoticon reactions got more promotion. But that change backfired, too, when incendiary content—posts that received many angry-face reactions, for example, like rage-inducing political stories—was getting too much promotion and souring the tone of the entire site. That they attracted more engagement didn't mean the posts were necessarily more worthwhile.

It wasn't only Facebook that moved from a chronological feed to an increasing volume of algorithmic recommendations. Almost every major social network followed the same path over the 2010s. Filterworld began taking shape in the middle of the decade when algorithmification intensified.

Facebook acquired Instagram in 2012, when it only had thirteen employees. In the years since, the photo-sharing app has become more like Facebook itself, moving away from a linear feed of photos uploaded by friends into a stream of videos, ads, and recommended posts. In March 2016, the Instagram feed began switching from a chronological to an algorithmic arrangement. The change was tested on small groups of users then rolled out to more and more, until it hit everyone. The increasingly out-of-order feed induced a sense of confusion and anxiety akin to the feeling of someone rearranging the furniture in your house without your knowledge. Before, by scrolling through the feed, you were moving back in time. But suddenly, a post from two days ago appeared at the top of your feed.

Early 2016 was also when Twitter became less chronological, briefly making the algorithmic feed the default when users first got on the app—a problem for a site that many people used as a real-time news ticker. (The chronological option was called "Twitter Classic," as if it were a beloved junk-food flavor.) Later, the app would swap users over to an algorithmic feed automatically after a while and force them to opt out of it. Although Netflix's content recommendations had long been algorithmic, 2016 was also when the streaming service began changing its home-page interface, prioritizing recommendations and individualizing it for each user.

Larger cultural consequences, unexpected by users and perhaps by the companies themselves, followed this shift—the way that damming a river changes an entire ecosystem. When feeds are algorithmic, they appear differently to different people: It's impossible to know what someone else is seeing at a given time, and thus harder to feel a sense of community with others online, the sense of collectivity you might feel when watching a movie in a theater or sitting down for a prescheduled cable TV show. The advent of Filterworld has seen a breakdown in monoculture. It has some advantages—more than ever before, we can all consume a wider possible range of media—but it also has negative consequences. Culture is meant to be communal and requires a certain degree of consistency across audiences; without communality, it loses some of its essential impact.

Intensifying the problem of fragmentation was the fact that recommender-system updates do not roll out at the same time to all users at once across an app. For a year or two after 2016, my personal Instagram feed remained rigorously chronological, while everyone around me complained about not seeing what they wanted. Eventually my feed switched over too, and I understood what they had been complaining about. We came to rely on our feeds working in certain ways, and when those changed, how we behaved as consumers also changed. We were stuck in the algorithmic flow, driven by whichever variables it was programmed to seek.

The rise of the algorithmic feed, like the Internet itself, came slowly and then all at once. Early in the 2020s, as I'm writing, recommender systems seem unavoidable, mediating our consumption of every form of digital media. Technology often appears to belong to the distant future right up until the moment the switch flips, and the leap forward becomes totally mundane, a simple fact of daily life.

In his sprawling early twentieth-century novel *In Search of Lost Time,* Marcel Proust excavated such subtle changes in personal sensibilities against the backdrop of evolving technology. In one passage, Proust's narrator describes the telephone as "a supernatural instrument before whose miracles we used to stand amazed, and which we now employ without giving it a thought, to summon our tailor or to order an ice cream." The telephone had only been invented in the late nineteenth century, when Proust's novel is set. By 1899, there were seven thousand telephone subscribers in Paris. And yet telephones had still become banal. Even during one of his first phone calls, the narrator becomes annoyed by the device instead of awed. Proust wrote: "Habits require so short a time to divest of their mystery the sacred forces with which we are in contact, that, not having had my call at once, my immediate thought was that it was all very long and very inconvenient, and I almost decided to lodge a complaint."

In 1933, the Japanese novelist Junichiro Tanizaki memorialized another moment of technological change when he wrote *In Praise of Shadows,* a book-length essay about electric lights arriving in Tokyo. The metaphorical switch had flipped; within Tanizaki's lifetime (he was born in 1886), electric lights had gone from unknown in his country to ubiquitous, thanks to the intrusion of the West beginning in 1867, in a wave of increasing globalization and subsequent clashes of cultures. The Westerner's "quest for a brighter light never ceases," Tanizaki wrote. In the essay, Tanizaki mourned the unique forms of Japanese culture that the old dimness of candlelight had inspired, from the gleam of gold leaf on a home's interior sliding door to the murky appearance of miso soup in a darkened restaurant: "Our cooking depends upon shadows and is inseparable from darkness."

Yet Tanizaki couldn't ignore the attraction of electricity and other new devices: porcelain toilets, heaters, and neon signs. "It was not that I objected to the conveniences of modern civilization," he wrote. As he described in his fiction, the novelist loved movie theaters and modern architecture as much as he appreciated tradition. *In Praise of Shadows* tracked how technology changed, culture adapted, and personal taste shifted in turn—a pattern we see throughout Filterworld in our own time.

With new technology, the miraculous quickly becomes mundane, any glitch in its function is felt as bothersome, and finally it becomes ignorable, the miracle forsaken. We forget that life wasn't always this way, that we couldn't directly speak to people across long distances, that ceiling lights didn't make every room bright, or that we didn't have our information and media automatically filtered by machines. Such is the presence algorithmic feeds now have in our lives; the algorithm is often unconsidered, part of the furniture, noticed only when it doesn't function in the way it's supposed to, like traffic lights or running water.

## CATCHING ALGORITHMIC ANXIETY

If the chess-playing Mechanical Turk was an (illusionary) encounter with miraculous technology that made decisions independent of a human hand centuries ago, we now undergo that experience dozens of times a day, in the digital spaces that we are accustomed to relying on. It's hard to overstate the ubiquity of machine influence. From what we can tell using public metrics, Facebook today has nearly three billion users. Instagram has around two billion. TikTok has over one billion. Spotify has over 500 million. Twitter has 400 million. Netflix has over 200 million. For all the people on these platforms, every interaction, every moment of passive consumption, is mediated by algorithmic recommendations. Even if some users can opt out of an algorithmic feed, their participation contributes to the data that fuels other users' recommendations. The dragnet is inescapable. Social networks and streaming services have become the primary way a significant percentage of the global population metabolizes information, whether it's music, entertainment, or art. We now live in an era of algorithmic culture.

Technology companies have long sought to achieve this massive scale. Monopolistic growth is more important to these entities than the quality of user experience and certainly more important than the equitable distribution of culture through the services' feeds. (A digital platform has none of the curatorial responsibility of, say, an art museum.) According to Silicon Valley ideology, the pursuit of scale far outweighs any negative consequence it might have, as a memo written by Andrew Bosworth, a deputy of Mark Zuckerberg's at Facebook, demonstrated in 2016:

> So we connect more people. That can be bad if they make it negative. Maybe it costs someone a life by exposing them to bullies. Maybe someone dies in a terrorist attack coordinated on our tools. And still we connect people. The ugly truth is that we believe in connecting people so deeply that anything that allows us to connect more people more often is *de-facto* good.

That statement is a stark illustration of the attitude that if people are using a platform, staying engaged and active, then it counts as successful—no matter what they are doing. That ongoing engagement is sustained by automated recommendations, delivering the next provocative news headline or hypnotic entertainment release. Today, it is difficult to think of creating a piece of culture that is separate from algorithmic feeds, because those feeds control how it will be exposed to billions of consumers in the international digital audience. Without the feeds, there is no audience—the creation would exist only for its creator and their direct connections. And it is even more difficult to think of consuming something outside of algorithmic feeds, because their recommendations inevitably influence what is shown on television, played on the radio, and published in books, even if those experiences are not contained within feeds. Filterworld spills out everywhere.

Trevor Boffone, a scholar of theater who took up work as a high school teacher, gave me an apt description of what algorithmic culture amounts to: "The films that do well are films that have TikTok followings; the Billboard Hot 100 is dictated by TikTok; you go to Barnes and Noble and you see a BookTok table," he said. (BookTok is a term for TikTok's community of literary influencers.) In other words, for a piece of culture to be commercially successful, it must already have traction on digital platforms. Boffone's career, too, has been shaped by algorithmic feeds. When he began learning TikTok dance moves with his teenage students and posting videos of them online, he quickly accrued hundreds of thousands of followers on

Instagram and other platforms. He appeared on national television, briefly becoming a viral character—the dancing teacher. Following his experiences, he published an academic monograph on dance performance, a subject that had quickly become more compelling to universities and editors with its rising public popularity on TikTok. "I've had more interest in one month of this year in my work than in the previous ten years combined," Boffone told me.

Boffone's experience follows a fundamental rule of Filterworld: Under algorithmic feeds, the popular becomes more popular, and the obscure becomes even less visible. Success or failure is accelerated. "A traditional Instagram post, the life of it is dictated by the first three to five minutes of the post," Boffone said. If a post gets engagement immediately, then it's likely to get more, and vice versa. This dynamic can be cruel. When I post an offbeat Instagram image or an obscure tweet and it doesn't get much action, that doesn't stop me from checking back multiple times for more likes, even though I know I haven't hit the algorithmic jackpot.

The absence of attention inevitably raises the question of what the feed *will* promote, tacitly encouraging safer choices, urging conformity. Who receives promotion is also a problem. It's often not the original creators of a meme or trend who get credit, attention, and thus financial gain from its popularity in an algorithmic feed. TikTok choreography itself is an example. The TikTok influencer Charli D'Amelio became famous in 2019 for her dance videos on the platform. But one of the moves she popularized and was often credited with, called the Renegade, was actually created earlier by Jalaiah Harmon, a Black teenager from Georgia. The Renegade was a series of front-facing movements perfect for the TikTok screen, with swinging punches and hip shakes—not too difficult a sequence, but also tough to memorize and thus rewarding to re-perform.

Harmon first posted the dance on an app called Funimate as well as Instagram. But TikTok's hyper-algorithmic feed accelerated it to mainstream fame, seeded by D'Amelio's following, even as it helped to erase Harmon's authorship, since D'Amelio didn't cite her. Content creators from marginalized groups, who don't have the same access to media and attention as, say, a white, private-school-educated, professionally trained dancer, like D'Amelio, have a harder time benefiting from the tides of Filterworld. (Since being recognized for her work, Harmon herself has gained three million TikTok followers.)

Given that these capricious systems control so many facets of our lives, from socializing with our friends to building audiences for our creative projects, is it any wonder that social media users feel paranoid? We're encouraged to overlook algorithmic processes, but their glitches remind us of their unearned authority. The ambiguity of algorithmic influence creates a feeling that has been labeled "algorithmic anxiety." Algorithmic anxiety describes the burgeoning awareness that we must constantly contend with automated technological processes beyond our understanding and control, whether in our Facebook feeds, Google Maps driving directions, or Amazon product promotions. We are forever anticipating and second-guessing the decisions that algorithms make. Algorithmic anxiety is not hypothetical or an abstraction: It's already prevalent. Technology companies are aware of it and have been manipulating the feeling in their users for years.

In 2018, Shagun Jhaver, at the time a PhD candidate at the Georgia Institute of Technology, worked with two Airbnb employees to conduct a sociological study of the company's users. They analyzed how the platform's hosts—who rented out their homes on the service for income—interacted with and felt about Airbnb's algorithmic recommendation, search, and ratings systems, which helped renters find and book their listings. Jhaver and the other researchers coined the term *algorithmic anxiety* for the hosts' "uncertainty about how Airbnb algorithms work and a perceived lack of control," the team wrote in their findings. Hosts worried that the search algorithm was unfairly ignoring them or prioritizing other properties. Jhaver noticed that the anxiety was ascribed more to the technology than the quality of the actual homes the hosts were renting out: "It was particularly to do with the algorithm itself rather than improving their listing and property in other ways," he told me.

Airbnb forces a "double negotiation" for the hosts, the researchers wrote, because they must determine what their guests are looking for in a listing as well as which variables the algorithms are prioritizing to promote their property more often. But hosts could not tell which variables actually boosted their listing. They believed factors like the number of reviews accrued, the quality of reviews, and the number of photos available would help their chances of promotion, but they were less certain as to whether the algorithm analyzed their pricing, home amenities, or length of tenure as a host. They had little information about how the systems worked. It was all a matter of perception. As one host in the study complained: "It's frustrating seeing the search: lots of listings that are worse than mine are in higher positions."

Quality is subjective, of course, but the host's sentiment speaks to how users can feel misunderstood and misjudged by algorithmic evaluations. "It's like an exam, but you don't know what's going to be on this exam, or how to score well on this exam," Jhaver explained. And it's not just the users who don't know what's going on. Jhaver continued: "At the end of the day, even the people who create the algorithms cannot tell you which factor was responsible for which decision; the complexity of the algorithm is so high that disentangling different factors is just not possible."

Failing to game the algorithm may cause an immediate drop in income for hosts, which they, as any worker, rely on remaining consistent. (The inconsistency of algorithmic promotion forces us to engage with it and stress about it even more, like repeatedly pulling a slot machine lever to hit the jackpot.) Gig-economy platforms like Airbnb have long promised flexible work and alternative ways of making or supplementing a living, but they also created a new form of labor in the need to stay up to date on changes in algorithmic priorities. Where hosts worry about Airbnb's search algorithm, artists similarly fret about Instagram's and musicians about Spotify's. The hosts' reaction to such algorithmic anxiety, the researchers found, was to develop "folk theories"—superstitious tricks that were meant to goose more algorithmic promotion and better search results—the same way I used to post my article links with fake wedding announcements. Some of the strategies included constantly updating their listings calendar, changing their profile details, and even opening the Airbnb website more often throughout the day. The tricks bring to mind a child putting a spoon under their pillow to cause a snow day and are perhaps equally as effective. As the researchers found, hosts "usually had doubts about whether such theories were true but despite their uncertainty still performed those actions in an attempt to influence the algorithm."

Algorithmic anxiety is something of a contemporary plague. It induces an OCD-ish tendency in many users toward hyperaware-ness and the need to repeat the same rituals, because when these rituals "work," the effect is so compelling, resulting in both a psychological dopamine rush from receiving attention and a potential economic reward if your online presence is monetized. It undergirds so many of our behaviors online: selecting the right profile picture, curating an attractive grid of photos on an Instagram account, choosing the right keywords on a marketplace listing. We worry that our posts either won't be seen by the right people or will be seen by too many if selected for virality, exposing us to strangers. There's an emotional fallout to this quest for attention: we end up both overstimulated and numb, much like a glassy-eyed slots player waiting for matching symbols to come up.

Algorithmic anxiety happens because there is a dramatically asymmetrical relationship between user and algorithm. For the individual user, trying to predict or dictate the outcome of the algorithm is like trying to control the tide. To continue the metaphor, all users can do is surf the wave that's already formed. There is little incentive for companies to assuage this anxiety because a user's confusion can be beneficial to business. When a company's product is ineffective or a user encounters difficulty, it can be blamed on the opaque entity of "the algorithm," which is perceived as external to both the users and the company itself, since they are likened to opaque "black boxes." Exploitation is disguised as an accidental glitch instead of an intentional corporate policy. In reality, a company like Facebook is wholly in control of their algorithmic systems, able to change them at will—or turn them off.

Algorithmic anxiety places the burden of action on the individual, not the business—the user must change their behavior or risk disappearing. Users sometimes complain of being "shadowbanned" when their posts or content on a platform suddenly lack the same level of engagement as before. Users often fear that their account specifically has been blocked without warning or recourse by some decision-maker; but the algorithmic priorities may simply have silently changed, and traffic is no longer flowing in their direction. The effect goes back to the Mechanical Turk; we can't always tell the difference between technology working and the *illusion* of technology working, but the perception may be just as impactful, in the end, as the reality.

In her 2019 dissertation titled *Algorithmic Anxiety in Contemporary Art,* the scholar Patricia de Vries defined algorithmic anxiety as a condition in which "the possible self is perceived to be circumscribed, bounded, and governed by algorithmic regimes." Her words feel breathtakingly accurate. The possibilities that we perceive for ourselves—our modes of expression and creation—now exist within the structures of digital platforms. The consequences of such anxiety include "algorithmic determinism, fatalism, cynicism, and nihilism," de Vries wrote. It builds to a sense that, since we users cannot control the technology, we may as well succumb to the limits of algorithmic culture and view it as inevitable. Many users have already entered such a state of despair, both dissatisfied and unable to imagine an alternative.

De Vries began observing this cultural shift as early as 2013, when she saw several museum exhibitions highlighting the work of artists who were critical of automated surveillance and data collection. While algorithmic feeds had only just begun entering mainstream experience, events like the 2010 Flash Crash, caused by algorithmic stock trading, and technology like facial recognition had implanted the word in news headlines. By the middle of the decade, when she developed her research, it became "this sort of object of our fascination," de Vries told me. The algorithm was a specter that haunted any encounter with digital platforms and their increasingly intrusive presence in our lives. That is not to say we understood what exactly algorithms were doing, per se: "Just as the fear of heights is not about heights, algorithmic anxiety is not simply about algorithms," de Vries said.

To move forward, we must disentangle the effects of algorithmic recommendations as technology from the ways that we have habitually adopted them as the primary gatekeepers of our online communication. Algorithms, after all, are inextricable from the data they run on, which has been created and is constantly refreshed by humans. Actual influence coexists with the fear of influence, which is equally manipulative. Algorithms entered our lives by promising to make decisions for us, to anticipate our thoughts and desires. Filterworld represents the establishment of the psychic world of algorithms—not just how they work, but how we users have come to rely on them, allowing them to displace our own agency, even as we come to resent their looming presence.

- - -

# CHAPTER 2

# The Disruption of Personal Taste

## THE AMAZON BOOKSTORE

One afternoon, in Washington, D.C., I walked southeast to George-town, which is one of the city's main shopping hubs. Its cobble-stoned streets and main thoroughfare by the river form something like an outdoor mall, with cutesy restaurants and cupcake bakeries sprinkled among the retail outlets of international fashion brands: Nike, Lululemon, Zara, Club Monaco. Shoppers gravitate to which-ever brands suit them best, perhaps based on a particular aesthetic or an implied lifestyle. The brand a customer picks says as much about them as it does about the brand—it's a reciprocal relation-ship between creator and customer, with the customer believing (or hoping) that the brand's ethos is representative of their own identity. A shopper doesn't go to Nike just because they want good running shoes; Nike casts an aura of youth and energy over everything it pro-duces, whether sneakers or brightly screen-printed T-shirts. Zara makes dresses, among many other clothing items, and through them projects a sense of cutting-edge style without the cost of traditional luxury brands. To buy a Zara dress is to participate in its image of efficient glamour—a nightly party. Every piece in the store refers to that sensibility. In other words, each store serves a particular sen-sibility, and consumers select from them based on their individual tastes.

But one Georgetown store stood out as different: Amazon Books, a brick-and-mortar bookstore operated by the enormous Internet corporation. Amazon began building physical bookstores in 2015, with its first location in Seattle. When it opened in D.C. in 2018, it was strange to stumble across its sans serif logo out in the real world (this was before its trucks became omnipresent on city streets and highways). The bookstore's interior was also unfamiliar. When I walked in for the first time, I was struck by the visual chaos—it didn't have a bookstore's usual atmosphere of meditative calm. Instead, it more closely resembled a grocery store. All the book covers were facing outward, side by side on the shelf like so many digital icons. And each book had a digital label below it showing its respective rank on the Amazon site, with numbers determined by user reviews, volume of sales, and even how many pages buyers of the book read through, a metric measured digitally by Amazon's Kindle e-readers.

The arrangement of the physical store followed the design of its website, with the "most popular" titles featured prominently up front. The books were not organized by author, their author's nationality, or even consistently by genre, but rather by how successful they were online—that was the algorithm Amazon Books used for determining the quality and value of literature. Engagement reigned supreme once again. Signs posted around the store explained why certain books were shown off: they were "top sellers," or they were rated "4.5 Stars & Above," or even "4.8 Stars & Above." Did the extra 0.3 stars on average really indicate that much about a book's worthiness? Other titles were "Most-Wished-For on Amazon.com" or else highlighted by how many preorders they had received online. Some walls of shelves were arranged into an analog recommendation system. On the left side of each shelf was a single book, labeled "If You Like ←," with a selection of books to the right, "You'll Love →." For example, Noah Harari's *Sapiens* spurred a recommendation of other nonfiction bestsellers like Jared Diamond's *Guns, Germs, and Steel* and Peter Frankopan's *The Silk Roads*. Most remarkable of all, however, was that each book was priced according to Amazon's website algorithm, which adjusts prices in real time based on supply and demand.

This was the opposite of independent bookstores, which have a well-deserved reputation for charm and personal quirkiness. Their shelf labels are unique or offbeat, presenting specialties: New Age, art monographs, local history. Their owners know their local clientele, subtly shaping the stock to reflect it. Some books may not sell particularly well, but the owners choose to keep them on display as a demonstration of the store's ideals and their personal taste.

It was hard to discern a sense of taste in Amazon Books; there was no spirit there with which I could identify. Instead, the overall narrative was driven wholly by the market and whatever provoked attention. The aesthetics on display were yoked to the need for superficial, immediate engagement, perhaps part of the reason for the late-2010s vogue for novel covers made up of brightly colored, semi-abstract, semi-figurative blobs. (They may have been eye-catching, but had nothing to do with the novels' content.) Though the Amazon store stocked many of the same books as other bookshops I frequented, the environment was unrecognizable and alienating. I couldn't see myself as a buyer, not only because of Amazon's destructive practices as an employer and as a monopolistic corporation, but because there was no coherent idea of an imagined shopper.

Like many things that operate at the scale of the Internet, the bookstore was inhuman. It made recommendations based on the mass of data produced by all Amazon customers. It was as if you could buy only the books that appeared on the *New York Times* bestseller list, but the list was operated by an untrustworthy company, one solely devoted to treating books as fungible objects to be offloaded as quickly as possible. Amazon measured books by sales the way Facebook evaluates content by likes, an approach antithetical to my romantic vision of a bookstore as a place to escape, to discover something new and surprising.

One reason the Amazon bookstore felt so strange was that it represented a blatant intrusion of the Internet's algorithmic logic into what we call "real life." We're bombarded by suggestions for songs, images, and television shows online; it's easy to accept the recommendations and the automatic mediation of algorithms when the experience happens on a screen, because these suggestions are so frictionless, fast, and unavoidable. But they are much more obtrusive when they take place in the physical world, where our choices are rarely dictated so obviously by machines. Maybe the Amazon store's uncanniness stemmed from how it confronted me with my own lack of freedom, demonstrating just how much algorithms push us into not thinking for ourselves.

The bookstore selection driven by the average of all of Amazon's data was curiously homogenous and ultimately boring. It had been aggressively filtered in advance to appeal to me—or at least myself as a generic consumer—with abundant reassurances that *other people* did like the books on display. But I wasn't excited or encouraged to page through any of them. Rather, I was overwhelmed, which might be the default state of consumers in Filterworld: surrounded by superabundant content, but inspired by none of it.

A joke written on Twitter by a Google engineer named Chet Haase in 2017 pinpoints the problem: "A machine learning algorithm walks into a bar. The bartender asks, 'What'll you have?' The algorithm says, 'What's everyone else having?'" The punch line is that in algorithmic culture, the right choice is always what the majority of other people have already chosen. But even if everyone else was, maybe you're just not in the mood for a whiskey sour.

My favorite bookstore has long been McNally Jackson, a collection of New York City–area stores whose first location was in SoHo (in 2023, the original flagship relocated six blocks away). Though it wasn't in any way personalized, it always felt like the store was there for me personally, like it understood what I was looking for, because its stock was both so broad and so specific. During my decade living in Brooklyn, I often took the L train into Manhattan and then the 6 downtown, walking the leafy streets to the McNally storefront, through the glass door into the vestibule, and then into the contained sprawl of the shop. Two equally sized tables in front formed its nucleus: on the left, a table for nonfiction, and on the right, fiction, with corresponding sets of shelves behind them. Many of the books stacked on display were recent releases, but there was also a selection of the books the store's staff decided were worth a closer look, a collective act of curation. An academic work of philosophy from a small press was nestled next to popular nonfiction; the fiction table didn't just hold novels but poetry, zines, fictionalized memoirs, and hybrid-genre books. The arrangements always seemed to say: *Just trust us.*

The contents of the McNally tables shifted on a weekly basis.

Behind each rearrangement I felt the hand that selected the book, an individual intelligence, rather than a singular formula. Browsing was a way of discovering new things; one could argue that Amazon's formula of "if you like this, you'll like that" functions similarly, but the connections at McNally were less direct and literal. They expanded the shopper's idea of what a particular category could contain.

If the Amazon bookstore represented the triumph of algorithmic logic, then McNally was the pinnacle of human tastemakers, the word we often use for the people who sort and select the culture that we consume. Booksellers are tastemakers, but so are librarians who recommend titles for their patrons, professional buyers for lifestyle boutiques, radio-station DJs, movie booking agents who advocate on behalf of films to theaters nationwide, and concert programmers who book bands for venues. These tastemakers all provide an interface between the creators of culture and its consumers. They constantly gather and judge new material to determine how and why it may resonate with audiences—a process that now falls under the broad banner of the word *curation*.

It's easy to overlook the fact that when consuming content through digital platforms, what we see at a given moment is determined more directly by equations than such tastemakers. With Netflix's home page, Facebook's feed, and Spotify's automated radio, there is no direct influence from editor, DJ, or booker, but, rather, a mathematical processing of crowdsourced data stretching to encompass every user on the site. The curation, such as it is, is automated, scaled up until it's beyond the grasp of any individual person. Through our algorithmic feeds, we get only the Amazon retail experience, not the McNally curatorial eye.

## GOOD TASTE

The "taste" of tastemakers means personal preference, the discernment that we all apply to figure out what we like, whether in music, fashion, food, or literature. We make constant decisions to listen to, read, or wear one thing instead of another. These choices are intimate, reflecting our ephemeral moods and the slow building of our individual sensibilities—of our senses of self.

Everyone has friends who they think of as having "good taste." My friend Mark, for instance, works as a theater designer but also has an enviable knowledge of music—it's not his job; it's his passion. Though many people leave the habit behind in adolescence and just recycle their past favorites, Mark listens to each buzzy new band and determines whether it's worth sharing with friends. Every few months, I ask him for a handful of suggestions. I don't always like all the albums he picks, but I know there's something worthwhile to listen for in the music. I trust his judgment, and he knows enough about my personal taste to determine which music might suit me best.

In other cases, there's the friend who always knows the right wine to bring to dinner, the friend tuned into the most relevant fashion brands, or the friend who recommends television shows worth watching. *Taste* is a word for how we measure culture and judge our relationship to it. If something suits our taste, we feel close to it and identify with it, as well as form relationships with other people based on it, the way customers commune over clothing labels (either loving or hating a particular brand). Intentionally bad taste might be just as compelling as good taste, as the author Rax King described in her book *Tacky:* "Tackiness is joyfulness." But in its origins, taste is a much deeper philosophical concept. It borders on morality, representing an innate sense of what is good in the world.

In the 1750s, taste was tackled in a French encyclopedia entry with notes from the philosophers Voltaire and Montesquieu, who together offer a good basis for its Western conception. Voltaire wrote, "In order to have taste, it is not enough to see and to know what is beautiful in a given work. One must feel beauty and be moved by it. It is not even enough to feel, to be moved in a vague way: it is essential to discern the different shades of feeling." Taste goes beyond superficial observation, beyond identifying something as "cool." Taste requires experiencing the creation in its entirety and evaluating one's own authentic emotional response to it, parsing its effect. (Taste is not passive; it requires effort.) Montesquieu, who was a baron and a judge in addition to a public intellectual, contributed "An Essay Upon Taste, in Subjects of Nature, and of Art," a literary sketch that was left unfinished when he died in 1755.

It's a beautiful, meandering piece of writing on what delights the soul. Taste, according to Montesquieu, "is nothing else but an ability of discovering, with delicacy and quickness, the degree of pleasure which every thing ought to give to man."

"Natural taste is not a theoretical knowledge," Montesquieu continued, "it's a quick and exquisite application of rules which we do not even know." The latter part of that statement strikes me: Taste is an abstract, ineffable, unstable thing. A listener to music or reader of a book cannot truly tell if they will enjoy something before they experience it; pleasure in a piece of art is never guaranteed. So when encountering an artwork, we immediately evaluate it by some set of mental principles, and, hopefully, find the beauty in it, feel affirmed, even if we can't quite describe what that beauty is or how exactly we determined it in the first place. Taste is supposed to be ambiguous. As the Italian philosopher Giorgio Agamben summarized in his 1979 monograph on taste, "Taste enjoys beauty, without being able to explain it."

Taste is a fundamental part of the self; developing or indulging it means constructing a firmer sense of self. It becomes the basis for identity. In 1906, the Japanese writer Okakura Kakuzo wrote *The Book of Tea,* a way of enshrining Japanese taste and communicating it, in English, to his friends and patrons in the United States, a group that included the art collector Isabella Stewart Gardner. Art itself was not meant to be generic or cater to a broad audience, Okakura argued in a discussion of tearoom design: "That the tearoom should be built to suit some individual taste is an enforcement of the principle of vitality in art." Okakura recounted the story of a statement by the seventeenth-century artist Kobori Enshiu. Speaking to his disciples, Enshiu complimented a fellow tea master's collection of tea ceremony implements precisely because few others appreciated them: "The great Rikiu dared to love only those objects which personally appealed to him, whereas I unconsciously cater to the taste of the majority." Enshiu derided his own taste as too mainstream to be truly great. Yet catering to "the taste of the majority" might be the single goal of algorithmic feeds—a majority based on data.

Taste is not necessarily wholly positive or efficient. In 1930 the Japanese philosopher Kuki Shuzo wrote an essay attempting to define a Japanese cultural value called *iki,* which amounted to a kind of urbane world-weariness, a pronounced ambivalence in all aspects of life. (W. David Marx, an American writer and friend of mine long living in Tokyo, compared it to aspects of New England WASPiness.) Love, money, and beauty could all be as easily lost as gained, and gaining may not always be better than losing. Absence must be appreciated as much as presence. "Iki is understood as a superior form of taste," Kuki wrote.

Montesquieu crucially argued that surprise, which can be alienating or challenging, like a particularly ugly wabi-sabi Japanese tea vessel, is a fundamental element of taste. "Something can surprise us because it excites wonder, or because it is new or unexpected," he wrote—it exists outside the realm of what we already know we like. "Our soul often experiences pleasure when it feels something it cannot analyze, or when an object appears quite different from what it knows it to be." Understanding this feeling of surprise can take time. Taste is not necessarily instantaneous and changes as you consider and digest the experience of an artwork: "We become aware of the presence of great beauty when something inspires us with a surprise which at first is only mild, but which continues, increases, and finally turns into admiration."

Citing the work of the Renaissance Italian painter Raphael, Montesquieu described the slow burn of a powerful artwork, whose elegance might emerge unexpectedly from initial subtlety. For me, it brings to mind Frank Ocean's 2016 album *Blonde,* which was released four years after his debut album *Channel Orange.* At first, I overlooked it. The tracks didn't sound like individual songs, more a wash of synthesized sound, and the lyrics were vague to the point of inscrutability, emotion only veiled and auto-tuned. But as I kept listening, pulled along by some undefinable quality within the music, I came to realize that the album's abstraction was the point, its elusiveness a portrait of modern alienation and the need to keep living despite it. Of course, *Blonde* was a major popular masterpiece of the early twenty-first century, a bestseller. But the album and the musician alike didn't play by the rules of algorithmic feeds.

If taste indeed must be deeply felt, requires time to engage with, and benefits from the surprise that comes from the unfamiliar, then it seems that technology could not possibly replicate it, because algorithmic feeds run counter to these fundamental qualities. When recommendation algorithms are based only on data about what you and other platform users already like, then these algorithms are less capable of providing the kind of surprise that might not be immediately pleasurable, that Montesquieu described. The feed structure also discourages users from spending too much time with any one piece of content. If you find something boring, perhaps too subtle, you just keep scrolling, and there's no time for a greater sense of admiration to develop—one is increasingly encouraged to lean into impatience and superficiality in all things. As the Korean philosopher Byung-Chul Han argued in his 2017 book *In the Swarm,* the sheer exposure of so many people to each other online without barriers—the "demediatization" of the Internet—makes "language and culture flatten out and become vulgar."

Building your own sense of taste, that set of subconscious principles by which you identify what you like, is an uphill battle compared to passively consuming whatever content feeds deliver to you. But the situation can't solely be blamed on the presence of algorithms. Today we have more cultural options available to us than ever and they are accessible on demand. We are free to choose anything. Yet the choice we often make is to not have a choice, to have our purview shaped by automated feeds, which may be based on the aggregate *actions* of humans but are *not* human in themselves.

In some ways, this shift to algorithms is convenient. It's tiring to interrogate your preferences all the time: researching which new cultural products are available to you; reading magazines or requesting book suggestions from friends; and making decisions about what and where to eat. It's a luxury form of labor that eighteenth-century French philosophers may have had plenty of time for, but in the much faster-paced contemporary world, most of us cannot afford. (Montesquieu didn't have Instagram to distract him from contemplating Raphael canvases.) Following the suggestions of the Netflix home page, for example, offers a shortcut.

Taste can also feel more like a cause for concern than a source of personal fulfillment. A selection made based on your own personal taste might be embarrassing if it unwittingly clashes with the norms of the situation at hand, like wearing athleisure to the office or bright colors to a somber funeral. I find myself mortified when I pick out a previously unexplored bar or restaurant for a group of friends, a choice I think will be a crowd-pleaser, and it turns out to have entirely the wrong vibe. (One such bar in D.C. turned out to have too many taxidermy animal heads on the walls for comfort.) In that situation, an automated recommendation from Yelp or Google Maps may have suited me better: the proof of democratic, average approval takes the pressure off making a choice that may prove too quirky. Yet at the same time, I wouldn't want those lowest-common-denominator rules to determine which books I read or television shows I watch. Culture isn't a toaster that you can rate out of five stars—though the website Goodreads, now owned by Amazon, tries to apply those ratings to books. There are plenty of experiences I love—a plotless novel like Rachel Cusk's *Outline,* for example—that others would doubtless give a bad grade. But those are the rules that Filterworld enforces for everything.

As taste requires surprise, it also thrives on challenge and risk, treading too far in a particular direction. Safety may avoid embarrassment, but it's also boring. Over the twentieth century, taste became less a philosophical concept concerning the quality of art than a parallel to industrial-era consumerism, a way to judge what to buy and judge others for what they buy in turn. This phenomenon— conforming too much with popular taste and thus insulating yourself from having a more inspiring, personal encounter with culture—is depicted in Georges Perec's 1965 novella *Things.* The story concerns a couple in their early twenties, Jerome and Sylvie, who work as marketing researchers, interviewing consumers with questions like "Why are pure-suction vacuum cleaners selling so poorly? What do people of modest origin think of chicory?" The couple are human data collectors. Their personal desires also resemble the results of a marketing survey: they like what they are supposed to like. Perec's sketch of their fictional aspirational apartment includes jade ashtrays, cane-seated chairs, Toile de Jouy wallpaper, Swedish lamps, and Paul Klee drawings. I admit, it still sounds nice to me today.

Yet the image of perfection entails a degree of emptiness. When taste is too standardized, it is degraded. "Their still-wavering taste, their over-hesitant meticulousness, their lack of experience, their rather blinkered respect for what they believed to be the standards of true good taste, brought them some jarring moments, some humiliations," Perec wrote. Such as when Jerome attempts to follow the fashion of the day by dressing like an English gentleman but succeeds only in a "continental caricature" of it, appearing like a "recent emigrant on a modest salary." He also wears through a pair of elegant British shoes by wearing them too often. Jerome and Sylvie have an idea of what they should like, but they don't quite understand why or how. Consumption without taste is just undiluted, accelerated capitalism.

There are two forces forming our tastes. As I described previously, the first is our independent pursuit of what we individually enjoy, while the second is our awareness of what it appears that most other people like, the dominant mainstream. The two may move in opposite directions, but it's often easier to follow the latter, particularly when the Internet makes what other people are consuming so immediately public. (If you didn't post about it, did you really watch a TV show?) Algorithmic feeds further reinforce the presence of that mainstream, against which our personal choices are evaluated. Taste is inescapable; it involves "the most everyday choices of everyday life, e.g., in cooking, clothing, or decoration," the French sociologist Pierre Bourdieu wrote in his 1984 book *Distinction: A Social Critique of the Judgement of Taste*. These choices can be symbolic of a range of things beyond just our aesthetic preferences, such as economic class, political ideology, and social identity. "Taste classifies, and it classifies the classifier," Bourdieu wrote. No wonder that we worry about what to like, and sometimes find it simpler to export that responsibility to machines.

Amazon created a device that was meant to approximate taste. It was called the Amazon Echo Look, and it could make all your fashion decisions for you. I tried it out after it launched in 2017. The Echo Look was a small white cylinder made of plastic raised up on a little arm, with a camera at its center like the lone eye of a cyclops. It was advertised as a means to take easy selfies of your entire outfit— simply stand the device on a shelf, then use voice commands to tell it to take a photo, while jauntily posing. The photo was then sent to your phone and stored in an app that built an encyclopedia of your wardrobe—you could scroll through your own clothes as if they were a private Instagram account (not unlike Cher Horowitz in *Clueless*). But the camera also judged your clothes with a function called "Style Check," using a combination of algorithmic analysis and human workers (recall Amazon's faux-automated Mechanical Turk) to tell you if the garments matched or if the combination was fashionable.

To see how the Echo evaluated style, I tried wearing two different T-shirt and jeans outfits—one set all black and the other all gray—standing in front of the Echo Look like it was my mother before picture day at elementary school. When I compared the two ensembles with Style Check, the black clothes fared better, scoring 73 percent stylish, out of the possible 100, while the gray outfit got only the remaining 27 percent. The system gave little explanation for the score: "The way you styled those pieces looks better," it said. Maybe monochrome black is an established fashion trope, whereas monochrome gray is less pleasing and thus more radical? I couldn't tell.

Other pithy judgments included "Better color combination" and "The shape of the outfit works better." Style Check also informed me that when wearing an oxford shirt, rolled-up sleeves are better than buttoned at the wrist, and popping your collar is a good idea (contrary to my own perception of taste, established in middle school rebelling against the peak of Abercrombie fashion). Blue denim is the best choice for jeans, according to Echo Look's algorithm. It offered evaluation, but no holistic understanding nor grounding in emotion. Style Check simply compared your choices to the net average of data in its archives. Your taste in fashion was best when it followed everyone else's. What's more, the Echo Look also offered instant purchases of clothing that matched its ideal dress code, sold by Amazon, of course, which profited from its vision of algorithmic averageness.

This is a bottom-up model of cultural preferences at odds with both the personal definition of taste and the pre-Internet system of tastemakers, individuals who handpicked what was cool and imposed it on everyone else. The hierarchy is best depicted in a scene—and now meme—from the 2006 film *The Devil Wears Prada*. Meryl Streep plays a facsimile of the *Vogue* editor in chief Anna Wintour, while Anne Hathaway is her naive assistant who is just learning the ropes of fashion media. In one moment, Hathaway wears a chunky blue sweater that she picked up on a whim at a department store sale, seemingly less for its stylishness than for its convenience. But Streep tells her that the decision was dictated for her well in advance, by fashion editors like herself. Streep's monologue is imperious: "That blue represents millions of dollars and countless jobs, and it's sort of comical how you think you made a choice that exempts you from the fashion industry when, in fact, you're wearing a sweater that was selected for you by the people in this room from a pile of 'stuff,'" Streep says. Human tastemakers picked it out.

Taste, in the end, is its own kind of algorithm that classifies things as good or bad. The equation that it is based on factors in personal preferences, preconceptions absorbed from marketing, and social symbolism, as well as the immediate experience of a piece of culture, and eventually produces a personal answer for whether you find the thing at hand enjoyable or repulsive. So it can be difficult to distinguish that organic social code from the software code of recommendation algorithms, though it is vital to do so.

Should the human fashion editor tell you what to like or should it be the algorithmic machine, in the form of the Amazon bookstore, Spotify feed, or Netflix home page? That is the central dilemma of culture in Filterworld. The former option is mercurial and driven by elite gatekeepers, a powerful group built up over a century of modern cultural industries, riddled with their own blind spots and biases including those of gender and race. (That group includes not just the mostly white fashion magazine editors of New York City but also Hollywood producers, record-label executives, and museum curators.) Yet the human flaws may become even more dramatic in an algorithmic ecosystem when the actions of mass audiences dictate what can easily be seen. Racism, sexism, and other forms of bias are a de facto part of that equation.

Online, users are often insulated from views and cultures that clash with their own. The overall digital environment is dictated by tech companies with ruthlessly capitalist, expansionary motives, which do not provide the most fertile ground for culture. While the magazine fashion editor may periodically use their ability to pick out and promote a previously unheard voice, the algorithmic feed never will; it can only iterate on established engagement. We users have less chance of encountering a shockingly new thing and deciding for ourselves if we like it. Fashion, to take one example, is often strongest as an art form when it doesn't follow the rules and chase averages. Part of its appeal lies in breaking with the social code: wearing something unexpected or strange, even at times challenging your own taste. It's something that no automated recommendation alone can approximate. Algorithmic feeds are a double-edged sword: A marginalized fashion designer might find a way to game the Instagram algorithm and spark their own popularity without waiting to be noticed by a white editor who might be biased against them. But they are then conforming to the tenets of a tech company even more powerful and more blinkered than the editor.

The Amazon Echo Look may have been an algorithmic bridge too far. Reviewers appreciated the device's innovation, more as a plain camera than a style aid. But it never became a popular product. In 2020, Amazon announced that the device was going to be discontinued and the camera and attendant app would cease functioning entirely. The company aimed to "apply AI and machine learning to fashion," an attendant statement said. The Style Check function was integrated into the Amazon shopping app. Perhaps its ultimate goal of collecting data about our tastes, to be leveraged in some future application with a perfected recommendation algorithm, was achieved after all.

## THE NORMALIZATION OF TASTE

The force of algorithmic pressure is not theoretical. It's not a gloomy dystopian future but, rather, a pervading force that is already influencing cultural consumers and creators. On the consumer side, the bombardment of recommendations can induce a kind of hypnosis that makes listening to, watching, or buying a product all but inevitable—whether it truly aligns with your taste or not. I noticed precisely that happening in an advice column published by the fashion critic Rachel Tashjian in her email newsletter *Opulent Tips*. Valerie Peter, a woman in her early twenties, had written to Tashjian in 2022, complaining that algorithmic feeds had made it harder to figure out her own style preferences. "I've been on the internet for the last 10 years and I don't know if I like what I like or what an algorithm wants me to like," Peter wrote, expressing an acute case of algorithmic anxiety. Instagram, TikTok, and Pinterest all felt like dead ends. "I want things I truly like, not what is being lowkey marketed to me," she ended her letter. I got in touch with Peter to find out what exactly had caused this crisis of taste, and we ended up discussing how the rise of social media fundamentally changed our relationship to culture.

At the time, Peter was finishing graduate school in electrical engineering and was living where she went to school, in Manchester, England. As a child, moving between Nigeria and Britain, she had been deeply interested in fashion and followed all the runway shows. Friends told her she should be a fashion writer, but she decided to pursue a more financially stable route and keep her passions for personal enjoyment. She had been on the Internet since an early age and joined Facebook in 2011, as a tween. Gradually, social media had come to feel inescapable; particularly during the pandemic, Peter began relying heavily on it as a connection to the outside world. "It has kind of slipped into real life as well," Peter said. Lately, trend cycles have accelerated into "microtrends" that come and go in a matter of weeks; she feels like she's missing out when friends cite a meme or video she hasn't seen. (The anxiety of not keeping up with the algorithm.)

In late 2021, Peter got caught up in one microtrend. A fad of leg warmers, fuzzy fabric tubes pulled up to the knee, suddenly took over her feeds—her Instagram explore page, TikTok "For You" feed, and Pinterest recommendations, all at once. It wasn't paid advertising, and yet it was everywhere. Before she was exposed to them online, Peter told me, "I would never think about leg warmers. I thought they were ugly, hideous, ridiculous." But soon enough she found herself buying a pair online with the click of a button, on an almost subconscious whim—"magically," she said. The purchase ultimately didn't change her mind; Peter wore the ill-fated leg warmers only a few times before she stashed them at the back of her closet. Buying them was "a choice that I'm not even sure I made," she said.

The algorithmic influence had felt invasive in social media feeds that she believed were largely organic, the way blatant product placement might intrude on an otherwise absorbing movie. Still, just like the Generic Coffee Shops I encountered around the world, no one entity had forced all the various influencers and platforms to conform to the trend; embracing leg warmers was simply a way to game the feed, to get more promotion and thus attention and followers. Once Peter engaged with so much as a single post about the leg warmers, the recommendations pounced and the content became inescapable. (Following the algorithmic logic of "if you like this one thing, you'll *definitely* like more and more of it.")

Peter had a similar experience with Van Cleef & Arpels jewelry, which became popular on TikTok after it appeared on a reality show, and astrology, a subject Peter briefly followed on Twitter and then lost interest in. But Twitter's recommendations kept serving tweets about astrology to her, often negative warnings, no matter how many times she requested them to stop. "I started fearing for my life every time Mercury was in retrograde," she said. "I don't want to see it, but I keep being shown it. This is ruining my life." Not only does the feed try to guess what you like, it may not understand when your preferences move on or evolve.

Algorithmic anxiety is fueled in part by the scourge of targeted online advertising, which uses the same kind of algorithms as the feeds. Your engagement is tracked by digital surveillance, and then you are served ads for products that match what you engage with, from brands that pay for your attention. Since ads are the primary way that many digital platforms and online publications make money, they are everywhere, interrupting articles, popping up with autoplay videos. Unlike a television commercial or a print magazine ad, they are personalized, and reiterate subjects you might prefer to ignore—because so many publishers sell their ads through the same software, like Google's AdSense, the same ads might appear on every website. I've experienced this kind of haunting with a piece of furniture, a credenza made by the German manufacturer USM. The piece's modernist grid of brightly colored metal shelves appears everywhere, catching my eye before I even realize it. Rather than making me desire the credenza more, however, I've grown tired of it, suspicious of my own preferences.

"A lot of culture is shaped around social media now; there are so many microtrends. Before you blink or decide if it's something you like or not, the feed has moved on to the next thing," Peter explained to me. She summarized the problem: "I just want to know that what I like is what I actually like." In other words, she was seeking confidence and stability in her own sense of taste. Though she knew she was partially responsible for her recommendations, the algorithmic acceleration of content online outpaced her everyday experiences to an absurd degree. "Not every interaction I have in real life would shape my choices. Why should my tiniest interaction with an influencer wearing leg warmers? They fed it to me," she said. There was more diversity and originality in a physical walk down the Manchester sidewalk than in her digital feeds, which all ran together.

I feel the same way about my personal design aesthetic, which tends toward the mid-century and minimalist—which are, after all, the generic styles of Instagram. I was already interested in the style before my time on social media, but the slow trickle of curated accounts that I followed has lately turned into a flood. My feed is full of unwanted recommendations of ever more accounts posting elegant room interiors: blandly clean, beige-walled, plant-bedecked homes in Mexico, Sweden, Japan. As with Peter's leg warmers problem, just because I enjoyed a sprinkling of this content doesn't mean I want to see it all the time. Instead of accomplishing the goal of sustaining my attention, the recommendations force me to confront the aesthetics' lack of context and meaning. It may be that the algorithmic feed will convince me that I don't like what I thought I liked, or at least turn my taste against it much faster than otherwise due to its oversaturation, the way a meal seems less appetizing when you eat it too often.

Algorithmic taste, in Peter's case as a consumer, was both boring and alienating. On the creator side, by contrast, ubiquity can be profitable. For a commercial brand like Van Cleef & Arpels, more attention on a particular product is an almost invariably positive thing. The wider an audience it reaches, the more of a product sells.

The bigger the meme, the better. Yet algorithmic recommendations also have a way of warping cultural creators' intentions for what they put out into the feed, changing their relationship to their own work as well. In many cases, neither side is happy with what is getting promoted.

In early 2018, a fifty-four-year-old musician named Damon Krukowski, the drummer of the 1980s indie band Galaxie 500, noticed something strange was going on with his old band's music on Spotify. Since the band bought back the rights to its music and moved it to its own label, Krukowski could see exactly how many streams its various tracks were getting. One track, "Strange" from its 1989 album *On Fire,* was getting played far more often than any other one from the band's discography—hundreds of thousands more plays. (Which also meant that the song was making more money for Krukowski and his former bandmates.) On a chart of streaming volume, the line for "Strange" diverged from the rest of the catalog, rising at a forty-five-degree angle. And that track hadn't been a single, had not received any marketing push or prioritization when it originally came out. "To me, it was totally random," Krukowski told me. Adding to the strangeness was the fact that the "Strange" boom was on Spotify alone; it wasn't nearly so popular on other streaming services.

For Krukowski, "Strange" was meant as kind of a joke: a loose parody of more popular music. His nickname for the track while the band was composing it was "Heavy Metal Ballad." It's an outlier on the otherwise lo-fi, shambling album. Galaxie 500's music is proudly introverted. They belonged to a scene of spotlight-shy, intellectual bands that were punk but also nerdy—the trio, with bassist Naomi Yang and guitarist Dean Wareham, began playing together as students at Harvard.

Galaxie 500 broke up in 1991 after releasing just three albums, but Krukowski continued his career as a musician and author and eventually settled in Cambridge, Massachusetts, with Yang, his partner. While managing the commercial rights of his band's catalog in the 2010s, he became a critic of the streaming industry. The only thing that had changed to possibly cause the "Strange" phenomenon was that in 2017, Spotify had made its autoplay option the default. So anytime the music that the user had chosen stopped—whether a track, album, or playlist—another algorithmically recommended song would instantly play.

"On the day that they switched the preset, it was the beginning of this separation of one song from the rest of our catalog," Krukowski said: "Strange" was being recommended by that system more often than any of Galaxie 500's other songs. Krukowski posted his observations in a newsletter, which attracted the attention of Glenn McDonald, who at the time worked as Spotify's "data alchemist." McDonald did an internal investigation and concluded that "Strange" had hit the algorithmic jackpot not because of Galaxie 500's unique musical style, but because the song was more similar to songs by other bands than Galaxie 500's other tracks. In many cases, if "Strange" played, the listener was unlikely to hit the Skip or Stop button, and so the recommender system registered it as an effective selection and offered it to ever more listeners.

When I asked Krukowski why he thought the song hit the mark, he identified the jokey qualities that made it not unlike the heavy-metal ballads that were popular in the eighties: a regular backbeat on the drums, a screechy guitar tone that was uncharacteristic for Galaxie 500, a lack of long solos, and a short run time, at three minutes and nineteen seconds. In other words, "Strange" sounds like a regular song. "It was fun to play together because we were allowing ourselves to bash a little more than usual," Krukowski said. "That's what the algorithm heard in the song." There was also an algorithmic feedback loop, in which what is popular becomes more popular. "Once it's out there being recommended a whole lot, then it gets recommended even more," he said. Given the priorities of Spotify's recommender system at the time, the content that was the most generic succeeded best.

This is how algorithmic normalization happens. *Normal* is a word for the unobtrusive and average, whatever won't provoke negative reactions. Whichever content fits in that zone of averageness sees accelerated promotion and growth, like "Strange" did, while the rest falls by the wayside. As fewer people see the content that doesn't get promoted, there is less awareness of it and less incentive for creators to produce it—in part because it wouldn't be financially sustainable. (The rule of culture in Filterworld is: Go viral or die.)

The bounds of aesthetic acceptability become tighter and tighter until all that's left is a column in the middle. While popular styles shift, like moving targets, the centralization and normalization persist. That's why when a particular pattern of tweet starts succeeding wildly, seemingly everyone on Twitter suddenly copies it: posting an open-ended request for recommendations, for example, or presenting an absurd joke as something your child (real or made up) said to you. Language itself gets normalized. "There's a pressure to be normal. That pressure is just saying: Be the same, whatever's familiar to you is safe and somehow makes you feel like part of the group," Krukowski said. "There's a horrible vanishing point to that, and that is fascism." He described the condition of Filterworld as a "black hole of normalcy."

Fascism means being forced to conform to the tenets of a single ideological view of the world, one that may utterly discount a particular identity or demographic. It is the mandate of homogeneity. Filterworld can be fascistic, in that the algorithmic feeds tend to create templates of how things are supposed to be, always informed by inherent biases—a bracketing of reality that is then fulfilled by users creating content that fits the mold. That bracketing includes forms of culture as well as identities. It might also be accurate to describe Filterworld as dictatorial or feudal: we all reside online within spaces we have no power over, following capricious rules that we don't approve.

Krukowski doesn't dislike his belated hit "Strange," but, he said, "I never thought it was a standout track. If you squint—which is what the algorithm does—and listen with your head turned to one side, through a gauze, you could mistake it for a different band." The song didn't represent the drummer's sense of what Galaxie 500 was trying to achieve creatively; what started as something of a musical joke unwittingly became emblematic of the band's work as a whole. The band had actually picked the slower, quieter "Blue Thunder" as the original lead single—a choice some of their label executives disagreed with.

With modern-day algorithmic recommendations, artists have much less choice in what becomes popular and even less control over the context that their work appears in. Spotify's interface, which highlights a band's most played songs at the top of the page, makes it harder to find and play a full album in its original order. Galaxie 500 can't intentionally resist the algorithmic decisions like they could push back against their label. Krukowski continued, "The weird thing with algorithms is that we're all under that pressure, whether we want to be or not. Even if we don't want anything to do with it, the algorithm is going to swoop in and pick your most 'normal' song and make you identified with that, instead of your most peculiarly 'you' track." The same process applies to artists, writers, and anyone online who has felt pressure to confine themselves to an arbitrary "personal brand."

And because Spotify implacably controls how listeners interact with the music, they do not have to incentivize musicians in the same way as major labels did, with rich record deals or other perks. "To have this pressure from an algorithm, they're not offering us anything in exchange," Krukowski said. Not even a stable living. "Strange" has fourteen million streams in its Spotify lifetime, while Galaxie 500's second-biggest song, "Tug Boat," has nine million. Yet the lifetime Spotify earnings of "Strange" have amounted only to fifteen thousand dollars. The trade-off of exposure for revenue, especially at the expense of the band's sense of identity, doesn't feel fair to the musician: "It's extractive." Yet such is the deal that so many creators have to make to fit in to Filterworld.

## CATEGORIZED BY NETFLIX

For most of my adult life, I didn't own a television. In college, I usually pirated the shows I wanted to watch, like *Mad Men,* and the illicit habit extended into the *Game of Thrones* era in the 2010s. I consumed most TV shows and films via the classic setup of a laptop propped up next to me in bed, my head tilted up by pillows to achieve the perfect viewing angle. Netflix launched the earliest version of its streaming service in 2007, but I didn't have my own account for a long time, and even then it was a user profile on my partner's parents' subscription. This mode of viewing content was intermittent and ad hoc. First, I had to know what I wanted to watch, which meant following suggestions from friends or recommendations found on social media or blogs. Then I had to seek it out and set up my computer, bathing in the cold light of the close-by screen in a darkened room. It was a long way from turning on the living room television as a child in the 1990s and watching whatever was on cable.

But my viewing habits changed during the onset of the COVID-19 pandemic in 2020. As news of quarantine set in and hints of global supply-chain slowdowns started, the one thing I made sure to acquire for my apartment was a large television, the first one I had ever bought for myself—a sixty-inch flat-screen that loomed in the living room like an alien, all jet-black shiny plastic. It replaced a chair in the corner. For a while, my partner, Jess, and I couldn't get used to its presence in our apartment, but then we had no choice: during lockdown there wasn't much to do besides catch up on the backlist of prestige TV shows. So I finally started my own Netflix account.

The Netflix home page, with its scrolling grid of thumbnails advertising each separate show or film, became another content feed, like Spotify, Instagram, or Twitter. How often I checked it in those days made me much more aware of how the interface was tailoring itself to what it perceived to be my preferences. It gradually brought particular categories of shows to the top of my home page: travel documentaries, cooking shows, and international mystery miniseries. These selections were gathered under taglines like "Top Picks for Kyle" and "Categories for You," promising personalization. Both the categorized rows, from top to bottom, and the individual shows, from left to right, are algorithmically ordered. As Netflix describes it in its official Help Center, "Our systems have ranked titles in a way that is designed to present the best possible ordering of titles that you may enjoy."

Netflix pioneered the filtering of culture through recommendation engines. Before it debuted its streaming service in 2007, when it was still just a system of mail-order rental DVDs, Netflix had Cinematch, a module on its website that recommended movies for users, based on other users' ratings (out of five stars), a form of social information filtering not far from Ringo, the early music recommendation system mentioned in the previous chapter. Cinematch launched in 2002. Over the years, the predictions proved to be accurate within half a star three-quarters of the time, and half of Netflix users who rented a movie that Cinematch recommended rated it five stars. In 2006, Netflix created a contest for machine-learning engineers to improve on the recommendations by 10 percent—building a better algorithm—for a chance at a $1 million prize. One developer in the contest told *The New York Times* in 2008 that he was having trouble with a specific set of movies, a problem that, once solved, could improve his algorithm's score by as much as 15 percent. They were films like *Napoleon Dynamite, Sideways, Lost in Translation,* and *Kill Bill: Volume 1*—quirky stories with polarizing aesthetics that a viewer could either really like or really hate. These films might fall into a category like "cult classics," their appeal not quite reducible into math despite their cultural importance. It's a quality that algorithmic normalization still works against, and thus tends to be missing in the Filterworld era.

In 2009, a team called BellKor in Chaos, led by AT&T Research engineers, along with another team called Pragmatic Theory, won Netflix's competition. Together they created a tool called Pragmatic Chaos that beat the original algorithm by 10.06 percent. One major innovation was incorporating "singular value decomposition," an algorithmic strategy grouping together movies that shared specific qualities, like romances or comedies. Added layers of singular value decomposition could sort for subtler factors, like action movies that don't feature gore. The idea of taste became a series of ever more granular preferences, liking A instead of B, rather than a deeper-seated, holistic sense of self.

Cinematch's line of "movies you'll love" thumbnails at the top of the Netflix website was a predecessor to the much more dynamic streaming home page Netflix viewers know and love (or hate) today. While Spotify's recommendations happen quickly and repeatedly, with the end of each song, the algorithms of TV streaming services are slower to act. The user chooses a new show to watch far less often, and most of the time the platform needs only to play the next episode of a series, a recommendation that requires no calculation. But Netflix nevertheless functions similarly to Spotify, guiding our choices toward particular content and shaping what we perceive as representative of a given genre, the same way that Galaxie 500's "Strange" became misleadingly representative of the band's music.

The search function within Netflix's app is slow and inexact; it's difficult to search by genres and impossible to filter by information like actors or directors. (This lack has given rise to an entire genre of search-engine-optimized articles published online that list what is and isn't on Netflix, like a telephone book for streaming.) The search results are also influenced by the previous actions of other users—it's not just an index of information but another recommendation feed, more likely to surface what other people already like. Users' intentions are all but discouraged by Netflix. The home page becomes the main method of discovery, influencing what viewers watch and when. More than 80 percent of streaming time from users was driven by Netflix's recommendation engine, according to a 2015 study by Carlos A. Gomez-Uribe and Neil Hunt. In a publicity video published by the company under Netflix Research in 2018, a machine-learning manager named Aish Fenton states: "Pretty much everything we do is a recommendation algorithm."

The Netflix algorithm factors in a user's viewing history and ratings; the actions of other users with similar preferences; and information about the content itself, like genre, actors, and release dates. It also includes the time of day the user is watching, what device they're watching on, and how long they tend to watch in that context. Netflix states that specific user demographics like age, ethnicity, and gender are not factored in—those variables might be perceived as adjacent to bias—but such identities can often be implied from other information about a user. Netflix ultimately combines content-based filtering and collaborative filtering. The home page becomes a magic mirror, requiring no input from the user to present what they might want to consume in that moment. It removes the burden of choice and the more intentional process of selection that had to happen in earlier eras of digital culture. Like so many aspects of Filterworld, the algorithmic interface presents itself as a neutral conduit, an open window or, more specifically, an accurate reflection and intensification of your personal taste. Yet it is far from neutral.

In 2021, a communication strategist named Niko Pajkovic published a paper on Netflix's recommender system in the new-media journal *Convergence*. "Algorithms are replacing the fundamentally human—or at least, the less digitally mediated—process of cultural meaning—and decision-making," he wrote. Pajkovic set out to test Netflix's impact on personal taste, and to do so designed a set of fake accounts with different archetypal personalities. The personalities ranged from "The Die-Hard Sports Fan" to "The Culture Snob" and "The Hopeless Romantic." The sports fan watched anything to do with strenuous physical activity, whether fictional or documentary, enjoyed superhero movies on the side but disdained romantic comedies. The snob pursued obscure art-house films and foreign directors, anything that would challenge their sensibilities. But they didn't watch much TV and hated reality shows. The romantic liked passion and high drama, moving between high- and lowbrow. Netflix asks new users to select a few things that match with their tastes, to shape initial recommendations, but Pajkovic didn't select anything, and the respective home pages for the different accounts started off, for the most part, identical. But that quickly changed.

Pajkovic logged in to each of the accounts in turn and watched the shows and films that were appropriate to the character's fictional taste, randomizing the time of day to eliminate that variable. As soon as the second day of viewing, personalization had started, and the accounts' home pages began to diverge. By day five, the romantic's account had a row advertising "Movies for Hopeless Romantics" and the snob's a row of "Critically Acclaimed Auteur Cinema." More generic home-page categories like "Familiar Favorites" and "Exciting Movies" also held personalized results, reflecting the same kind of content: romantic comedies for the romantic and athlete documentaries for the sports fan. Perhaps this strategy of slight misdirection is flattering to the consumer: You don't always want to be blatantly reminded by the text labels on the home page that all you watch are romantic comedies.

The Netflix algorithm slots users into particular "taste communities," of which there are more than two thousand. And there are more than seventy-seven thousand "altgenres" or niche categories, which include "Cerebral French Art House Movies," "African-American Action & Adventure from the 1970s," and "Emotional War Dramas Based on Real Life." Users are often unaware of how they've been categorized, as well as unaware of the full array of these various niches. The user doesn't choose these categories intentionally; they just see the algorithmic results as their home page narrows to themes that they're most likely to start watching.

Even more striking than the recommendations themselves, Netflix also algorithmically changes the thumbnail art on all its content to tailor it to the specific user. That trick began in late 2017 under the label of "artwork personalization." Pajkovic observed it happening to his test accounts. At the end of two weeks of watching, all of the thumbnails on the page looked similar to each other: "Of the first 10 titles suggested for the Hopeless Romantic, which were spread across the top two rows, five of them presented artwork images containing a romantic embrace (e.g., a couple kissing or staring into one another's eyes)." Similarly, the sports fan's home page was covered in images of individual male figures performing dramatic actions: throwing a fist, tending a soccer goal, riding a bull. In screenshots, the spreads look almost nauseating, the content homogenous, like a restaurant menu of only hamburgers.

At times, the images were also misleading. For the Netflix-produced series *Outer Banks,* the sports fan received a thumbnail of two characters carrying surfboards to a body of water, while for the romantic it was a close-up of two characters about to kiss. Both hewed toward the accounts' specific preferences, as evidenced by their watching history. But neither image really represented the show, which was an action-driven mystery dealing with disappearances and murders. Users have observed, with justifiable anxiety, how Netflix's home page only displays thumbnails with their same skin color, despite theoretically not tracking their race. The year 2018 saw a controversy in which some people observed that the rom-com *Love Actually* was recommended to them with prominent imagery of the Black actor Chiwetel Ejiofor, who plays only a minor part in the film. By changing the show's thumbnail in such an aggressive way, the platform is manipulating the users, not recommending what they might like but altering the presentation of the same content to make it appear more similar to their preferences. The algorithmic image selection is pushing you to watch something that you might not have otherwise cared about—particularly if it had been labeled honestly—on the off chance that it does end up working for you. It's the opposite of the interface's message of personalization, and the opposite of the cultivation of personal taste, since it's a manipulation from the start.

Pajkovic discovered another manipulation with an account that he used to watch a random selection of content, as a control for the experiment. On its home page, that account ended up being served all eight films in the *Fast & Furious* franchise—in fact, *Fast & Furious* films were recommended to every one of Pajkovic's accounts, though there wasn't necessarily a justification beyond the fact that Netflix was paying a high fee to license them. The algorithm "defaulted to recommending content with a high likelihood of producing user engagement and did so under the guise of personalization," Pajkovic wrote. You might like *Fast & Furious* films because lots of people like them generally, but that's not the same as *Fast & Furious* being a target of your specific preferences. Ultimately, such Netflix recommendations are less about finding the content that suits a user's preferences and more about presenting what's already popular or accessible, an illusion of taste. In 2023, Netflix was streaming fewer than four thousand films, a lower total than what one of the larger Blockbuster stores stocked before that company disappeared, often upwards of six thousand films. The recommendations create an illusion of diversity and depth that doesn't exist in reality.

The hollowed-out meaning of taste in the Filterworld era has something in common with the way engagement is measured by digital platforms: it's a snap judgment predicated mostly on whether something provokes immediate like or dislike. Taste's moral capacity, the idea that it generally leads an individual toward a better society as well as better culture, is being lost. Instead, taste amounts to a form of consumerism in which what you buy or watch is the last word on your identity and dictates your future consumption as well.

Pajkovic's made-up Netflix users aren't completely normal cases—few consumers focus so closely on a specific category, and so home pages are likely to be more diverse. But the mechanism of recommendations and the tailoring of the thumbnail images serve to flatten our perception of culture and limit the possibilities for expanding our horizons. In guiding us into particular categories through soft coercion, the Netflix algorithm ends up defining our taste as only one fixed thing, made more rigid by every successive interaction on the platform, moving deeper into a pigeonhole. Even when the recommendations are accurate, they can become limiting. As Pajkovic wrote, "Feedback loops reinforce a user's preexisting preferences, diminishing their exposure to a diverse range of cultural offerings and denying art, aesthetics and culture of its confrontational societal role." That lack of confrontation is concerning. It's not that great art needs to be inherently offensive; rather, when everything conforms to established expectations, we miss out on culture that is truly progressive and uncomfortable, that might subvert categories rather than fit neatly into them.

Spotify works similarly to Netflix, bracketing users into predefined categories of taste, and like other platforms, its algorithm is most often flawed, biased, and non-neutral. In September 2019, the country music star Martina McBride attempted to create a country music playlist on Spotify. The platform can automatically recommend songs to add to a playlist. McBride discovered that the algorithm offered lists of songs only by male country artists fourteen times in a row, refresh after refresh, before it came up with a single female musician. McBride was shocked, posting on Instagram: "Is it lazy? Is it discriminatory? Is it tone deaf? Is it out of touch?"

Jada Watson, a professor at the University of Ottawa who studies country radio airplay, tried the feature for herself and ended up with a similar result: She went through twelve refreshes of all men. Even though, for research purposes, Watson uses Spotify solely to listen to women artists, she found that "within the first 200 songs (19 refreshes), only 6 songs (3%) by women and 5 (3%) by male-female ensembles were included (all emerging after 121 songs by male artists)." The recommendations clearly didn't have much to do with what else she listened to on Spotify. McBride discovered that the playlist-recommendation function wasn't based on the user's listening habits at all, but on the title of the playlist. So, per Spotify's algorithm, one might assume that country music is equated with men, a formula that still held even when Watson made a playlist called "Country Music by Musicians with Vaginas." A biased algorithm defined the genre in a biased way. It's a "very narrow perspective of what country music means," Watson told me. Despite its message of personalization, Spotify in this case created a vacuum of diversity.

In a 2014 post on a blog run by Microsoft Research, a scholar named Christian Sandvig coined the term "corrupt personalization" to describe such flawed recommendations as the manipulative Netflix movie thumbnails and homogenous Spotify playlists. "Corrupt personalization is the process by which your attention is drawn to interests that are not your own," Sandvig wrote. The recommendation system "serves a commercial interest that is often at odds with our interests." In the case of Netflix, the misleading images and the omnipresent *Fast & Furious* suggestions may serve to increase user engagement and encourage people to think they're getting value out of the service and thus continue renewing their subscriptions, maintaining the company's growth.

Other examples of corrupt personalization include Amazon suggesting its own in-house brands before other results in its marketplace and Google Search prioritizing the company's other products, like Google Maps, as the best sources of information. The company profits, but the user may suffer, and it degrades the overall cultural ecosystem. As Sandvig wrote: "Over time, if people are offered things that are not aligned with their interests often enough, they can be taught what to want. . . . They may come to wrongly believe that these are their authentic interests, and it may be difficult to see the world any other way." The Internet has been increasingly enclosed into a series of bubbles, self-reinforcing spaces in which it becomes harder to find a diverse range of perspectives. This idea is familiar from politics—liberals mainly consume digital content that reflects their beliefs, as do conservatives—but it applies to culture as well. In the matter of personal taste, knowing what you like is difficult, but it's equally hard to know when you don't like or don't want something when it's being so strenuously presented as "For You." In Filterworld, it becomes increasingly difficult to trust yourself or know who "you" are in the perceptions of algorithmic recommendations.

In 2011, the writer and Internet activist Eli Pariser published his book *The Filter Bubble,* describing how algorithmic recommendations and other digital communication routes can silo Internet users into encountering only ideologies that match their own. The concept of filter bubbles has been debated over the decade since then, particularly in the context of political news media. Some evaluations, like Axel Bruns's 2019 book *Are Filter Bubbles Real?*, have concluded that their effects are limited. Other scientific studies, like a 2016 investigation of filter bubbles in *Public Opinion Quarterly*, found that there *is* a degree of "ideological segregation," particularly when it comes to opinion-driven content.

Yet culture and cultural taste have different dynamics than political content and ideological beliefs online; even though they travel through the same feeds, they are driven by different incentives. While political filter bubbles silo users into opposing factions by disagreement, cultural recommendations bring them together toward the goal of building larger and larger audiences for the lowest-common-denominator material. Algorithmic culture congregates in the center, because the decision to consume a piece of culture is rarely motivated by hate or conflict. Jingjing Zhang, a professor at Indiana University who studies recommendation algorithms, found evidence for the theory of homogenization when she collaborated on an experiment about personalized music recommendations, presented at the 2012 Dublin Conference on Recommender Systems.

Students were presented with songs that they were told had been recommended to them based on their personal taste, as indicated by a star rating—but the ratings were actually artificial and arbitrary. Students were then asked how much they would pay for a given song; the higher the star rating, the more they were willing to pay. Each added star resulted in a 10 to 15 percent increase in willingness to pay for the song. The experiment showed how the perception of recommendation could skew the perceived value of a given piece of culture, making it seem more likable or significant. The flaw intensifies due to the self-reinforcing loop of algorithmic recommendations. Over time, the system will "provide less diverse recommendations," as Zhang told the podcast *Planet Money*. Eventually, she said, it will "provide similar items to everybody, like, regardless of personal taste." Hence the homogenization we are experiencing today.

## COLLECTING CULTURE

App interfaces that present the appearance of recommendations can be as important as actual recommendations in determining what culture we consume and how we feel about it. Interface design falls under the tech industry label of "user experience": the micro-interactions that happen as a user navigates, searches, and clicks. The user experience of today's platforms tends to be overwhelmingly passive. You're not supposed to look under the hood too much, just consume what's already in front of you—theoretically, the algorithm knows you better than you know yourself, though that's patently untrue. If we can always rely on the Netflix home page, Instagram's Discover page, or the TikTok "For You" feed to show us something that we're interested in, then we have less impetus to decide for ourselves what to look for, follow, and, perhaps most important, save. We often build our senses of personal taste by saving pieces of culture: slowly building a collection of what matters to us, a monument to our preferences, like a bird constructing a nest.

But the more automated an algorithmic feed is, the more passive it makes us as consumers, and the less need we feel to build a collection, to preserve what matters to us. We give up the responsibility of collecting. Over the past two decades, the collecting of culture—whether films on DVD, albums on vinyl, or books on a shelf—has shifted from being a necessity to appearing as an indulgent luxury. Why would I bother worrying about what I have access to at hand when digital platforms advertise their ability to provide access to everything, forever, whenever I want? The problem is that there is no guarantee of permanence in what digital platforms offer—the appearance of totality is a facade, buttressed by recommendations—and their interfaces are constantly changing. The confusion induced by a suddenly changed interface is a common experience in Filterworld.

One morning in late 2021, I opened Spotify on my laptop and found myself suddenly lost. I was used to performing a specific set of clicks to access the music I like—in this instance, a 1961 jazz album by Yusef Lateef called *Eastern Sounds.* Many weekday mornings working from home during the pandemic I would put the album on first thing, much to the annoyance of Jess, who often laughed at its repetitive, discordant opening notes. But that day I couldn't find the album, or the full list of albums that I had saved with the Spotify Like button, which was the software's principal way of keeping them in one place. My muscle memory didn't work. The collection had been rearranged without giving me any notice or choice in the matter. It felt like a form of aphasia, as if someone had moved around all the furniture in my living room overnight and I was still trying to navigate it as I always had. A new "Your Library" tab in Spotify's moody black-and-green interface hinted at everything I was trying to find, but instead it opened a window of automatically generated playlists that I didn't recognize. The next tab over offered podcasts, which I never listened to on the app. Nothing made sense.

As all forms of media have moved into streaming, when everything seems to be a single click away, it's easy to forget that we can also have physical, non-algorithmic relationships with the pieces of culture we consume in our personal time. We store books on bookshelves, mount art on our living room walls, and keep stacks of vinyl records. When we want to experience something, we seek it out: finding a book by its spine or pulling an album from its case. The way we interact with something, and where we store it, also change the way we consume it, as Spotify's update forcibly reminded me. The same thing happened with Twitter when it added its own algorithmic "For You" feed and Instagram when it moved the button to post a photo, at one point replacing it with the button to watch TikTok-style videos.

All these changes make me crave the opposite: a fixed, stable, reliable way of accessing whatever culture you want. Which is exactly what earlier forms of collecting and consuming culture once offered. We took that stability for granted. In 1931, the German cultural critic Walter Benjamin wrote an essay called "Unpacking My Library," describing our relationship with physical cultural objects. In the essay, Benjamin narrates removing his book collection from dusty crates, where the volumes had been enclosed for years. The volumes are splayed loose on the floor, "not yet touched by the mild boredom of order," all set to be rearranged on shelves once more. For Benjamin, the very possession of these books formed his identity as a reader, writer, and human being—even if he hadn't read all of them. They sat proudly on his shelves as symbols, representing the knowledge that he still aspired to gain or the cities to which he had traveled. Accumulating books was his way of interacting with the world, of building a worldview that he furthered in his critical writing.

Benjamin's library was a personal monument, the same kind that we all construct of things we like or identify with, building our sense of taste. Its importance lay in its permanence—collections are made up of things that we own, that don't go away unless we decide they should. "Ownership is the most intimate relationship that one can have to objects," Benjamin wrote. "Not that they have come alive in him; it is he who lives in them." In other words, we often discover, and even rediscover, ourselves in what we keep around us. But that codependence or co-evolution of collection and person wouldn't happen if the order of Benjamin's shelves and the catalog of his books kept changing every few months. That's what Spotify's interface updates and algorithmic changes felt like to me: a total disruption of the pieces of art and culture that shaped me.

In Filterworld, our cultural collections are not wholly our own anymore. It's as if the bookshelves have started changing form on their own in real time, shuffling some material to the front and downplaying the rest. It reminds me of a sleight-of-hand magician who subliminally encourages you pick a specific card—even as the magician lets you believe it's your own choice. And this lack of agency is undermining our connections to the culture that we love. We don't often think about bookshelves on their own, separate from what they contain, but they are great devices. They display books or albums, and you can choose from among the displayed options in a relatively neutral way. The collector is the only one who decides how to arrange their possessions, ordering books by author, title, theme, or even color of the cover—and they stay in the same places they're put. That's not true of our digital cultural interfaces, which follow the whims and priorities of the technology companies that own them. If Spotify suddenly gives the category of podcasts a prominent new placement, for example, it's because the company has decided that podcasts are going to make up more of its revenue in the future. The interfaces follow the company's incentives, push-ing its own products first and foremost, or changing familiar patterns to manipulate users into trying a new feature.

Benjamin wrote that collectors have a "feeling of responsibility" to their collections. But it's very difficult to feel such ownership for what we collect on the Internet; we can't be stewards of the culture we appreciate in the same way as Benjamin. We don't actually own it and can't guarantee accessing it in the same way each time.

You can accrue a laboriously curated digital library of music only to have it thrown into disarray when the app changes. Or your col-lections can be lost entirely when a streaming service shuts down. Digital interfaces tend to change without warning and without record; each redesign erases its previous iterations. There's no way to access older, favored versions of Spotify or Instagram the way it was possible in decades past to stick with an outdated software ver-sion by declining updates. The apps now mostly exist in the cloud, accessed online by the user, and the company wholly controls how they work. This instability only intensifies the cultural flattening going on, since users can't store or revisit their past experiences within their original context. All that exists is a relentlessly changing digital present tense.

The disappearance or overhauling of a particular app throws the content gathered there to the wind. The Internet is not like a bunch of eight-track tapes that can be played again with the proper technology and experienced in full once more. Building a collection online more closely resembles building a sandcastle on the beach: eventually the tide washes in, and it's as if it never existed in the first place. Such is the feeling I get when I look back at my accounts on older platforms like Tumblr, where over the early 2010s I collected 408 pages of anime GIFs, fragments of poems, and elegiac video-game screenshots, or when I scroll back to the photo albums I posted on Facebook around 2007, a feature that has since faded out, at least as it was originally intended.

The shifting sands of digital technology have robbed our collec-tions of their meaning. They appear only as nostalgic ruins, the re-mains of once-inhabited metropolises gone silent. Many of the images I once shared on Tumblr are now broken links. I could have downloaded these collections in their prime and made sure I could always access them, but that wouldn't capture the meaning of their flow and the social exchange that they once represented. What I see when I look at my Tumblr archive that's still extant online is a glimpse of a slower, more intimate, linear, and coherent digital space than what now exists in the turbocharged feeds of the algorithm era. Tumblr was more like a bookshelf. It reminds me that things were once different, but doesn't give me much hope of recapturing that meditative pace.

As a teenager, I had a binder of music on CDs that I kept in the family car I usually drove. Some I had purchased; others were mixes that I assembled and burned myself, codifying my personal taste. I still have that binder, and looking at it now—the very nineties rubberized edges and heavy-duty fabric—gives me a sense of nostalgia and a memory of the music contained therein. With Spotify, there's no CD binder I can take with me. As I've used the platform longer, the interface changing shape, I've found myself becoming a more passive user, saving fewer albums and thinking less about their themes and stories as cohesive creations. But what's worse for me as a collector and cultural consumer is ultimately better for the platform: I'll keep subscribing to Spotify because it's the only way I'll have access to my music.

While we have the advantage of freedom of choice, the endless array of options presented by algorithmic feeds often instills a sense of meaninglessness: I could be listening to anything, so why should any one thing be important to me? The constructive relationship between collecting and culture goes in both directions. When we find something meaningful enough to save, to add to our collection, the action both etches it a little deeper into our hearts and creates a context around the artifact itself, whether text, song, image, or video. The context is not just for ourselves but for other people, the knit-together, shared context of culture at large. That's what Benjamin described when he wrote, "The phenomenon of collecting loses its meaning as it loses its personal owner." Collections need individual caretakers, whose voices and tastes they express. The mass of Spotify isn't a coherent collection; it's an avalanche.

The user can sometimes feel like a hapless victim of that avalanche. Streaming services separate between two styles of consumption to analyze their users, as executives have described to me. There are "lean-in" moments, when the user is paying attention, choosing what to consume and actively judging the result. And there are "lean-back" moments, when users coast along with content running in the background, not worrying too much about what it is or what plays next. Algorithmic recommendations push us toward the latter category, in which we are fed culture like foie-gras ducks, with more regard for volume than quality—because volume, sheer time spent, is what makes money for the platform through targeted advertising.

As consumers become increasingly passive, failing to exercise distinctly cultivated tastes, artists are forced to contend even more with algorithmic pressures, because working through the feed is the only way they can reach the scale of audience and engagement that they need to make a living. They need to reach us where we are, and where we are is leaning back in the feed, not paying too much attention, both accepting of the newest algorithmic recommendation and likely to flip away at a moment's dissatisfaction. There is no choice but to adapt.

## CREATORS CONFORMING TO THE FEED

TikTok was a platform that I joined late but hungrily. It was well into 2020, and after many months of pandemic quarantine, I felt like I had exhausted all possible forms of online entertainment. But I had never tried TikTok: I thought it wasn't for me, that as a millennial instead of a member of Gen Z, I wasn't part of the intended audience. But I was desperate for activity, so I downloaded the app onto my phone and opened it to the main feed. My virgin feed was immediately populated with video clips, seemingly at random. The algorithm was throwing darts at the board of my personal taste to see what landed—surveiling what I kept watching and what I skipped over by swiping. A few themes started to emerge: skateboarding tricks, cute dogs, and musicians playing guitars. It was hypnotic, not least because I didn't have to do anything. I could just lean back and let my brain almost subconsciously decide what was interesting. Gradually, new themes would emerge in the feed: travelogues, cooking videos, crafts constructed with rudimentary tools in the wilderness. Over just a matter of weeks, a spread of generic categories that most people enjoy refined themselves into a series of specific interests that I shared with a smaller group. This was the algorithmic feed at work, sorting my preferences into categories of taste and then serving up those subjects, over and over. It was the most personalized and accurate feed I had ever used; as such, it felt both pleasurable and horrifying.

TikTok is run by a Chinese company called ByteDance and has a Chinese equivalent, Douyin, but it didn't launch in the United States until 2018. That's when ByteDance acquired another Chinese social network called Musically, which had launched in 2014 and was best known for teenagers posting lip-synching music videos, with a pre-established strong user base in the United States. Musically merged into TikTok, which became popular for its quick video clips of music or dance, a holdover from its predecessor. At first TikTok videos were just fifteen seconds long at most, an echo of the brief-lived but beloved video app Vine; then the limit was lengthened to a minute, and then ten minutes. What also set TikTok apart was its primary "For You" feed, which is almost entirely algorithmic. Users were not encouraged to choose who to follow; they just trusted the decisions of the equation. (As opposed to the likes of Twitter and Facebook, which remained somewhat chronological and based on follows.) The gimmick worked; in 2021 TikTok passed a billion monthly active users and took its place as a successor in the line of massive social networks that host our digital lives. Its success meant that all-algorithmic feeds increasingly became the default, and it began to create a new era of digital fame and cultural success as well.

One category of video I started to see in my feed was quick, narrative-less montages of everyday life: glimpses of coffee being poured, beds being made, light coming through windows of apartments. These were mostly anonymous, the creator holding their phone in front of them and assembling a portrait of their surroundings. Pop music provided the soundtrack: familiar songs that imbued the moment with a cinematic ambience. The format seemed particularly suited to the pandemic, when domestic surroundings had to be "romanticized"—as TikTok users put it—since there were no other spectacles at hand. In one TikTok, a man filmed himself swimming in a lap pool that was on the top floor of a tall apartment building. The soundtrack was Frank Ocean's "White Ferrari," a soft, elegiac song about driving late at night.

This was my introduction to the work of Nigel Kabvina, who at that point was an unknown twenty-five-year-old living in Manchester, in the north of the United Kingdom. When I saw his swimming video, Kabvina had only a few thousand followers. In the following two years, he would reach over four million followers and enter into the very top echelon of TikTok creators, thanks to the "For You" feed's ability to rocket a video instantly to millions of viewers, even if the account is relatively obscure. (There's no need to have an established audience if recommendations are so dominant, though it doesn't hurt.) Kabvina succeeded by aggressively catering to the feed, subordinating his own taste—his creative expression—to the limits of algorithmic promotion. But in the beginning, he was just messing around. In our first conversations, he explained that in making the videos he was trying to capture certain feelings, an ephemeral atmosphere that the format of a TikTok was particularly good at capturing. It was a way to counteract the stress of quarantine; Kabvina's bartending job at a chain of specialty cocktail bars had vanished.

Kabvina also began making cooking videos in his apartment, quick clips in which he assembled elaborate dishes, often a brunch for his roommate. He incised baroque patterns into avocado toast; burned rosemary and trapped the smoke under a glass; and even froze ice into a crystalline bowl for cereal. I watched as his account gained followers, first tens of thousands and then hundreds of thousands. His videos were a hit; an active community with its own inside jokes grew in the videos' comment sections. By August of 2021, Kabvina had reached a million followers and decided to pursue TikTok full-time. He quickly netted sponsorship clients like Google and Sainsbury's, the British grocery chain.

I met Kabvina in person in London one day in winter, while he was on a business trip from Manchester. I asked him to pick a place to meet and he chose Swift, a famed cocktail bar with a branch in Soho—"a must when traveling to London," he texted me. We first sat upstairs in a subway-tiled storefront and then snuck into a booth in the cozy basement. I took Kabvina's recommendation on a cocktail to start with, too: an Irish coffee, which was a specialty of the house and ideal for our late-afternoon meeting time. He wore an unobtrusive all-black outfit and had a wide, easy grin. I recognized his face only because he had recently started showing it on TikTok, whereas previously he had filmed himself only from the shoulders down. Kabvina's TikTok audience had become big enough to financially sustain him, though its vast scale still bemused him. "Imagine going to your kitchen and making a cup of tea and imagine thirty people walking into the room staring at you intently. Then try to imagine a million," he said. Every month, his TikTok videos were getting forty million views. Kabvina's videos, the algorithmic feed, and the rapacious audience formed a feedback loop. He called it "instant gratification": "I can post on TikTok and in ten minutes I can check back and see thirty thousand people have watched it."

Little in Kabvina's background would have suggested him for social media fame. He was born in Malawi, and his father attended an engineering college in the United Kingdom on an exchange program in a town outside of Manchester. When Kabvina was six years old, in the early 2000s, his father moved him and his mother to Manchester. The city was cold, both in temperature and temperament. Though they moved into a small Malawian community, the family faced racism from British locals. "People threw stuff at our house; people would spit on me. When you're a kid you're desensitized to it," he said. The atmosphere contributed to a sense of alienation. As a child Kabvina was unenthusiastic in school until he encountered Mr. Clark, a math teacher whose no-nonsense style agreed with him, and Kabvina began improving on tests. One day, another student in the math class said he wanted to be an accountant, and Kabvina decided to follow his lead. At the same time, his mother, who had a strong perfectionist streak that her son inherited, was working part-time as a baker. She set Kabvina on a path of hyper-independence: he picked his own groceries, made his own packed lunch for school, and ironed his own clothes. He especially enjoyed cooking, but guessed that his parents would never approve of it as a career path. Kabvina studied math and accounting in college, and took up film studies as well—all strengths for his future TikTok career. But a job offer at UBS in London was derailed by bureaucracy, and he ended up back in Manchester, where he fell into bartending and found he enjoyed it. He progressed from trainee bartender to winner of cocktail competitions and bar manager.

Unusually for the mid-2010s, social media didn't factor into Kabvina's life. He wasn't into Instagramming his food at restaurants, though he liked taking the photos for his own personal archive. His friends, mostly older bartenders, disdained the Internet and chided Kabvina whenever he pulled out his phone while they were hanging out. *We're in the moment; you're capturing it, you're ruining it,* they said. *Back in my day we used to talk to people.* His hesitancy was partly due to the entrenched British sense of shame and a reluctance to look silly in public—which is coincidentally the act that the TikTok feed prizes most.

The pandemic lockdown of 2020 changed everything. Kabvina's apartment, on the fourteenth floor of the first high-rise built in Manchester, which has a pool, gym, and sauna on the eighteenth floor, provided a perfect studio for his evolving shoots. The floor-to-ceiling windows made for ideal lighting, without the need for electric spotlights. And the clean geometry of a recent renovation provided a kind of monochrome photo backdrop against which his food presentations stood out. The generically luxurious apartment reminded me of an essay that the writer and software engineer Paul Ford wrote in 2014 called "The American Room." In it, Ford describes the archetypal background of a YouTube video, the kind often shot in the odd beige corner or basement of some suburban house. "For most of us life happens against a backdrop of intersecting off-white walls," Ford wrote. But the archetypal TikTok room, its successor, is fancier. The walls are still white, but the room is coherently decorated and lit by sunlight instead of fluorescents. It complies with the unspoken but ubiquitous aesthetics of Instagram.

Kabvina built his own narrative arc into his TikTok account, creating a social-media-era hero's journey. He studied the most popular accounts. Influencers like Charli D'Amelio and Emily Mariko became famous in part for getting famous, starting from anonymity. "The biggest trend I'd notice is . . . [followers] want a protagonist to take them on this journey," Kabvina said. He also carefully optimized his cooking videos according to the data TikTok gave him. Avoiding too much speaking or text made them appealing to a global audience—his food needed no translation. (It was a successful strategy; Mariko also became famous for her speech-less cooking videos.) The TikTok app reveals to creators at which point in a video users tune out and flip to the next video. If viewers were skipping at nineteen seconds, Kabvina would go back and examine the underperforming section, and then try to avoid its problems in the next video. Such specific data allowed him to optimize for engagement at every moment.

Kabvina liked the granular feedback and the iterative process to improve his work, perhaps a holdover from his math background. "I see creators get frustrated with the algorithm; they're assuming something's wrong," he said. "It's a lot easier to blame the algorithm than to try to say, 'My content isn't that good.'" For independent creators, the algorithm takes the place of bosses and performance reviews; it's a real-time authority gauging your success at adapting to its definition of compelling content, which is always shifting.

Kabvina has established his own equation that he judges his work by. He takes the number of views a particular video gets, then takes 10 percent of it. That's how many likes a video needs to qualify as successful: at least one-tenth of the viewers have to be compelled enough to take the action of hitting the Like button. Artists have always evaluated their work based on numbers, whether on-air radio plays, movie tickets sold, or museum exhibition attendance. But before Filterworld, creative taste—which is the way that artists evaluate their own work, as much as how consumers evaluate their appreciation of it—has never been so influenced by data and the granular measurement of attention.

## AMBIENT CULTURE

While Nigel Kabvina thrives on the pressure of an algorithmic feed and keeps surfing it to higher follower numbers and opportunities for sponsored content, the same forces are acting on all kinds of creators. Just as algorithmic recommendations slot users into categories of consumption, supplanting their personal tastes, they also sort cultural output into categories, which creators run up against. These categories are the house styles of Filterworld, in which greatness is defined by optimization rather than dramatic creative leaps into the unknown. Culture is continuously refined according to the excesses of data generated by digital platforms, which offer a second-by-second record of what audiences are engaging with and when and how. The preset styles are omnipresent and stultifying. Homogenization is beginning to alienate consumers rather than entertain them, and the entity to blame is "the algorithm." In recent years, an underlying sense has emerged that algorithmic culture is shallow, cheap, and degraded in the washed-out manner of a photocopy copied many times over. This, too, is a form of algorithmic anxiety: the feeling that, when such a human endeavor as making culture is so automated, authenticity becomes impossible.

Complaints regarding this pervasive shallowness have popped up increasingly often and with increasing intensity. I've taken to collecting them to document the growing antipathy. The poet Eileen Myles said that it is impossible to separate the creative process from digital technology: "You may not use social media, but it's using you. You're writing in tweets, like it or not." The playwright and novelist Ayad Akhtar described our "click-bait consciousness," trained to interact with anything in the feed designed to be triggering. "The worship of algorithms is mutilating creative industries," the television writer Cord Jefferson complained. "Culture is no longer made. It is simply curated from existing culture, refined, and regurgitated back at us. The algorithms cut off the possibility of new discovery," wrote Paul Skallas, an anti-technology lifestyle influencer, bemoaning the 2010s' plague of movie sequels and endless continuations of Marvel superhero franchises. Skallas labeled this lack of innovation "stuck culture." "Algorithms are limiting the future to the past," the futurist Jarod Lanier said. As the late British philosopher Mark Fisher wrote, "The twenty-first century is oppressed by a crushing sense of finitude and exhaustion. It doesn't feel like the future."

This perception that culture is stuck and plagued by sameness is indeed due to the omnipresence of algorithmic feeds. But it's not that innovation isn't happening; it's that innovation is improving only in the direction of the feed, encouraging the development of products that serve the structure of digital platforms, as Nigel Kabvina's cooking videos do. The perfect piece of algorithmic culture, after all, is almost intentionally uninteresting. Its emptiness can at times be literal. In 2014, a band called Vulfpeck uploaded an album of ten tracks of silence on Spotify and titled it *Sleepify*. A digital riff on John Cage's 1952 composition *4'33"*, each track was titled with an increasing number of Z's. Using other digital platforms like Twitter, the band encouraged their listeners to play it on repeat while they slept, earning the band streaming royalties from Spotify, which had no way of telling whether a user was truly paying attention to the music or not. The soporific album earned at least twenty thousand dollars in streaming royalties, but Spotify requested that the band take it down, because it "violated their terms of content." (In response, the band recorded a track called "Official Statement" and uploaded that, too.) Though it eventually disappeared, like all content that goes up against digital platforms, and despite being a literal void, *Sleepify* found a kind of success.

Though it emerged in the twentieth century, one of the most relevant concepts for culture in the twenty-first century is the composer Brian Eno's coinage "ambient music." Eno named the new genre in the liner notes of his album *Music for Airports* in 1978. Ambient music "must be as ignorable as it is interesting," he wrote. "An ambience is defined as an atmosphere, or a surrounding influence: a tint." Eno made music that was intentionally ambient. *Music for Airports* was a collection of slow, soft synthesizer compositions that flowed in and out like waves slowing ebbing as they hit beach sand, a fitting atmospheric sound for a transient, ethereal space like an airport. When you listen to the album, it lightly colors your sensory environment without getting in the way—you can do work while listening to it, or carry on a conversation, or meditate on it as an artwork. It rewards all forms of attention, adapting to any purpose. In Filterworld, culture is becoming more ambient. Like *Sleepify*, it's designed to be ignored, or, like the Marvel movie franchise, no single moment or fragment of it is particularly significant because there is always more to be consumed. When we embrace ambience, we lose the meaning of the finite and the discrete.

The TikTok "For You" feed is a good example of this tendency.

The feed flows by without the user needing to pay attention to any one thing too closely, since another is always about to load, personalized to some degree by their previous actions. There is nothing to alienate personal taste but also nothing to deeply compel it. Such feeds encourage the quality of ambience because they allow for a consistent baseline of engagement; the user never stops the flow. Yet consuming it for too long at a stretch, like during a TikTok binge, leads to a feeling of depersonalization: Are you becoming the person the algorithmic feeds perceive you as, or were you already?

The successor to Brian Eno's *Music for Airports* is the YouTube stream "lofi hip hop radio—beats to relax/study to," which was created by a DJ named Dmitri going by the username ChilledCow in 2015. It's a 24/7 stream, like a live radio channel, of mid-tempo, acoustic-inflected electronica that often sounds hazy or nostalgic, like music from the future coming through a staticky radio. The channel has played for stretches of over twenty thousand hours at a time and has over twelve million subscribers; it might be one of the most popular music outlets of our era. And yet the music is utterly forgettable: the songs are almost indistinguishable from one another, and the music's unobtrusive consistency makes it perfect, as the title suggests, for relaxing or studying—or literally sleeping. (An anime-style animation of a girl wearing large headphones studying at her desk, inspired by a Studio Ghibli movie, provides the appropriate visual mood.) As Eno suggested, it can be ignored or actively listened to—but it mostly gets ignored.

Videos like Nigel Kabvina's early atmospheric clips and speechless cooking feats impart a mood without concrete meaning, which is left up to the consumer's interpretation. They can mean, or not mean, anything. Many streaming television shows are ambient, too, deemphasizing narrative in favor of compelling atmosphere, tacitly leaving room for the viewer to look at their phone while watching without missing too much. Debuting on Netflix in 2020 during pandemic quarantine, the dramedy series *Emily in Paris* may as well have been a screen saver of Paris, celebrating its heroine's accomplishments of posting scenes from her fabulous life in the city on social media. When we're not watching streaming television or hypnotized by social-networking apps, podcasts piped in through

AirPod headphones provide ambient chatter, noise that represents social stimulus without real-life social contact.

In so many cases, the culture disseminated through algorithmic feeds is either designed to produce a sensory void or to be flattened into the background of life, an insidious degradation of the status of art into something more like wallpaper. While personalized feeds create algorithmic anxiety, the only salve they provide is this form of ambient culture, which can feel personal without actually being so—if you don't have to think too much about the art you're consuming because it's so bland, you don't need to worry about if it truly represents you or not. Like a corporatized form of Buddhism, the implied answer to anxiety is to learn not to desire differentiation in the first place, to simply be satisfied with whatever is placed in front of you. The cultivation of taste is discouraged because taste is inefficient in terms of maximizing engagement.

While the obstruction of taste and the tactic of corrupt personalization may feel like individual problems—users must work harder to identify what they truly like—it also quickly scales up into massive social issues. When millions of consumers are subtly misled and thus ultimately fed what they consume, certain kinds of culture are choked off from exposure and financing. That is because the flow of capital changes and moves more easily to things that adapt to algorithmic feeds. The effect is blatant in the context of selecting TV shows to watch or clothes to buy, but it also influences larger-scale actions in our lives, like the restaurants we go to, the places we travel, and how we interact with our neighborhoods and community members.

■ ■ ■

# CHAPTER 3

# Algorithmic Globalization

## SEEKING THE GENERIC COFFEE SHOP

Filterworld is not limited to digital experiences on our screens. It is a pervasive force that shapes the physical world, too. Because algorithmic systems influence the kinds of culture we consume as individuals, molding our personal tastes, they also influence what kinds of places and spaces we gravitate toward. And where our preferences go, businesses hoping to sell us things or grab our attention will follow, catering to those preferences. The same way that Netflix, Spotify, and Instagram algorithmically prioritize certain kinds of digital content that fit with each platform's structure, other apps direct our attention toward places that similarly meet the platforms' incentives. Airbnb guides users toward home rentals that match the algorithmic reflection of their desires; Google Maps highlights a personalized set of local institutions by emphasizing them on the digital map; and Yelp and Foursquare collate user reviews and engagement into ranked lists of restaurants, bars, and cafés. It's strange to think of a "feed" existing outside of a screen, but these apps work like an algorithmic Netflix home page for physical space. You can scroll down the list and select the experience you want to have. These apps make our IRL experiences just as frictionless as our digital ones.

For most of the 2010s, I was a religious user of Yelp, an app for finding and reviewing restaurants and other local businesses. The red-and-white interface became a trusted source of recommendations. When I lived in Brooklyn, I would open it every other week to see if new cafés had opened near my apartment or to check in on reviews of places I hadn't been yet. I also turned to the app when I was on reporting trips and needed a place to work or pass the time between meetings. In Berlin, Kyoto, and Reykjavík, I searched for coffee shops, and quickly scrolled through Yelp's list, which was sorted by the cafés' star rating—a reflection of how much the app's other users had liked each spot.

I often typed "hipster coffee shop" into the search bar as a short-hand because Yelp's search algorithm always knew exactly what I meant by the phrase. It was the kind of café that someone like me, a Western, twentysomething (at the time), Internet-brained millennial acutely conscious of their own taste, would want to go to. Inevitably, I could quickly identify a café among the search results that had the requisite qualities: plentiful daylight through large storefront windows; industrial-size wood tables for accessible seating; a bright interior with walls painted white or covered in subway tiles; and Wi-Fi available for writing or procrastinating. Of course, the actual coffee mattered, too, and at these cafés you could be assured of getting a cappuccino made from fashionably light-roast espresso (which has fruitier flavor notes than traditional dark roast), your choice of milk variety (including whole, soy, almond, hemp, and oat, in a proliferating list), and elaborate latte art (a rosette pattern poured into the top of the coffee with steamed milk, which turned into a kind of hipster brand logo). The most committed among the cafés would offer a "flat white" (an Australian cappuccino variant) and avocado toast, a simple dish, also with Australian origins, that over the 2010s became synecdochic for millennial consumer preferences. Infamous head-lines blamed millennials' predilection for expensive avocado toast for their inability to buy real estate in gentrifying cities.

These cafés had all adopted similar aesthetics and offered similar menus, but they hadn't been forced to do so by a corporate parent, the way a chain like Starbucks replicated itself. For a corporation, strict uniformity ensures efficiency, familiarity, and dependability across its locations—driving customer loyalty and profitability. Instead, despite their vast geographical separation and total independence from each other, the cafés had all drifted toward the same end points. The sheer expanse of sameness was too shocking and new to be boring. I felt bemused and dislocated by it, the way it feels slightly unreal to take an overnight flight and land in a different country. It seems too easy.

Of course, there have been examples of such cultural globalization going back as far as recorded civilization, from the homogeneity of marble temples and bathhouses dotted across ancient Rome's empire to various omnipresent symbols of colonialism and global migration: the eighteenth-century ubiquity of the milky British cup of tea, the sameness of the Irish pub or the Chinese restaurant opened by immigrants. In fact, the French sociologist Gabriel Tarde complained about homogeneity in 1890 because of the travel industry emerging across Europe with the rise of passenger trains. As he wrote in *The Laws of Imitation:*

> The modern continental tourist will find, particularly in large cities and among the upper classes, a persistent sameness in hotel fare and service, in household furniture, in clothes and jewelry, in theatrical notices, and in the volumes in shop windows.

Places that connect gradually grow to resemble each other in certain ways simply because of their interconnection, in the sense of the movement of products, people, and ideas. The faster the exchange, the faster the similarity sets in. But the twenty-first-century generic cafés were remarkable in the specificity of their matching details as well as the sense that each had emerged organically from its location. They were proud local efforts that were often described as "authentic," an adjective that I was also guilty of overusing. When traveling, I always wanted to find somewhere "authentic" to have a drink or eat a meal. If these places were all so similar, though, what were they authentic to, exactly? Authenticity usually implies a direct connection to a certain root, a stable source for history and meaning. What I eventually concluded was that they were all authentically connected to the new network of digital geography, wired together in real time by social networks. They were authentic to the Internet, particularly the 2010s Internet of algorithmic feeds.

In 2016, I wrote an essay titled "Welcome to AirSpace" for the Verge, describing my first impressions of this phenomenon of sameness. "AirSpace" was my coinage for the strangely frictionless geography created by digital platforms, in which you could move between places without straying beyond the boundaries of an app. The word was partly a riff on Airbnb, with its ability to enable global travel, but it was also inspired by the sense of vaporousness and unreality that these places gave me. They seemed so disconnected from geography that they could float away and land anywhere else. When you were in one, you could be anywhere.

My theory was that all the physical places interconnected by apps—the contemporary equivalent of Tarde's pan-European trains—had a way of resembling one another. In the case of the cafés, the growth of Instagram gave international café owners and baristas a way to follow each other in real time and gradually, via algorithmic recommendations, begin consuming the same kinds of café-related content. One café owner's personal taste would drift toward what the rest of them liked, too, eventually coalescing into a net average. On the other side of the business equation, Yelp, Foursquare, and Google Maps drove customers like me—who could also follow the popular aesthetics on Instagram—toward cafés that conformed with what they wanted to see by putting those cafés at the top of searches or highlighting them on a map. To court the large demographic of customers molded by the Internet, more cafés needed to adopt the aesthetics that already dominated on the platforms. Adapting to the norm wasn't just following fashion but making a business decision, one that the consumers rewarded. When a café was visually pleasing enough, customers felt encouraged to post it on their own Instagram in turn as a lifestyle brag, which provided free social media advertising and attracted new customers. Thus the cycle of aesthetic optimization and homogenization continued.

I recently experienced this overall effect in Newport, Rhode Island, an historic seaside resort town, founded in part on piracy, where most of the local design is styled with vintage nautical artifacts. The vibe is like a particularly luxurious pirate ship. When I looked for a spot to take a break from the heat, a café called the Nitro Bar was given particularly prominent placement with a big dot on my Google Maps app because I was algorithmically predicted to like it. Instead of maritime, it had the perfect AirSpace aesthetic, with pendant lamps, floating wooden shelves, and a copper-plated tap system on the marble countertop, which dispensed the latest in nitro cold brew drinks. Photos highlighted by Google gave me a preview of what the interior looked like, and I also flipped to its Instagram account, which had over twenty thousand followers. Thus reassured of its generic quality, I walked over to the café in the physical world and gratefully ordered a cappuccino, which came with perfect latte art. It felt less like I had stumbled across the café than it had found me. The algorithmic recommendations had approximated my taste based on my previous data, automated it, and then served it back to me. They provided a physical shortcut, rerouting my path toward the Nitro Bar. The rest of the cafés on the downtown street—kitschier, less polished, perhaps more historic—I could safely ignore.

When I found one of these coffee shops, whether to grab a quick dose of caffeine or work for a prolonged period, I felt comforted and paradoxically at home. I was certain that I could do my best writing there because I was free of distractions and I could rely on having everything I liked, which may not have been true of a less generic, more chaotically designed café. It was also a form of pretension: I felt that I fit in in these outposts. They reflected my tastes and aspirations, as someone who traveled a lot and took a cosmopolitan pride in working everywhere. But identifying with a literally empty symbol also struck me as weird.

In a way, the perfect generic café was like the blank space of a fresh Word document or a website background: what filled it was what you projected upon it. At times finding them felt like a pilgrimage, similar to an architecture tourist seeking out Gothic cathedrals. When a café executed the generic aesthetic particularly well, or innovated with some added novelty, I was giddily pleased and relished the well-balanced blankness. Patti Smith has written that as she got older, she still went to cafés to write and ordered a cappuccino each time, but didn't need to actually drink the cappuccino;

its presence on the table next to her notebook was enough to spark creativity. For me, the space itself was inspiration enough.

Coffee shops provided a perfect test case for my theory of digital geography. They were spaces of consumption, in which members of a certain demographic, who were also very active on the Internet, expressed their personal aspirations by spending money. The café space integrated aesthetic decisions across architecture, interior design, and tableware. They showcased trends in both beverages and food. They included a particular selection of music with soft ambient soundtracks, like lo-fi beats. Each café comprised a temple to all forms of contemporary taste—they were total works of art, to use Wagner's term for a fully immersive aesthetic creation that engages every sense. Cafés turned out to be my canary in the coal mine for examining the impact of the Internet on cultural tastes and consumption patterns. They were where its influence was felt most blatantly.

Just as early Western coffee shops in the seventeenth century provided a venue for the proliferation of democratic and egalitarian ideas, by mingling different classes in one physical space, the cafés of the 2010s also created a form of social organization. They offered a casual gathering point for the growing economy of "gig workers" and digital creative laborers, people whose schedules didn't align with the usual nine-to-five of the traditional office, and who lacked the infrastructure of an office entirely. (I was very much one of those people, drifting between various Brooklyn cafés to write piecework articles, getting to know the faces of other regulars.) In addition to being connected by digital platforms, this geography was also serving those who found work on digital platforms, whether drivers on Uber or freelance graphic designers on Fiverr.

When my AirSpace essay was published in 2016, readers embraced the term I had coined, observing it in their own day-to-day experiences. They emailed me examples of cafés that were "AirSpacey" and marveled at how ubiquitous the style was. Though it was particularly identifiable in cafés, the same sensibility could be found in coworking spaces, start-up offices, hotels, and restaurants—all spaces where time was temporarily spent and aesthetic was flaunted, where physical space was turned into a product.

As years passed, however, I realized that AirSpace was less of a specific style than a condition that we existed in, something beyond a single aesthetic trend. Like all fashions, the visual style of that moment in the mid-2010s decayed. The white subway tiles began to look too cliché, the way the laminate countertops in my childhood home felt like the nineties, and they were replaced by brightly colored or more textured ceramic tile. The early rough-hewn style of high Brooklyn lumberjack, with its repurposed industrial furniture, gave way to careful Scandinavian-ish mid-century modernism, with spindly-legged chairs and wood joinery. In the late 2010s, the dominant aesthetic grew colder and more minimal, with cement countertops and harsh geometric boxes in place of chairs. Accoutrements like lights made from rusty plumbing fixtures were left behind in favor of houseplants (succulents especially) and highly textured fiber art, evoking West Coast bohemia more than hardscrabble New York City. The association with Brooklyn gradually faded out (after the 2020 pandemic, Brooklyn itself was seen as less desirable than downtown Manhattan), and the generic style became less associated with a place than with digital platforms, like Instagram and the insurgent TikTok. In a 2020 essay, the writer Molly Fischer labeled it "the millennial aesthetic"; it was also embraced by start-up companies like the mattress seller Casper and the coworking space chains WeWork and The Wing. Fischer asked, "Will the millennial aesthetic ever end?"

The elements of style—Edison bulbs versus neon signs—turned out to be less important than the fundamental homogeneity, which became more and more entrenched. The signs changed, evolving one step at a time over the years, but the sameness stayed the same. Even in the nineteenth century, Tarde predicted that in the future stylistic difference would be based not on "diversity in space" but "diversity in time."

Each new aesthetic shift became pervasive in turn. Within my old Brooklyn neighborhood of Bushwick, a dim, industrial-chic coffee shop called Swallow whose furniture often resembled a flea-market sale was once the height of fashion, but it was outpaced by Supercrown, a glossier space with matching stools and an expansive skylight. After Supercrown shut down, Sey Coffee emerged a few blocks away. It's a spartan environment in which succulents—some even embedded in the walls—outnumber comfortable chairs. Its exposed brick walls have been painted white. At one point, its rear held an entire ceramics studio, which produced the café's cups, redolent of wabi-sabi. It is not a space in which to linger, but it is aesthetically perfect. You almost have to Instagram it, capturing your cappuccino in bright daylight on the polished concrete of the bar. Sey embodied that frictionless, easily shared aesthetic developed for digital platforms.

Sometimes people expressed annoyance at the very presence of subway tiles in coffee shops. But I think it was the sameness of Air-Space that was off-putting, not exactly the style itself. Homogeneity in a diverse world is uncanny. There could be a disappointment with finding the expected aesthetic in yet another place—a burgeoning boredom—as well as a sense of intrusion, that the influence of digital platforms was extending somewhere that it had not theretofore reached, a sign of Filterworld's expansion.

A South African woman named Sarita Pillay Gonzalez noticed the aesthetic in Cape Town in the late 2010s, when she was working there at an urbanism nonprofit. Gonzalez saw it as a form of gentrification, or even an echo of colonialism in a postcolonial country. Generically minimalist coffee shops were popping up on Kloof Street, in Cape Town Central. Gonzalez identified them by their "long wooden tables, wrought-iron finishings, those lightbulbs that hang, hanging plants," she reeled off the list when I spoke with her. The aesthetic itself was propagating into different venues as well: beer halls, gastropubs, art galleries, Airbnbs. "It's not just coffee shops; even people who are renting out or renovating historical homes, a lot of them are also hewing to that aesthetic, too," Gonzalez said. She had noticed a similar transformation in northeast Minneapolis while she was living there around 2016, where warehouse buildings were turned into coffee shops, microbreweries, and coworking offices, the common indicators of a gentrifying neighborhood.

According to Gonzalez, the style marked "a globally accessible space. You're able to hop from Bangkok to New York to London to South Africa to Mumbai and you can find that same feel. You can ease into that space because it's such a familiar space." The homogeneity contrasted with the general hipster philosophy of the 2010s, namely, that by consuming certain products and cultural artifacts you could proclaim your own uniqueness from the mainstream crowd—in this case a particular coffee shop rather than an obscure band or clothing brand. "The irony of it all is that these spaces are supposed to represent spaces of individuality, but they're incredibly monotonous," Gonzalez said. Her comment echoed another paradoxical message of Filterworld and algorithmic recommendations: You are unique, just like everybody else.

Not only the spaces but the customers were homogenous, Gonzalez observed: "If you go into the cafés, they're predominantly white. But it's historically a neighborhood for people of color. It's definitely associated with the gentrifying class of people." Only certain types of people were encouraged to feel comfortable in the zone of AirSpace, and others were actively filtered out. Gentrification is a form of flattening, too—a fact visible not least from the aesthetics of renovated buildings that take over affordable neighborhoods, the bricks painted gray, the wooden railings turned into tension wire, the sans serif address numbers mounted next to the door. It required money and a certain fluency for someone to be comfortable with the characteristic act of plunking down a laptop on one of the generic cafés' broad tables and sitting there for hours, akin to learning the unspoken etiquette of a cocktail bar in a luxury hotel. The Air-Space cafés "are oppressive, in the sense that they are exclusive and expensive," Gonzalez said. When whiteness and wealth are posed as the norm, a kind of force field of aesthetics and ideology keeps out anyone who does not fit the template.

## THEORIES OF FLATNESS

In the early 2000s United States, I grew up with the idea that the world was flat. Those years saw the dawning mainstream awareness of globalization, the way that colonialism and capitalism had led to a planet that was more interconnected and felt smaller than ever before. The major culprit for this popular idea was the *New York Times* columnist Thomas Friedman's 2005 book *The World Is Flat*. It felt like common wisdom: flatness meant that people, goods, and ideas flowed across physical space faster and easier than ever. It was a turbulent moment in history, but even 9/11, and the enduring wars that followed, drove home a certain visceral lesson that America wasn't so distant or separate from the rest of the planet. "The world is flat" thus became an ambivalent lesson: You can consume plentiful products manufactured in China, but what happens in China might also affect you personally.

In his book, Friedman wrote about various "flatteners," forces that were knitting the planet closer together. Several of these were digital technology: affordable Internet browsers like Netscape; workflow software that enabled collaboration between international businesses and factories; and search engines like Google, which expanded access to information. "Never before in the history of the planet have so many people—on their own—had the ability to find so much information about so many things and about so many other people," Friedman wrote. The book mostly addressed the macroscopic level of nations and corporations (which were rapidly becoming more similar). The "playing field" was being leveled, which meant that any company could compete against any other no matter where they were located. Hierarchies were being flattened, so a small company or a freelancer could compete with much larger enterprises. Just as highways interconnected the United States, the fiber networks of the Internet created "a more seamless global commercial network," Friedman wrote, and "helped to break down global regionalism."

Not only were industries and economies being flattened in the new globalized order, but culture trended that way as well. The nascent Internet exerted a pressure to share, and it connected individuals on a microscopic level in the same way that countries and corporations were being connected. "Everyone wanted everything digitized as much as possible so they could send it to someone else down the Internet pipes," Friedman wrote. The pipes have since grown much larger and faster.

Filterworld is the end point of Friedman's flat world, because the same forces are increasingly acting on every aspect of our personal lives, down to the level of the subconscious. Beyond dry statistics about manufacturing orders or consumer demand, images and video began flowing across the world faster than ever, particularly with the rise of social media, which encouraged users to generate their own content. Social networks only came to the fore after Friedman's book, but similar to Netscape, they democratized access to online digital media—making it possible to create it as well as consume it. Flickr, which gave users the ability to upload, publish, and organize photographs on individual accounts with a rudimentary social network, launched in 2004 and targeted amateur photographers. YouTube was founded in 2005. It allowed anyone with a powerful enough Internet connection to upload and share video clips. Instagram followed in 2010 and created a larger culture of sharing snapshots from newly mainstream iPhone cameras. These became globalized, too.

Nothing epitomized the shift more than "Gangnam Style," the music video from the South Korean rapper Psy, directed by Cho Soo-hyun, that premiered on YouTube in the summer of 2012. The four-minute-long video was from the outset an internationalized artifact, emerging from the format established by American MTV, the synthesizer palette of European club techno, and the pan-Asian popularity of the Korean pop music industry. But the video was also deeply specific, building on a song that satirized the wealthiest neighborhood in Seoul, sung primarily in Korean. (Except for the epic English-language refrain: "Eh, sexy lady.") In December of 2012, "Gangnam Style" became the first YouTube video to pass a billion views. It eventually exceeded four billion.

When the song and video became popular, I remember feeling bemused at how easily I could consume K-Pop, as smoothly as watching any American music video. It was thanks to YouTube that the experience was so frictionless, and due in part to the platform's algorithmic recommendations that so many people saw it. (Remember that in Filterworld, attention begets attention.) Two thousand and twelve was also when YouTube integrated the variable of "watchtime" to its algorithm, meaning "which videos you watched and for how long," according to a company blog post, leading to better-targeted recommendations. Suddenly, via digital platforms, much of the world was watching the same thing. And that was just the early days of digital globalization. Now, a decade later, there are over thirty YouTube videos with over three billion views—a symbol of just how much YouTube has absorbed audiences' attention away from TV as well as how widespread its user base has become.

Globalization is often used as a term in relation to the availability of commercial products like smartphones; political ideas like democracy; and intervention in international conflicts like the American-led Iraq War. But such interconnection has also led to a more mundane and pervasive flattening of individual experiences. In the United States, I use the same devices, access many of the same social networks, and connect to the same streaming services as an Internet user in India, Brazil, or South Africa. Friedman's model of increased international competition has resulted in only a few overall winners, which profit hugely from their monopolization of the internationalized digital space. (Individuals and small businesses compete, but mainly with each other for purchase in the landscape of much larger platform companies, like wolves competing for territory.)

In fact, for more than a decade before *The World Is Flat*, cultural theorists were already describing how globalization, particularly the accelerated version caused by the Internet, breeds sameness and monotony. There was also a rising anxiety about this sameness, a disaffection with the cultural consequences of globalization. In 1989, the Spanish sociologist Manuel Castells conceived of the "space of flows," which he defined as "the material arrangements that allow for simultaneity of social practices without territorial contiguity," as he wrote in a 1999 article. In other words, Castells argued, electronic telecommunications infrastructure like the Internet enabled shared culture to be collectively developed across distances rather than relying on physical proximity. The culture that formed was the same across the disparate places that the telecommunications networks covered. It was a departure from physical geography, which Castells labeled the "space of places."

Many different aspects of human society began to follow the logic of the space of flows more than the space of places, including "financial markets, high-technology manufacturing, business services, entertainment, media news, drug traffic, science and technology, fashion design, art, sports, or religion," Castells wrote. The significance of geography thus receded further. In 2001, Castells wrote that the space of flows "links up distant locales around shared functions and meanings . . . while isolating and subduing the logic of experience embodied in the space of places." Where you were physically mattered less, both to your experiences and your affinities, than which channels of media you were consuming.

If geography was becoming less significant, then zones of transportation and movement mattered more. In 1992, the French philosopher Marc Augé wrote a book titled *Non-Places*, which studied the sensory experiences of highways, airports, and hotels: zones that had become reliably similar the world over. They lent a distinct, paradoxical sense of comfort to the modern nomad, who belonged to the placeless zone. In non-places, "people are always, and never, at home," Augé wrote. The book's introduction narrates a French businessman driving to the Charles de Gaulle airport, zipping through security, shopping duty-free, and then waiting before the plane boards. The personality-less space of the airport attains

> something of the uncertain charm of the waste lands, the yards and building sites, the station platforms and waiting rooms where travelers break step, of all the chance meeting places where fugitive feelings occur of the possibility of continuing adventure.

The procession to the flight and then the numbing experience of flying itself involves a kind of stripping-away of the self and surroundings until everything becomes smooth and uniform. It's a recognizable feeling—that slight separation from reality that happens when the plane takes off, or the clean burst of anonymity when opening the door of a hotel room for the first time. "The space of non-place creates neither singular identity nor relations; only solitude and similitude," Augé writes. He describes "the passive joys of identity-loss." Even the magazine the fictional businessman reads on the plane references "the homogenization of needs and consumption patterns" in the "international business environment."

In the 1990s and 2000s, there was a kind of optimism or utopianism to the march of globalization and this etherealization of experience. If the planet was brought closer together, with new airports and international hotel chains, perhaps people would understand each other better. The flattening of geography was something like the universal language of Esperanto: it might represent a simplification, but at least it would be familiar to everyone. There was an argument to be made that sameness was more efficient, not only for comfort's sake (at least for the wealthy Western traveler) but for the nurturing of capital as it flowed from one place to another in the form of investments or infrastructure. Set patterns were more predictable and could scale up faster. Chaotic diversity was unprofitable, just as personal taste makes for inefficient digital consumption.

The Dutch architect Rem Koolhaas was fluent in this international convergence. His firm, Office for Metropolitan Architecture, worked across Europe in the nineties and became known for daring conceptual buildings that weren't always actually built. Koolhaas's designs were otherworldly. OMA's 1996 Hyperbuilding, which looks like several skyscrapers crashing together at sharp angles, could be built anywhere as a "self-contained city for 120,000," as the firm's description ran: "The building is structured as a metaphor of the city: towers constitute streets, horizontal elements are parks, volumes are districts, and diagonals are boulevards." The characterlessness of the architecture, its easy merger into the burgeoning realm of non-places, was a purposeful part of the design—an aesthetic that embraces the generic. Koolhaas described his philosophy in a 1995 essay titled "The Generic City," which is one of those short pieces of writing that you read once and it never leaves your mind. Its sharp declarations of aesthetic and architectural theory have proven prophetic in the twenty-first century. "Is the contemporary city like the contemporary airport—'all the same'?" the essay begins. "What if this seemingly accidental—and usually regretted—homogenization was an intentional process, a conscious movement away from difference toward similarity? What if we are witnessing a global liberation movement: 'down with character!'"

Koolhaas's generic city is the place that all urban residents inhabit, with gentrified AirSpace buildings and coffee shops; co-working spaces serving tech workers; and the same set of restaurants and bars. It is the familiar place we arrive at, stepping off a plane, rolling through an airport, and taking a car to a loft-style hotel, where we check in using our phone. Koolhaas poses the international flattening of identity as something that can be positive, or at least include its own advantages: "The stronger identity, the more it imprisons, the more it resists expansion, interpretation, renewal, contradiction." Take Paris, for example: "Paris can only become more Parisian—it is already on its way to becoming hyper-Paris, a polished caricature." A place's uniqueness only attracts more tourists, which gradually grind it into dust with the increasing flow of travelers, who arrive to consume its character as a product and leave it ever more degraded. Difference just gets in the way; it creates friction in a world that is increasingly frictionless, whether in its cities or in its music. The ability to flow is the key to power in the new era, as the Polish sociologist Zygmunt Bauman observed with his circa-2000 concept of "liquid modernity": "It is the most elusive, those free to move without notice, who rule." The same is true in Filterworld for those who are willing to take up whichever content and aesthetics algorithms are prioritizing in a given moment, not anchored by any one identity.

One must take Koolhaas's writing with a degree of irony and a tolerance for the absurd. The architect has an artist's tendency to make grand pronouncements that he doesn't entirely back up with facts or data. His essays are best read as provocations, brief, ecstatic visions of how architecture might work or how people might live in it in the future. Koolhaas saw the decline of local identity as a consequence of the Internet, even from the perspective of 1995: "The Generic City is what is left after large sections of urban life crossed over to cyberspace," he wrote. "It is a place of weak and distended sensations, few and far between emotions, discreet and mysterious like a large space lit by a bed lamp." (The line evokes the now-universal experience of staring at your phone in a dim bedroom, scrolling through feeds.) In this description, there are shades of how Manuel Castells explained the space of flows draining meaning away from the space of places, as more of life and culture took place between or across physical locations than within them.

The generic city or the space of flows, or the flattened world, gradually creates its own context with its own norms and expectations. It "induces a hallucination of the normal," Koolhaas wrote. A "hallucination" because it isn't purely organic, it is a vision induced by technology, like a fever dream, and "normal" because it is a homogenized template, a repeating pattern whose ubiquity establishes its own normalcy. The generic city has spread implacably, unchecked.

Gayatri Chakravorty Spivak is a literary theorist who was born in Calcutta, India, in 1942 and is considered one of the pioneers of postcolonial theory. Coming from outside of the West but educated in Western institutions like Cornell University and Cambridge, hers is a unique prism through which to survey and critique the aftermath of the twentieth century. "After 1989, capitalism triumphant has led through to globalization," she wrote in her 2012 collection *An Aesthetic Education in the Era of Globalization*. By evaluating everything solely in terms of financial productivity, capitalism has turned so many aspects of life into "nearly complete abstraction," she wrote. One consequence is "the mind-numbing uniformization of globalization." The world is flat, per Thomas Friedman, but flatness has revealed itself to be stultifying.

I referenced one of Spivak's aphorisms in this book's introduction: "Globalization takes place only in capital and data. Everything else is damage control." We talk about politics, culture, and travel becoming globalized, but on a more fundamental level, Spivak is correct that what really flows across the planet are various forms of money and information: investments, corporations, infrastructure, server farms, and the combined data of all the digital platforms, sluicing invisibly like wind or ocean currents between nations. We users voluntarily pump our own information through this same system, turning ourselves into flowing commodities, too.

This history of flatness is important because it shows that flatness has a history. The homogenization of Filterworld is not just a phenomenon of our own moment; it is a consequence of changes that happened long before algorithmic feeds and is just as likely to intensify in the future. After all, each time a grand flattening is announced the world somehow finds a way to get even flatter.

Thinkers like Augé, Koolhaas, and Spivak all cited software as a metaphor to describe how geographical places and nations came to resemble each other in an era of overwhelming global interconnection, and as a factor in how such homogenization happened. But in the era of social media, the same effect has occurred at the level of the person, including both cultural consumers and cultural creators, who all log in to the same set of apps. In the place of physical hotels and airports, we have Twitter, Facebook, Instagram, and TikTok as spaces of congregation that erase differences. Moving past Koolhaas's "Generic City," there is now also the generic global consumer, whose preferences and desires are molded more by the platforms they use than where they live. In some cases, we conduct our lives more in the space of flows than the space of places. We are only beginning to understand how, along with our world, we are now flat, too.

As someone who hangs out online and acts as a sieve for culture-as-content in my career as a journalist, I am a participant and an accelerant of this system. It's not that I particularly enjoy it or that I want the homogenization to spread further. But most of Filterworld's inhabitants are either unwilling or unwitting. Simply by trying to make a living or entertain ourselves we accelerate the flattening.

## GENERIC CAFÉ OWNERS

While I was traveling in Kyoto on a research trip for my first book in 2019, between visits to temple rock gardens I also traversed the city's coffee-shop scene. In early-twentieth-century Japan, a culture of *kissaten* emerged: quiet tearooms that served coffee and excluded alcohol, catering to groups of writers and intellectuals seeking calm environments. Coffee had been officially imported to the isolated country only in the late nineteenth century, after it was first introduced by Dutch traders. The Japanese cafés were modeled on Parisian ones—though Paris was a place few Japanese people traveled to at the time, save the wealthy and the academic intelligentsia, who were beginning to read and translate French authors.

I got a recommendation from a friend living in Tokyo to visit Rokuyosha, a *kissaten*-style café that opened in Kyoto in 1950. It was difficult to find, down basement steps on a busy street with an unobtrusive wooden sign mounted onto mottled turquoise-and-brown square ceramic tiles, which I later discovered were custom made for the shop. Descending into the shop itself was like entering a kind of womb: the interior was surfaced in ornamented dark wood paneling, with leather-padded benches and two-person booths lining the hallway-sized space. No more than ten people at a time could fit comfortably inside. I ordered a pour-over coffee and a homemade donut from the elderly couple who ran the place from behind the bar, using a voice not much above a whisper, since the café was silent. Like the other guests, I sat in my own booth, paged through a book, and wrote in a notebook. No one inside was looking at their phones, in part, I felt, because the space still seemed to exist in the time that it was originally built. It rewarded attention to the physical details and the atmosphere, beyond what could be picked up in an iPhone photo. The dematerialization of portable technology and the Internet just didn't suit it.

Rokuyosha contrasted with a café I found elsewhere in Kyoto. Weekenders was a place I discovered on Google Maps by searching for cafés; it was marked by a large dot on my iPhone, which I could still use all the time because I had paid Verizon for Internet access abroad. (I would have been lost without it.) It was located at the edge of a nondescript parking lot in the city's downtown—a space of constant movement—in a small two-story building. (Its original location opened as one of Kyoto's first espresso shops in 2005.) The architecture was in a traditional Japanese mode, with sliding-panel doors, rough plaster on the walls, and hanging rice-paper globe lamps. (This Japanese aesthetic had also been adopted by the San Francisco coffee-shop chain Blue Bottle, which installed lanterns and ikebana-esque flower arrangements in every city it landed in. When Blue Bottle opened its first, slightly recursive Tokyo café in 2015, it was extremely popular.) But Weekenders also had hints of the AirSpace Scandinavian influence, with its open shelving and clean blond-wood countertops. Such a café is another space in which we are "always, and never, at home," as Marc Augé wrote— a recognizable part of the international non-place.

I had ordered a cappuccino, and when it was placed in front of me, I pulled out my phone to take a photo of the porcelain cup balanced on the edge of the counter, which was a long, roughened piece of stone, incorporated like *spolia* in a medieval Italian church. Of course, I intended to share the photo online later. "People come here just for the Instagram," the barista told me in English, a slightly dry tone creeping in to his voice. I recall my acute sense of embarrassment taking the picture. I was performing a cliché. But with its unobtrusively minimalist interior and soft daylight, the café seemed to ask for it. Looking up Weekenders's Instagram account now, its tagged photos over the course of years are a litany of the same self-satisfied image, the image that I took: a single coffee resting on the countertop.

The reduction to a single, archetypal, repetitive image wasn't an accident. It was the end point of a longer process. In the early 2010s, a new phenomenon emerged called an "Instagram wall." In part, it was an outgrowth of the street-art movement of the 2000s, a gentrification of graffiti that saw clean, officially sanctioned murals take over city walls, particularly in neighborhoods where decrepit warehouses were plentiful. Street art became an attraction in and of itself, like an outdoor art gallery. When I lived in Bushwick, I saw constant groups of French tourists being guided along the sparsely populated streets of the industrial neighborhood as if it were the Louvre, marveling at murals that eventually were replaced by hand-painted paid advertising.

While street art was originally a guerilla activity, Instagram walls were spots designed for people to stop and take photos in front of, to post on Instagram. They were also referred to as "Instagram traps." Some were just bright-colored graphic patterns that provided a perfect backdrop for a photo—the lambent pink walls of the Mexican architect Luis Barragan's 1948 home became a de facto Instagram wall, attracting tourists. Others created a scene that the photo subject became a part of, akin to those painted-cartoon wooden props with cutouts for people to poke their faces through and pretend to be a farmer or a football player. The epitome of the Instagram wall, one of its most popular tropes, was a pair of angelic wings unfurling to the left and right of an empty space where a person would stand, often stretching their arms upward as if taking flight. Just have a friend step back and take the photo, then post!

The peak of this phenomenon might have been a brunch-focused restaurant called Carthage Must Be Destroyed. It opened in my then neighborhood of Bushwick in 2017, on a block full of forbidding warehouses. The interior was bare—exposed brick and plumbing, communal wood tables—but it had a single, aggressive design gimmick: Everything was painted pale pink. The door was pink, the counter was covered in pink tile, the espresso machine had pink housing, and the dishes were glazed-pink ceramic. The menu wasn't particularly distinctive, offering the usual array of toasts, avocado and otherwise (its co-owner Amanda Bechara is Australian), so the main attraction was the aesthetic. The moment press photos were released, everyone wanted to go to "that pink restaurant."

The space was optimized for consumption as a digital image. At the time, "millennial pink," a slightly darkened blush color, had been made ubiquitous by the Internet. It was even sometimes known as "Tumblr pink," associated with the early multimedia social network where it took root. It could be found on Nike sneakers, Glossier makeup products, and Away suitcases. Apple's "rose gold" devices released in 2015 were even part of the trend. Carthage might as well have been the Millennial Pink Experience, an immersive Instagram wall. Visitors spent so much time taking photos that the restaurant had an official policy to disallow snapshots of the space as a whole—photos of your own food only. The policy didn't really work; it all but demanded customers snap a few illicit pictures and post them. Instagram remains full today of evidence of theoretical rule breaking.

These installations became utterly exhausting to encounter by the end of the decade. So-called Instagram Museums arose that made the taking of the photo the intentional goal of the experience, as if the only point of going to the Louvre was to take a selfie in front of the *Mona Lisa*. There wasn't even a restaurant menu to distract from the act of digital image making. The Museum of Ice Cream that opened in San Francisco in 2017 offered dessert-themed immersive installations, and the Color Factory, also from 2017, surreal monochromatic rooms for dramatic portraits. Each failed as compelling visual art because they required the presence of the subject and the taking of a photograph to make sense—outside of digital platforms they were incomplete; the production of the content was all that mattered. In that, they served a very clear purpose. Instagram walls or experiences attracted visitors to a locale and kept them engaged by giving them an activity to perform with their phones, like a restaurant providing coloring books for kids. It was a concession to the fact of our growing addictions—you can't just go somewhere; you must document your experience of it. And as visitors posted those photos online and ideally tagged the business or location, the photos became a kind of decentralized online billboard, a form of free advertising and digital word of mouth. The Instagram walls perpetuated themselves.

The installations were a physical form of search-engine optimization. Rather than including keywords on a website, the Instagram walls ensured that as many photos of a place as possible would exist on digital platforms, building a wider footprint. The more posts there were, and the more often they happened, the more promotion algorithms would also pick up on the place and display it to more potential customers. The walls spoke to the looming fact that even physical places have to exist as much on the Internet as they do in real life.

Though the walls have become cliché, the way they work has been dispersed into every aspect of spaces and places, which began to optimize for what we called "Instagrammability." A restaurant might include a living plant wall embedded with a neon sign of its name, easily visible from every table and thus an ideal target for documentation and sharing. A particular dish might be so elaborately visual that it functions more as an image than as food. That's how a New York City bar called Black Tap became famous around 2016 for its elaborate milkshakes, which came so encrusted with candy and other accessories (even an entire piece of cake) that they were barely edible but looked appropriately dramatic in a photo for Instagram. In fact, the shakes were designed not by a chef but by the restaurant's social media manager. They were first served only at special events for social media influencers, but became even more popular with regular customers, who could turn them into content just the same. They were more meant to be photographed than finished; the excess of ingredients created unsustainable physical waste.

Standing at Weekenders in Kyoto, I felt that the entire coffee shop had become a kind of Instagram wall, a recognizable prop with which to document your tastes as a consumer. Posting a photo was a way of showing that you took part in the aspirational international non-place, the always-and-never home of the hypermobile twenty-first-century creative traveler. I appreciated the effect—after all, I had sought out that experience of sameness and achieved it. But there was also something missing: I wasn't surprising myself with the unfamiliar during traveling, just reaffirming the superiority of my own sense of taste by finding it in a new place. Maybe that's why it felt hollow.

The influence of technology on culture is often subtle. It can be so pervasive or change things so quickly and completely that you miss the connection between cause and effect. It simply becomes the new reality. To make sure my hunch about generic cafés was correct, I set out to talk to a series of coffee shop operators around the world to figure out why they designed their cafés the way they did. Many of them described the standard AirSpace aesthetic of industrial minimalism. Tim Wendelboe, the Norwegian coffee pioneer who opened his first café in 2007, told me that its signature Nordic minimalism was partly a consequence of budget: he recycled the material that was already in his building, a former salon, and used the reclaimed wood to build a bar counter. Xanthe Ang, of Singapore's Chye Seng Huat Hardware, likewise referenced the shop's "hardware heritage"—it's located in an Art Deco–era shophouse, with high, garage-like ceilings and metallic light fixtures. Greg Schuler of Mallorca's Mistral Coffee noted his design's embrace of "raw elements": bare tile floors, exposed ductwork, and plywood shelves.

In a 2018 academic collection titled *Global Brooklyn: Designing Food Experiences in Global Cities,* the editors Fabio Parasecoli and Mateusz Halawa reference "decentralized sameness." The homogenous template of 2010s cafés or restaurants "lacks any forms of centralized coordination," they wrote, but instead operates on network dynamics, with each node in the network broadcasting as well as receiving its aesthetics. The major network through which this distribution takes place is Instagram, a fact that the café proprietors emphasized. The pressure to conform was real.

Over the past decade, Instagram became "the lens in which we view the global specialty café world," Trevor Walsh, the marketing manager of Pilot Coffee Roasters, a chain of minimalist cafés in Toronto, told me. "We want to have design choices that play into nice photos, an environment that would be a shareable moment." Posting photos to Pilot's Instagram account and having customers share their experiences was a way to connect with cafés and coffee-industry colleagues in other cities. But the platform also created a pressure to keep up. "There's this constant urgency to be producing content. We are constantly feeling like we have to be in people's phones, be in people's desktops," Walsh said. They had to fill the algorithmic feed.

Simply existing as a coffee shop isn't enough; the business has to cultivate a parallel existence on the Internet, which is a separate skill set entirely. "It almost feels like, you must have a social media acumen, you must be savvy in this area that is adjacent to your business, but not directly embedded in your business, in order to be successful and visible," Walsh continued. That means achieving metrics like plenty of tagged photos on Instagram and positive user reviews on the business's listing on Google Maps. The end point of this pressure to have a digital presence was a form of restaurant that only existed online. "Ghost kitchens" were listings for simple delivery food, like burgers or pizza, that had brand identities on Uber Eats or DoorDash but no physical location; they were run out of another restaurant or an industrial group kitchen. The food existed as digital content first and traveled through the same channels.

Social media acumen requires awareness of each platform's recommendation algorithm as much as anything else. Walsh observed that some companies may have great stories to tell, but they "are not attempting to keep up with these algorithmic patterns that will allow them to be visible to a larger audience." Maybe they don't post often enough, or they don't keep up with shifts like Instagram promoting videos more than still images, a particularly stark change that occurred around 2022 as the platform attempted to mimic Tik-

Tok. Algorithmic promotion can also fall through, even if you think you know how to hack it. As Walsh told me, "We've put a lot of time and energy into creating beautiful content. But as a result of that algorithm, we find we're not necessarily hitting as many eyeballs as we think we could or should, and sometimes that can be a little disheartening." Popularity has less to do with how the coffee tastes than how it looks in an Instagram photo. Online appearance outweighing almost all else is a law that now applies to all kinds of businesses: bars, bakeries, fashion boutiques, and even art museums. (In the last case, it helps that galleries were already designed as spaces for looking at stuff, creating a perfect visual framing that could be translated to Instagram.)

"I hate the algorithm. Everyone hates the algorithm," said Anca Ungureanu, the owner and founder of Beans & Dots, a coffee company in Bucharest, Romania, with its original location in a former printing plant. Her goal was to build "something that did not exist at that moment in Bucharest"—a space that was, at least aesthetically, nonlocal. It draws an international crowd; when someone searches Google for specialty coffee shops in Bucharest, Beans & Dots pops up. Ungureanu developed an Instagram account full of cappuccino snapshots and accrued over seven thousand followers but grew frustrated when she felt that the platform was taking away her ability to access her audience through the feed. When her café started selling coffee online, Facebook and Instagram seemed to throttle their reach—unless they bought ads and boosted the social media company's own profits. It felt like algorithmic blackmail: pay our toll or we won't promote you. The tools that had served the café to grow and access new customers were suddenly being turned against it. Facebook and Instagram "don't let you take advantage of the community you've already built. From a certain moment onward, things are unfair," Ungureanu said.

Other café owners made the same complaint, like Jillian May, the cofounder of Hallesches Haus in Berlin, a café and boutique general store that opened in 2014. In its high-ceilinged, austere space set with arched windows, visitors can buy watering cans, lamps, and ceramic planters as well as coffees or salads. It has almost thirty thousand Instagram followers. Yet "there have been fewer and fewer likes over time proportional to our user numbers," May told me. "The same kind of photo that was posted five years ago would get a thousand likes, while today it receives only one hundred to two hundred likes." She feels the app is "pushing its users to pay for boosting posts, which we are not comfortable doing." That discrepancy feels like a broken promise for a social network that was premised on democratized, user-generated content. We users are what makes social media run, and yet we also aren't given full control over the relationships we develop on the platforms, in large part because algorithmic recommendations are so dominant.

May observed an effect that might be called follower inflation. High follower numbers correlate less and less to actual engagement over time, as the platform's priorities change and as some active accounts leave, or the same content tricks stop working. It's a familiar feeling for all of us who have been on Instagram over the past decade. While it might hurt your ego to receive fewer likes on a selfie, it's a real financial problem when that follower footprint is how a business makes money, whether it's a café attracting visitors or an influencer selling sponsored content.

Pursuing Instagrammability is a trap: the fast growth that comes with adopting a recognizable template, whether for a physical space or purely digital content, gives way to the daily grind of keeping up posts and figuring out the latest twists of the algorithm—which hashtags, memes, or formats need to be followed. Digital platforms take away agency from the business owners, pressuring them to follow in lockstep rather than pursue their own creative whims. There's a risk as well in hewing too closely to trends. Cliché is not desirable. If a trope is too stale, the algorithmic audiences won't engage with it, either. That's why the perfect generic coffee shop design keeps changing slightly, adding more potted plants or taking a few away. In the algorithmic feed, timing is everything.

The other strategy is to remain consistent, not worrying about trends or engagement and simply sticking to what you know best—staying authentic to a personal ethos or brand identity in the deepest sense. Rokuyosha, the basement café in Kyoto, is just such an institution. It can afford to let its customers simply drift to its level, if they so desire. It has no Instagram account. In a way, coffee shops are physical filtering algorithms, too: they sort people based on their preferences, quietly attracting a particular crowd and repelling others by their design and menu choices. That kind of community formation might be more important in the long run than attaining perfect latte art and collecting Instagram followers. That's what Anca Ungureanu was trying to do in Bucharest. "We are a coffee shop where you can meet people like you, people that have interests like you," she said. Her comment made me think that a certain amount of homogeneity might be an unavoidable consequence of algorithmic globalization, simply because so many like-minded people are now moving through the same physical spaces, influenced by the same digital platforms. The sameness has a way of compounding.

## TOURISM BY ALGORITHM

Recommendations on Yelp or Google Maps reshape the geography of a city by slightly redirecting the steps of individuals: a visitor walks to one café instead of another, or easily finds the neighborhood with the kind of restaurants they like even though they are new in town. It's easier to search and flip through the attractions of a place like a slideshow and choose where to go, perusing them as a form of content. After finding a desirable spot, they perhaps call a car to deliver them there frictionlessly, taking advantage of another on-demand algorithmic marketplace. That slight redirection also shifts the flow of money and attention, privileging some locations over others. If the algorithmic promotion lasts, the growth is self-reinforcing as attention once again begets attention.

Filterworld offers an increasingly airtight bubble in which to traverse the world, your attention smoothly routed from one object to the next, your physical movements guided toward each destination through apps. I've experienced this shift in travel myself. Yelp recommendations gave way to Airbnb rentals, which made it easier to feel less like a tourist than like a temporary resident in a cool neighborhood in any global city. Uber gradually expanded into more countries, so I could hail a taxi using the same familiar app and interface across a greater swath of the world. With the recent expansion of mobile payments, I can tap my phone to pay for things at a store or even get on the subway in New York City, London, or Lisbon. (Cryptocurrency promised, although did not really deliver, a government-independent money that could be spent frictionlessly anywhere.) Such tools have a way of making places feel slightly meaningless, since they can be so easily navigated by phone. The city becomes a backdrop to the omniscient screen, falling into the space of flows. Geographical differences give way to digital similarities, which can sometimes be very inconvenient when too many people are following the same algorithmic pathways.

In the mid-2010s, Los Angeles residents discovered that the map app Waze, which offered driving directions based on real-time data from other cars automatically filtered into an ideal route, was ruining otherwise quiet neighborhoods. When traffic was bad on the highway, the app would reroute drivers through residential streets in an attempt to get them to their destinations faster. "The algorithm is God," a 2018 article in *Los Angeles Magazine* proclaimed. The trick worked while not too many people were doing it, but then it caused its own problems. The neighborhoods of North Hollywood and Studio City became crowded with cars and trucks, which got stuck on steep hills and tight corners. It turned out that the Waze algorithm was treating such smaller streets as having the same capacity as much larger ones; it made recommendations as if the streets could handle the flow of another hundred cars, though of course they could not. The traffic caused noise pollution and accidents, to the point that the local government began negotiating with Google to get the data changed. Neighborhood residents took to fighting back against the algorithm themselves, logging in to Waze to report fictional accidents and roadblocks, thus signaling to the app that an alternative route past their house wouldn't save any time. Hacking the algorithm made an immediate change in their physical environment.

In this case, attracting the algorithm's attention caused an overflow. The machine saw the residential roads as convenient solutions for the equation it had to solve, though the solution had its own discontents. (Local happiness was not a variable the algorithm considered.) I observed the same thing happening around my partner Jess's parents' home in Westport, Connecticut. An hour outside of

New York City, many commuters drive past Westport on their way farther north or east. When the I-95 highway is crowded, Waze or Google Maps (whose parent company acquired Waze and began incorporating its data in 2013) sends the drivers through the quaint center of the two-hundred-year-old town, on roads meant only for local traffic. The two-lane bridge becomes blocked, and the short traffic lights barely let through a few vehicles before turning red again. In the end, no time is saved, and the quality of life downtown suffers.

It's only because of the app itself that this strange movement can happen with such speed and intensity, another kind of "decentralized sameness," but of action rather than aesthetic. Waze passively directs drivers, who may not even be aware of a looming slowdown ahead, to take the alternate route that it determines to be optimal. The presence of the generally reliable app replaces our need for decision-making and the judgment that it requires. (While highway choice is not really a matter of cultural distinction, it's an echo of algorithmic recommendation's supplanting of personal taste.) I rely heavily on Google Maps to guide me to my destination, having long since forgotten any driving directions I once memorized. Consulting maps of highways is a distant memory from childhood; I have fully surrendered to automated navigation. The Waze algorithm is a new agglomeration of capital and data that warps the world around it in unexpected ways. It both generates the real-time traffic data, through the omnipresence of personal smartphones, and leverages it to create driving recommendations, calculated by traffic patterns, gas efficiency, and tolls. Yet the driver is largely unaware of these variables and how they are being weighed; they only experience the end result.

The entire nation of Iceland experienced something like the Waze highway effect, albeit a version that it intentionally cultivated. It's an organic Instagram trap. The island is as unlikely a destination to attract humans as just about anywhere on the planet. Floating by itself in the northern stretch of the Atlantic Ocean, it's made up of active volcanoes, forbidding glaciers, and precipitous fjords. In fact, until around the ninth century CE, it was entirely uninhabited. A Swedish Viking named Garðar Svavarsson was the first to navigate around the entire island in 870, and the earliest settlements in Reyk-javík followed shortly after in 874. (Its name translates to "cove of smoke," so called because the chieftain Ingólfr Arnarson noticed steam from geothermal vents before landing at the site.) When the island's population was first officially measured in 1703, there were a little over fifty thousand residents. Even today the population numbers under four hundred thousand, with one of the lowest densities in the world at around eight people per square mile. And yet Iceland has regularly attracted over two million tourists per year (five times the number of locals), who stay at least one night in the country. Tourism accounted for 35 percent of the nation's export revenue in 2019, reaching a peak just before the COVID-19 pandemic halted international travel. It was larger than any other industry, meaning that Iceland's most profitable product was selling itself, offering experiences of a once-inaccessible place.

Tourism wasn't always such a cornerstone industry for Iceland. Travelers only exceeded the local population around the year 2000, and growth really took off around 2010. From that year, the chart goes exponential, like the spreading of a meme. Ironically, it was a disaster that kicked off the twenty-first-century tourism boom. The first cause was the eruption of the volcano Eyjafjallajökull in March 2010, which grounded flights across Europe for a week in April, since the volcanic ash filling the air would damage airplane engines. (As far as Iceland itself was concerned, the eruption happened in a very isolated farming community and required the evacuation of only around eight hundred people—no big deal.) Such a dramatic news event was covered across the world, and all those TV news spots ran photos of Iceland, which wasn't usually the subject of such global media exposure. Suddenly, many millions of people were seeing the pristine landscape, the glaciers looming in the distance, the torrential waterfalls, the natural hot springs. "Because of the volcano eruption, the whole world suddenly had its eyes on us," Karen María Jónsdóttir, who works in tourism innovation for the city of Reykjavík, told me.

The other cause of the tourism boom, according to some Icelanders, was Instagram. Over the years following the eruption, millions of people would attempt to re-create those idyllic Icelandic landscape photos for their own accounts. Posting your vacation photos online was the twenty-first-century update to the archetypal 1970s at-home slideshow. Seeing a great travel photo, especially in a social space online, induces a visceral sense of FOMO, the fear of missing out. You want to know where it was taken, how the person got there, and where they stayed while they were there. And thanks to Instagram's hashtags and location tags, with their attendant landing pages, it was very easy to tap a link and see the most popular algorithmically recommended photos from a given location. Of course, Iceland wasn't beautiful because of Instagram, the way cafés were intentionally designed to be Instagram-ready. It was beautiful because of various accidents of geology and geography. But Instagram framed and highlighted its natural assets, and the platform's recommendations propelled iconic images of Icelandic hot spots to the top of the feed for hundreds of millions of users, turning those images into the de facto representations of the country.

The same way that Damon Krukowski of Galaxie 500 found his band's music identified more with its algorithmically propelled top song on Spotify than the singles the musicians had chosen to represent themselves, the Instagram feed began to create a new public identity for Iceland. Michael Raucheisen, who has worked for the airline Icelandair for decades, explained to me that social media began driving Icelandair's perception of what tourists were looking for and how to attract them. "The visuals that we saw from passengers were almost more astounding than the photos we had in our stock," he said. The airline began publishing photos sourced from Instagram in its in-flight magazine. "The fact that people all over the world can share the beauty of Iceland on their social media channels makes our job a lot easier," Raucheisen said. Again, it wasn't that Instagram created the tourism, but it gave the tourism industry an enormous opportunity. Icelandair offered cheap flights and layover deals designed to help travelers stop by. New, modernized hotels were built around Reykjavík. Bars popped up themed for the visitors, with names like American Bar Reykjavík.

Social media attracted new demographics of tourists, too, who behaved in unexpected ways. In the decades before the boom, most tourists to Iceland were from neighboring Nordic countries as well as Germany and France. The travelers tended to stay for long periods of time, planning expeditions in far-flung parts of the country. More recently, the major groups have changed to American, British, and Chinese. They stay for shorter lengths of time—some drawn in by the layover offers, stopping on their way to somewhere else, often mainland Europe—and they stick closer to Reykjavík. Bus trips leaving from city hotels send tourist groups out to the major sights, the geysers, and waterfalls, before depositing them safely back at their rooms. Algorithmic recommendations were shaping those itineraries, too. Online travel agencies, or OTAs, like Kayak and Booking .com, were growing over the 2010s, accounting for hundreds of millions of travel bookings per year. The websites were a combination of search engines, user-generated review websites, and recommendation systems, giving flights, hotels, and cities average ratings out of five stars as if they were so many Netflix shows to choose from. The more tourists who were routed through these channels, the more their pathways through the nation became homogenized, like Waze routing cars through downtown Westport. An optimized version of Iceland emerged for consumption.

Much like the denizens of Generic Coffee Shops, the algorithmic global travelers were a privileged set. Being able to move freely across the world necessitated the right passport (likely an American one) as well as the right gender expression and skin color. Black users, to name just one example, long had difficulty using Airbnb because of racist hosts, who would deny their booking requests, until the platform eliminated profiles that displayed users' faces. Not everyone is able to easily be perceived as generic or fit into seemingly frictionless spaces. Convenience for one group of users doesn't mean convenience for all of them.

At the top of its list of "most popular" attractions in Reykjavík, Booking.com puts a "Full-Day Tour of the Golden Circle," a circuit of Iceland's most famous sights, including the Haukadalur geysers, the Gullfoss waterfall, and Þingvellir National Park, the site of the first Icelandic parliament in 930 CE. The tour was liked by 96 percent of visitors, as the site displays prominently under the search results. (By contrast, only 69 percent liked the listed three-hour whale-watching tour—the implicit message being, don't bother.)

How the OTAs sort these offerings have an outsize impact on which ones tourists select, and thus which businesses, like hotels and tour operators, survive. When I spoke to Skarphéðinn Berg Steinarsson, the director general of the Icelandic Tourist Board, he was quick to criticize the services. "Their financial reward comes from quick sales and simple products. They are endlessly promoting top ten lists, because that's a simple product," Steinarsson said. The incentive isn't to offer a particularly unique experience; it's to convince the most website visitors possible to click the Buy button, to engage with the content.

Such feeds of suggested information are superficial and inspire quick, passive decision-making; as Internet users, we have been taught that the top results are the best ones. But we are missing the depth, the lesser-known spots. In 2006, the *Wired* editor-in-chief Chris Anderson published his hit book *The Long Tail*, arguing that the breadth of the Internet made it possible for niche businesses, products, and content to thrive. Popularity was a curve rising exponentially toward the left side of a graph; Anderson predicted that the long, flat part of the curve, with diverse but relatively unpopular things, would be able to sustain itself in a new way, because consumers would always be able to find the specific thing that they were seeking online. Anderson observed the self-perpetuating effects of algorithmic recommendations even on Amazon in the early 2000s, as they drove sales of a previously obscure book from 1985, *Touching the Void*, which eventually hit bestseller lists. "The mass market is turning into a mass of niches," Anderson wrote.

In the Filterworld era, this effect has proven true in some ways. TikTok certainly enables a career in niche content production; one creator I enjoy following sustains herself by making videos about daily life on an Arctic island. But now-ubiquitous algorithmic recommendations have also made the left side of the long-tail graph that much larger, as they route even uninterested consumers toward the standardized set of content that has already proven popular. Leaked data from the video-game streaming platform Twitch suggested that only the top .01 percent of Twitch creators were able to earn the median U.S. income. Anderson may not have considered that attention would equate so closely with profit, driven by advertising rather than, say, book or DVD sales. "Mass culture will not fall, it will simply get less mass," Anderson predicted. We know now this is not the case. If anything, mass culture lately appears more aesthetically homogenous than ever.

Steinarsson mourned for the long tail of Icelandic tourism against the tide of OTA recommendations. "There are so many places that are not on those lists and never will be on those lists," he said. "How deep do you have to dig before you start seeing places that would really be something special?" The tourists' experiences are flattened, not because they have no other option but because the digital platform has made it incredibly convenient to simply follow in the steps of everyone else, a turbocharged, more coercive version of the old-school tourist guidebook. Both OTAs and Instagram have contributed to turning Iceland into a symbol of "overtourism," the term coined by travel-media entrepreneur Rafat Ali in 2016 and increasingly used to describe places that are being damaged or irrevocably altered by the sheer volume of travelers moving through them. Digital content promises to be scalable: the same file can serve an infinite number of consumers, as long as the server space exists to host it. Larger audiences don't change the experience. But physical places are not scalable.

In 2019, on a story assignment, I traveled to Iceland to experience its tourism boom, which was hitting a peak just prior to the pandemic halting global travel altogether. I stayed in an Airbnb rather than a hotel, selecting an apartment in the small stretch of downtown Reykjavík. Through the Airbnb search function I made sure the apartment was close to an industrial-chic coffee shop called Reykjavík Roasters, which I had identified in advance on Google Maps. The Airbnb was modeled on an industrial loft, with floor-to-ceiling windows opening to a view out over the miniature skyline. For decor, the identity-less apartment had a huge print of a photograph of the Brooklyn Bridge, which made me feel like I hadn't gone anywhere after leaving New York. Even though I had selected for that kind of aesthetic, the standardization seemed excessive for one of the more physically isolated places in the world.

My first expedition out of Reykjavík was the daylong bus trip around the Golden Circle. It felt like a throwback to elementary-school field trips, the group of us tourists sitting in our seats expectantly as an extremely stoic tour guide repeated the basic facts of where we were headed. Gullfoss, the enormous waterfall, was an awe-inspiring sight, a crack in the earth that 110 cubic meters of water flow through per second. The sheer volume of water and the roar that filled the air like speaker feedback at a concert would have been impressive enough even without the setting: rock crags covered in verdant green moss extending into fields. But much of my group was looking at the view through their phone cameras. The vista that they were capturing, down to the angle, was the same one that appears over and over again on the falls' Instagram page. They were further replicating the image, ensuring its dominance as a generic symbol of Iceland.

It reminded me of Don DeLillo's 1985 novel *White Noise,* in which the college-professor protagonist travels into the countryside with his colleague Murray to see "The Most Photographed Barn in America." Nothing makes the barn particularly remarkable except its notoriety—a fictional pre-Internet meme. Observing the crowd of photographers around the barn, Murray says, "We're not here to capture an image, we're here to maintain one. Every photograph reinforces the aura." "No one sees the barn," he concludes. "They are taking pictures of taking pictures." In Filterworld, it becomes hard to separate the nature of something, or its reality, from its popularity in terms of attention. Popularity alone often gets confused for meaning or significance, as in the case of DeLillo's barn.

Gullfoss has had to defend itself from photographers—as well as defend the photographers from themselves. Fences have popped up along the path running past the waterfall to prevent tourists from getting anywhere close to the edge or stepping onto the local moss, which can take a century to grow back. There have been fatal accidents around Gullfoss, echoes of American hikers falling off cliffs to their deaths while taking selfies. "If you fall over, it's impossible to find you. You're just gone," Steinarsson, the head of the tourism board, said. "What is that picture going to do for you?" he asked me. The only logic is if the photograph matters more than the sight itself.

The sheer volume of tourists arriving in Iceland has been slowly ruining what the tourists came to see in the first place: the island's natural grandeur. At some sites like the Haukadalur geysers, the relentless plodding of feet has turned the ground into mud. In the summer off-season, it usually has a chance to dry out, but tourism is increasingly year-round and the turf doesn't have time to recover. "If there's too much traffic there it would simply spoil," Steinarsson said.

Tourism driven by digital platforms causes a literal flattening, in the physical damage of so many feet and vehicle wheels, as well as a metaphorical flattening. As I have pointed out with other forms of culture, online ubiquity has a way of denaturing its subject, wearing away its essence into something more easily consumable, or else simply causing it to be consumed until it is gone. In Filterworld, uniqueness is an ephemeral product that gets seized on by algorithmic recommendations, recommended more and more until whatever was unique or special about it is either ruined or becomes cliché. The Greek island of Santorini, for example, famous for its white buildings and blue domes, had to post signs in 2019 demanding that visiting Instagrammers stop trespassing on rooftops to capture the perfect photo. The rooftops weren't just digital content; they were local residents' homes. A TikTok video from Santorini in 2023, during a post-pandemic resurgence of tourism, observed that this flattening had only intensified, with crowds lining up on the rooftops. "Just going somewhere to visually consume it because it's beautiful is not really what tourism should be about," the poster, Nikki Gibson, said in voiceover.

This process of Instagrammification was visible in two Icelandic hot springs that I visited. The first, the Blue Lagoon, is an established site for selfies. Conveniently located near the airport, it's a set of picturesque glassy buildings around a sprawling pool set amidst dark, jagged volcanic rock. The steam rising from the light-blue water against the alien landscape makes for a perfect photo backdrop. Though the Blue Lagoon is not a fully natural hot spring—it's heated by the runoff of a geothermal power plant—I had a perfectly pleasant time there, bobbing in the hot water, swimming up to the bar, and taking photos with my phone in a plastic case attached to a necklace that I bought to keep it dry. I daubed my face with whitish Icelandic clay and took a selfie that I posted on Instagram. All around me visitors were doing the same thing. You never forget you're a tourist at Blue Lagoon, which sees around a million guests annually. It's not a bad thing, but it can feel strange for travelers who pride themselves on seeking out more "authentic" experiences in which they try to be surrounded by locals. (Though it is good at curing jet lag.)

The other hot spring I visited was billed on my extended bus tour as the "Secret Lagoon," though its local name is Gamla Laugin, or simply "the old swimming pool." In fact, it is the oldest in Iceland; the pool, fed naturally by geysers that replace its water every twenty-four hours, was first built in 1891. In 1909, it hosted Iceland's first swimming lessons. After many decades of disuse, it reopened in 2014 with one single-story building housing lockers and showers. Unlike the Blue Lagoon, it was not designed to be photographed. The water was dark, not light blue, and it was surrounded by a bed of flat stones and mossy hillocks, with a tiny boardwalk running through the burbling geysers. A decrepit stone shed without doors or windows remained from the pool's historical use, giving it a sense of age and permanence. It felt local. I was a little embarrassed that our tour group of a dozen foreigners, arriving on a weekday mid-afternoon, seemed to be disrupting the routines of a handful of older solo swimmers. But I enjoyed the peaceful atmosphere and the sense that the place didn't demand anything from me other than appreciating it. I sank into the water and swam to the edge with plenty of space around me. No one was waving a phone around.

Though I was happy I made it there, I also felt the looming threat of a flood of tourists like me detracting from Gamla Laugin's uniqueness, turning it into another Blue Lagoon, a place to shoot TikTok videos and attract Instagram comments. The most common comment on a dramatic travel Instagram shot is always "Where is this?," implying another question: How can I get there, too? A certain ambivalence has always been a part of travel, knowing you're a tourist but also craving direct contact with a different place. Yet algorithmic recommendations have automated that process of word of mouth and turned tourism into a conveyor belt that intrudes much deeper into local cultural ecosystems—making places, or at least the experience of them, more similar in the process. The world is just potential fodder for content that attracts a few likes, makes money for digital platforms, and then evanesces, unlikely to ever be seen again. Wanting for a moment to avoid that cycle, I left Gamla Laugin and never posted anything about it.

## AIRBNB MIGRATION

During the COVID-19 pandemic, the same algorithmic forces that shaped tourism quickly began to shape movement within the United States as well. Within a matter of weeks, the ways in which many people evaluated real estate flipped. Dense cities had been increasingly desirable places to live, but with overloaded hospitals and the claustrophobia of quarantine, density became far less appealing. In 2020 and 2021, there was a marked population shift to suburban and rural areas, according to the US Census Bureau's estimates. Picturesque spots like Bend, Oregon; Portland, Maine; and Whitefish, Montana, boomed, and property prices rose in turn. In the Northeast and mid-Atlantic region, the focus was on upstate New York, the broad stretch of land from the Hudson Valley to the Pennsylvania border. During the chaotic months of summer 2020, if you couldn't buy a new countryside house, the next best thing was to rent one as an escape, and the fastest way to do so was on Airbnb. The algorithmic marketplace made moving as easy as clicking a button—but the speed and scale at which it happened meant that rentals became unaffordable, too. If you were fast enough and could pay enough, geography was frictionless; if you couldn't, you were stuck, and likely stuck with higher risk for catching COVID.

In the summer of 2020, I booked an Airbnb in the Catskills with a group of friends so we could all trek in from different cities: D.C., Boston, New York. I noticed that the houses with the most AirSpace aesthetics—cleanly renovated with white walls, equipped with minimalist furniture and brass fixtures—tended to book the fastest and cost the most. My group eventually found a large house in Hunter, New York, that sported a Chesterfield sofa from the direct-to-consumer brand Joybird and black-painted Shaker chairs along the slablike wood dining table. We were lucky to get it—

a woman had just canceled her summer-long rental, and I booked it twelve hours later. In fact, the house was set in a compound, with two smaller cabins on the grounds, which two Brooklyn families had booked for months on end to get out of the city. The Airbnbs existed because of COVID-19. "We went into mad pandemic time just trying to renovate them really quickly, because so many people wanted long-term rentals," the property's owner, Deirdre Patton, later told me. Patton had rented out the cabins on the platform before she even uploaded photos to the listings.

The suddenness of migration led to some strange phenomena across upstate New York. Renovations were rushed, and houses were thrown onto the marketplace with barely a piece of furniture in them, with conspicuous issues like broken plumbing or holes in the floors. City renters unused to full kitchens had accidents like leaving a pie to burn in an oven and setting off the fire alarm, as the founder of one rental company told me. A kind of turbo-gentrification was happening as New York City's population rushed northward, occupying the already low housing stock. Homes were selling for more than 20 percent over asking, according to one Realtor. It wasn't just upstate New York; those suddenly able (and forced) to work at home could work from anywhere. The options included popular remote-work destinations like Mexico City, Lisbon, and Bali, which saw influxes of new long-term visitors. These were "digital nomads"—people who hold down lucrative remote jobs or freelance gigs while traveling, working from their laptops in picturesque, relatively affordable locations.

This pandemic migration would have still happened without Airbnb, of course, but the platform accelerated and exacerbated it by making it so easy for a renter to find exactly the space they were looking for, and by motivating owners to put their homes on the marketplace to begin with. In a way, Airbnb had created the expectation of such immediate movement. One of the company's prominent slogans was "Belong Anywhere," with a campaign that began in 2014. "Experience a place like you live there," was another slogan. The underlying message was that you don't have to be a tourist anymore; you can playact the life of an actual local by staying in their home.

Airbnb was launched in 2008 by Brian Chesky and Joe Gebbia,

roommates and former classmates at the Rhode Island School of Design who had both studied industrial design, along with Nathan Blecharczyk, a developer. After college, they moved to San Francisco and had the idea of laying out an air mattress in the living room of their apartment to rent it out as a very lo-fi bed-and-breakfast. They landed their first customer during a design conference in the city, when hotels were crowded and visitors had few affordable options for overnight stays. This scenario underlies the platform's promise of intimacy and belonging: It was supposed to be about spare space, an act of almost charitable sharing that had the veneer of net social positivity. Strangers might get to know each other, and owners (or surreptitious renters) could financially support themselves by monetizing rooms that weren't always necessary. That intersection resulted in a company now worth over $80 billion, with over 150 million users. Airbnb might be the massive digital social network with the most direct physical consequences.

In practice, the company built such a lucrative market that many of the listings were short-term rental only—no one lived in them, lending apartments and even some entire streets the atmosphere of a hotel, like Marc Augé's non-place run amok. In its early years, Airbnb sent professional photographers to document properties, ensuring that the listings all shared the same cold, wide-angled, aggressively bright aesthetic, the better to be appealing as Instagram-like digital images. Ancillary cottage industries popped up, like Airbnb managers, who tidied the properties between customers, and design consultants, who could advise on decoration that would appeal to the platform's demographic. Natascha Folens, one such consultant, told me in 2016 that owners should embrace "the industrial look and the mid-century." "As long as it doesn't look cluttered and old," she added.

When I scroll backward through the history of my decade-old profile on Airbnb, I see grids of similarly spare, white-walled spaces: the hilltop Lisbon apartment where Jess and I had to pay a late fee to get in; the Seville courtyard with dramatic wooden shutters; the woodland glass box in upstate New York owned by a model-turned-restaurateur; the sterile lofted studio in Tokyo contained in its own tiny building even in the midst of the dense city; the immaculate Parisian apartment near Montmartre with its perfect collection of art books. I had been to all these places, but in a sense, they were one place, contained within my account, not belonging to anywhere at all. These real cities still persisted, of course. Normal people carried out their lives in them with a density and individuality that no one trip could ever encompass. But my encounter with the places had been limited, and I had been guided toward experiences that reinforced my own point of view, the taste profile built up by all my personal data online. I felt that I had inhabited an Instagram version of each destination—a shallow, superficially interactive image that ultimately did not reflect reality. In fact, the image occluded reality, made it harder to find. That feeling—that truth and authenticity are evasive and we are discouraged from seeking them by a series of digital mediations—seems to be at the heart of Filterworld.

In recent years, anti-Airbnb graffiti has popped up on the walls of cities where it is a dominant force. "Stop Airbnb and tourism" and "Our cities turn into commodities" in Athens. "Fuck Airbnb" in Venice. "One Airbnb tourist kicks out 2 to 3 students out [sic] of our city," in Coimbra, Portugal. (These were protests against algorithms as well as the overall dominance of American Silicon Valley companies.) Barcelona and Berlin became known for strict regulation of Airbnb, limiting who could rent out their spaces on the platform and for how long. There was a backlash against Airbnb as a company, protesting its aggressive fees and lax approval of unreliable hosts. Maybe hotels, the original generic experience, were coming back into fashion? But I've never given up Airbnbs. I'm too attracted by that abstract promise, to live an authentic life that's different from your own for a few days, imagining being a sculptor in Lisbon, say, or a Tokyo musician. For me, the illusion of tourism is more total if I stay in a real apartment—though of course it remains an illusion.

Airbnb as a company is aware of its flattening effects. In late 2021, I spoke with Chesky, now the CEO of Airbnb. It was a Zoom call; Chesky was at his home in San Francisco, though the background had been blurred out into nothingness by a filter. He spoke quickly and implacably, the tone of a man who already knows his thoughts on everything. "I'm trying to learn the lessons of overtourism. I don't per se think there's too much tourism in the world; I think overtourism is mainly too many people going to the same place at the same time," he said. "If you could design the perfect picture, you would fairly equally distribute people across many places across many dates, and you wouldn't overload any one place." Chesky was born in upstate New York, though a less romanticized area than the archetypal Hudson area that city dwellers flocked to: "Not a lot of people are going to my town, but it's actually pretty nice."

Chesky said that Airbnb was focused on solving this problem of "travel redistribution." Since tech platforms rarely address the enormity of the social changes they have caused, preferring to deemphasize their own power, it surprised me that he admitted Airbnb had an effect not just on how people travel, but on where they go, actively influencing the destination. "We point demand to where we have supply, to cities that want it," he said. Like other kinds of content in Filterworld, geography suffers from a problem of discovery. It's hard to find a particular place to travel when there are so many options; recommendations must serve up interesting finds while also suggesting what is familiar and recognizable. Users tend to stick to predetermined paths, as Chesky explained: "We have one hundred thousand cities and towns on Airbnb. People don't keep one hundred thousand destinations in their head; they keep about ten, and the ten are the ones that they see Netflix shows about. Everyone wants to go to Paris because of *Emily in Paris*."

I asked Chesky what he thought the consequences were of so many people traveling to the same places, routing through his digital platform, their choices and tastes influenced by what they found there. "You hit on one of the central questions of our time: What is our relationship to place? Is there more or less nationalism in a world where people can freely move across countries?" he asked. Chesky ultimately sees the shift as positive: "The optimist in me hopes that the implication of all this is that the world feels a little bit smaller. If you can make the physical world smaller, that's almost entirely a good thing. I think that's the endgame." Yet that vision of smallness is under the auspices and control of Airbnb, following the template the company has set and the conditions that it profits under. Smallness implies homogeneity and a move toward uniformity, most likely under a Western default, under the ideology of the tech industry. The trade-off that Chesky implied was that the more movement there was, the less identity there would be. Identity, too, is a matter of content.

■  ■  ■

# CHAPTER 4

# The Influencer Economy

## CHASING LIKES

For me, the Internet has always been inextricable from labor. Life online is an admixture of work and entertainment, very often both at once—which is predictable given that the Internet evolved to commodify the culture that emerged on it. Even before I went to college, social media was a marker of adult professionalism: in the summer of 2006, you could get on Facebook only once you had a college email address from whichever school you were going to attend, something accepted students didn't receive until the summer before their freshman year. So when I finally got a Facebook account, it was primarily a space for networking, getting to know the other students who were going to be part of my class at Tufts University. We quickly formed a Facebook group for the graduating class of 2010, which seemed at that point far in the future. We listed our hometowns, debated what we wanted to major in, and planned IRL meetups. Because of our shared affiliation, the social network had brought us together in advance, in a digital space—a form of social organization that felt rare at the time, merging the Internet and life offline. One very consequential life event emerged from that Facebook group: it was where I first interacted with my partner, Jess, and we began messaging about our shared taste in music.

During my junior year of college, the Internet also provided some of my first opportunities for paid work in the field I wanted to make a career in: writing. I had contributed reviews of art exhibitions to the *Tufts Daily* newspaper, and I joined Twitter in 2008, when the platform was more like a sparsely populated café than a roaring stadium. Then as now, Twitter's most addicted user base is journalists, who can't help but tweet the way wolves can't help but howl. Twitter gave me my first exposure to the media industry and the nascent world of online publishing. (Elon Musk may have changed Twitter's official name to X in 2023, but the original is far too set in my mind.)

Meanwhile, *The Atlantic*, which was still primarily a print magazine at the time, had recently launched themed blogs on its website, covering broad areas like culture and politics. Though individual writers including Ta-Nehisi Coates maintained themed blogs of their own to gather their thoughts on specific subjects, these verticals published many different writers, including freelance contributors. The freelancers tended to be emerging young writers, since they had to be willing to write for online-only media and hungry enough to accept very low fees. A friend at Tufts who had interned for *The Atlantic* one summer introduced me to an editor, and she accepted a few of my pitches. They were little arguments about cultural news and trends, what would now be called "hot takes," since they were based more on ephemeral opinion than on reporting or research. For *The Atlantic*, I wrote about why one singer-songwriter was better than another; later I weighed in on the gender symbolism of tote bags for the *The Guardian*, collected artworks that had gone viral for *Vice*, and extolled the benefits of online friendship for *The New Republic*. The pieces lived and died quickly, some sparking discussion in Facebook or Twitter feeds and others sinking without a trace.

Looking back on this early archive doesn't exactly fill me with pride, but it was what the digital ecosystem of the time demanded. Readers like hot takes because they're voicey and provide an opinion against which one can shape one's own; editors and writers appreciate them, too, because they're fast to write, cheap to commission, and easy to publish online. If you worked fast enough, you could go from zero to published in an afternoon. For these I was paid a pitiable but still-desired fee, in the low hundreds of dollars (*The Atlantic* started out at fifty dollars). The way twentieth-century writers must have felt about seeing their very first piece run in print, it was a thrill to have my byline appear in pixels under *The Atlantic*'s digital banner and in its signature typeface. It gave the text an authority that I didn't know it could have when I was drafting it in a Word document alone in the living room of my student apartment in Boston. (Digital spaces evoke memories just like Proust's madeleine: as I write this, I'm getting a whiff of the still, hot summer air, the bright sun, and the stiff cushions of the IKEA couch where I wrote and edited my first stories.) Of course, I also shared my articles on Twitter, where I followed a nascent crowd who were mostly engaged with the art world. It was my first brush with the constant contemporary labor of online self-promotion. Not only did you have to publish something; you had to market the piece and yourself at the same time.

Popularity contests are a perennial feature of culture. (In prehistory, surely there were cave paintings that were hyped up more than others and inspired Neanderthal queues, one viewer at a time.) Collectors of ancient Chinese painting habitually added their names to favored paintings by stamping them with seals—akin to an approving tweet or a thumbs-up like. Masterpieces acquired bunches of stamps over centuries, with some even layered on top of the painted landscape itself. In Western art, an elaborate frame with an insignia around a painting might speak to its importance, as would a bestseller-list label on a book or an album "going platinum"— all symbols of a high cultural value, or at least a high economic appraisal. These signals have always guided what consumers are likely to consume and thus appreciate. The bestseller label, for example, might encourage a shopper to give a book a second glance or flip to the first page. Artists have always had to be marketers of a sort, evolving public personas that served as calling cards for their work, as Jackson Pollock and Andy Warhol did. The difference today is that in Filterworld, the metrics—the number of likes, the pre-existing attention—tend to speak louder than the piece of culture itself. Not only do they act as a measure of success, but they create success, because they dictate what is recommended to and seen by audiences in the first place. It's as if a Chinese artist in the twelfth century had to acquire a large enough number of stamps before he could show his work.

I quickly learned to judge my success on the Internet almost solely in terms of numbers, which proliferated in the early stages of mainstream social media. The number of thumbs-ups on a Facebook post or Tweet was a representation of how many people it reached, how many people were inspired to click a button by your little self-promotional bulletin or opinionated missive. But was that a representation of a post's quality? Should we evaluate ourselves by this arbitrary new metric? The questions loomed, but given the utility of new social networks and the instant reach they afforded, it was easy to ignore such quandaries and just keep posting.

Suddenly, users could tell how every little piece of content compared to every other one. The numbers could not be escaped, popping up next to everything you read or watched. Even if the count of likes, shares, retweets, or faves was an artificial measure of value imposed by the platform itself, they still became the fastest and easiest way to judge what popped up in the infinite feeds of content. More was always better: if a YouTube video had a lot of views, perhaps it might be insightful or at least funny. Virality equaled quality—other people liked this, so you will, too. For creators, whether writers or aspiring Instagram influencers, metrics were the goal, the incentive, and the internal compass evaluating what worked and what didn't. Particularly in journalism, the higher the numbers, the more important something seemed to be. It was a truism: more likes meant more people had seen something. Each like was a vote in the seemingly meritocratic Internet, where anyone could upload content but certainly not everyone could inspire audiences to pay attention.

The law of virality—likes as an indication to the algorithm that specific content deserved more promotion—was particularly relevant for the early days of digital media. Publications' websites began to add shortcut buttons near the headlines of stories to share an article on Facebook, Twitter, and a proliferating list of other platforms. Then the buttons were updated to have their own tiny numbers, showing how many likes or retweets an article had gotten even before the reader had encountered its contents. Likes became the currency of the Internet, and journalists were forced to chase them. (Not that we needed much encouragement to do so.)

As a writer, I closely monitored the clicks on my articles. I was proud when my stories netted more likes than others'. When I tweeted links or shared my stories on Facebook, I noticed which posts got the most responses. The most successful tended to be the stories that impacted readers' personal lives or crystallized a complaint or problem they were having. When I made authoritative or dramatic statements, the reaction was dramatic in turn. I would recruit friends and colleagues via our always-on Gchat windows to prime my success by liking something right when it went up. It was a relief, years later, when these buttons fell out of favor and the visible numbers disappeared from article pages. But every time I have published an article over the past decade, I have fretted over just how many people were hitting Like and Retweet. I could try to game the system and be aware of which approaches might create extra engagement on social media, but ultimately the result was out of my control.

The tyranny of likes is in part a function of the algorithmic ecosystem we exist in online. Each button press is another data signal to be absorbed, a small sign that you're paying attention to a piece of content that can then be used to train machine-learning systems to serve you more of that thing. Computers don't track our eye movements—at least not yet—and so buttons like the thumbs-up or emoji reactions serve as a proxy for our reaction to content. These are convenient shortcuts for self-expression but also, inevitably, provide more grist for the mill of targeted advertising. We participate in our own surveillance by signaling our preferences so publicly.

It wasn't just articles that were measured by likes. So were Instagram selfies, Facebook status updates about vacations or weddings, and Medium blog posts announcing new business ventures. Medium, a minimalist blogging platform launched by a cofounder of Twitter in 2012, at one point adopted "claps" as its governing metric. Users could press a button to clap for a piece and click it as many times as they were inclined to—up to fifty claps. For a time, the number of claps also dictated the fees that Medium paid to writers who used its platform, a literal equation of likes to value. Over time, a kind of inflation of likes occurred. Each one had less and less value. By 2020, hitting Like on something wasn't so much a sign that you enjoyed it as just that you had perceived it—it had broken through the overall noise of the Internet. It was common for journalists to put a proviso in their social media bios reading "Likes don't equal endorsements" to guard against misinterpretation. Though you don't always press the Like button because you actually enjoy a post, liking is the only function available to you.

Every social media user has an innate sense of what will get liked. As with classical beauty or geometric proportion, the formula is inexact and yet always identifiable. Provocation inspires likes, since the like is a gesture of allegiance and agreement, a symbol of whether the user is on the side of the troll or the trolled. Outrage gets likes because the likes signal sympathetic outrage: You are mad, too, because how could anyone not be? Hence a common format of post claiming that not enough people are talking about a given subject: a war, a disaster, a bad policy, a bad person. The ignorance alone is an outrage! Sex gets likes, for reasons that don't require explaining. The politician Ted Cruz's Twitter account once liked a pornographic video, a lusty act that was blamed on a staffer. (In 2015, one article offered a warning in the headline: "A PSA for Dudes: Everyone Can See You Liking Teen Girls' Bikini Pics on Instagram.")

Then there are more acceptable emotions used to elicit likes. Humor plays well, both because you like the joke and because you want to pass it along to others, so sharing begets more sharing. Relatability works because it allows the widest possible audience across social media to recognize themselves in something. Relatable content includes eating habits, complaints about your own laziness, and common childhood experiences. ("Did you ever . . . ?") I once tweeted, "sorry I responded late to your email I was unjustifiably terrified of opening it," a momentary reflection on my own inbox anxiety. The line was neither particularly funny nor eloquent, but nearly 150,000 people liked it—by liking it, they were saying it themselves, in a way. A writer friend habitually saved her most banal observations to tweet on weekends, on the basis that it was then when audiences were looking for something particularly relatable. It often worked, regularly netting tens of thousands of likes. Finally, recognizability, in the sense of nostalgia or familiarity, is perfect for driving likes and engagement. You like because you know what something is; you are more likely to like a clip of a TV show that you've seen many times before than a clip of one you haven't seen, which would require sitting through the video and evaluating it.

These like-inspiring emotions are some of our basest human instincts, which makes sense because they also must occur in the space of an instant, before we continue scrolling. There is no room here for ambiguity, subtlety, or unsurety—you can't hit a button to show that you're still mulling something over, that you haven't come to any easy conclusions yet. Absolutes are the order of the day. Twitter has long been the feistiest arena on social media, where the action boils down to a daily contest for likes. Perhaps it's because the space is so minimal—only a few sentences at a time—and the methods of interaction so limited: retweet, like, reply, ignore. In ancient Roman gladiatorial contests, the emperor dictated the loser's fate with a hand gesture, thumbs up for a death sentence and thumb pressed down to the fist for mercy. On Twitter, the assembled users fill the metaphorical colosseum, and we're all raising our hands in real time to pass judgment with our likes. (Facebook still uses a thumbs-up icon, though it no longer means death.) We like someone's broadside against another person because we agree with the critique. We like a smart rejoinder—a "dunk"—because we agree with the person being critiqued. And each action is reinforced by the algorithmic feed, distributed to others to decide their own judgments.

The tyranny of likes is so complete that in 2016 the artist Nick DeMarco, who was part of an Internet art scene in the early 2010s, came up with a game called "0 Likes on Instagram." It was a Dadaist reversal of the usual rules of social media: instead of posting the most attractive, compelling photo, you had to post as neutral an image as possible. It couldn't even be ugly, since that would receive too much of a reaction, or your followers might like it ironically. "The game is deceptively simple yet infinitely complex," DeMarco wrote in a set of official rules. I tried it myself at the time; it was even harder when Instagram was smaller and you knew a few friends would certainly see your posts, before the feed was too algorithmic and occupied by too many accounts from brands and strangers. Total mundanity worked best, like an off-kilter photo of the sidewalk or a random wall. Sometimes I could get a single like, but never the true goal of none. DeMarco proposed an alternative of posting with a friend over the course of a day and trying to get the lowest number of likes overall, like golf strokes: "A winner is determined by whoever has the fewest likes at the point when the competitors split up." It's an amusing quest, but it also underlines the extent to which all activity on the Internet is driven toward the goal of more and more likes.

I got on Twitter in 2008 because I saw a news story that an American student studying abroad had been jailed in Egypt and had used the site to alert his family. I was about to study abroad in China, so I figured it might prove useful. It did, but not for so dramatic a reason. It kept me in touch with what my friends back home were doing, and the nascent online art world. For a long time, Twitter remained a segmented part of my life, a constant professional water cooler that filled my days with ambient chatter, a role that might have been filled by office colleagues for a non-freelancer. Something shifted over time, however; Twitter seemed to occupy an increasing amount of psychic space, to both play host to and drive the cultural discussions of the day. The 2016 election of Donald Trump, a hyperactive Twitter user, as president was likely the turning point. Not only were algorithmic feeds becoming more pervasive, but social networks became host to the parallel public-opinion battles of "the resistance," the loose liberal coalition against Trump that adopted, to an extent, the right's predilection for online trolling. Trump's use of Twitter, until he was banned in 2021 after the Capitol riot, only intensified its presence: the algorithmic feed ensured as many users as possible saw his tweets, even if they hated their originator. Twitter didn't just contain the news; it *was* the news.

The platform's gravity inexorably shaped what and how I wrote. As I used it to promote my writing and test out my ideas to see how audiences responded, I learned the mechanics of what worked and what fell flat. Authoritative statements hit, as did one-liner jokes and provocative arguments on any side of an issue. We Twitter users of the mid-2010s developed an argot of references and shorthands that shaped the platform's real-time discourse. During my peak periods of usage, when an idea came into my mind, it arrived subconsciously made for Twitter, restricted to a hypothetical 280 characters. I was no longer aware of the translation between thought and tweet; my brain had been completely trained on the dopamine hits of social media attention, like Pavlov's dog salivating at the ringing of a bell.

The likes were not the only reward; they existed in a wider online attention economy that bled into the offline economy at large. Likes lead to attention. Attention leads to new followers; followers who liked and shared my work in turn. More followers led to a veneer of personal authority: I was a voice to listen to in my field, a writer worth looking out for. And that reputation got me commissions from editors, part-time gigs, and full-time jobs, which drove me back to the beginning of that loop. Getting more likes felt like what I was supposed to be doing; it felt like work, and I was getting better at my job.

Beyond the social media presences of individual people, businesses and cultural productions had to attract likes, too. A fashion brand might measure its success in Instagram likes, because more likes meant more customer engagement and potential buyers. Accounts made for new movies or television shows would likewise be oriented toward likes, because they were a measurement of marketing success: if you could get more followers for the account of the *Twilight* sequel *New Moon,* then more fans were excited for it and the debut would attract more viewers. Such is the pressure to be likable, optimizing for the appropriate algorithmic feedback.

This is not a new pressure; it's basic human psychology to want to be liked, and we ultimately like what is most similar to us, the same way that mirroring another person's body language in conversation can make you appear more convincing or empathetic. Likability binds society together with the shared incentive to not offend or alienate. Yet interpersonal likability has not been a common metric of culture, particularly the kind of innovative art we have prized over the past century or two. Art itself—not to mention artists as people—tends not to be bound by the quest for likability, and yet likes are what the current tyranny of quantification prioritizes most. In Filterworld, what is likable succeeds and what is not likable is doomed to fail, particularly in any arena of culture where audiences are requisite for survival. And because our American cultural landscape is almost entirely subservient to capitalism, that means more or less all of it.

## THE EMPTINESS OF ALGORITHMIC CULTURE

In 2021, Martin Scorsese, creator of films both artistically and commercially successful, published an essay in *Harper's,* a magazine better known for hosting niche literary criticism than acting as a stage for world-famous directors. In the essay, Scorsese recounted his personal appreciation for Fellini, the mid-century Italian director of sprawling, grandiose productions, but he also took the opportunity to decry the state of contemporary cinema. In the era of streaming video, films had been flattened into the category of "content," Scorsese wrote. Content "became a business term for all moving images: a David Lean movie, a cat video, a Super Bowl commercial, a superhero sequel, a series episode." Scorsese goes on to describe the architecture of our cultural ecosystem—the content that we consume is being filtered by algorithmic recommendations, which operate based on what we've already seen and the subject matter or genre of the content at hand. "Algorithms, by definition, are based on calculations that treat the viewer as a consumer and nothing else," he wrote. There is only one way to interact with content: ingest it and like it.

That blanket category of content and the algorithmic prioritization of familiarity has undermined the medium of film, Scorsese argued: "The cinema has always been much more than content, and it always will be." What gets lost is the deeper art form of cinema, the medium that changed his life and the lives of so many others, the aesthetic and even moral challenges that come through the silver screen. Watching great movies was not always comfortable; the experience went beyond banal consumption and aspired to interrogating social norms and enabling viewers to discover new senses of self.

Scorsese used the example of Fellini's films as the opposite of digestible content and the pinnacle of filmmaking as art. Fellini's 1963 film *8½* is the pinnacle of the director's oeuvre for Scorsese, a fragmentary, self-referential meditation on the life of an artist. Scorsese described the moment the movie debuted: "People argued over it endlessly: the effect was that dramatic. We each had our own interpretation, and we would sit up till all hours talking about the film—every scene, every second. Of course, we never settled on a definite interpretation." It was so strange and unfamiliar that Scorsese had to digest it slowly, incorporating its influence into his own later movies. The paranoia that I hear in Scorsese's essay is that the art of the twenty-first century no longer holds up to such scrutiny. Instead, it's cheap and ephemeral, wafting through your life without leaving any discernible mark. (The passion of his writing shows just how much Scorsese was marked by Fellini, an impact that he was still processing six decades later.) That may be because to fit into digital feeds, in order to attract those pernicious likes and further promote itself as much as possible, culture has to be content first and art second—if at all.

Scorsese's complaints can be chalked up to his position as an elder statesman of his medium; some may even find his position retrograde. The world has changed since his youth; he no longer needs to think about what is new, because his reputation and level of access mean he can create whatever he wants. But others shared his sense of ennui and anxiety, echoing Scorsese's lament that something about algorithmic recommendations has robbed culture of its innate meaning. In an interview with NPR, the producer Barry Diller commented, "These streaming services have been making something they call 'movies.' They ain't movies. They are some weird algorithmic processes that has created things that last 100 minutes or so." "Much of culture now has the hollow, vacant feeling of having been made by algorithm," wrote the critic Dean Kissick, one of the more incisive commentators on contemporary culture, in 2021. "Algorithmic" has become a byword for anything that feels too slick, too reductive, or too optimized for attracting attention: a combination of high production values with little concern for fundamental content.

I feel that emptiness, too. By the late 2010s and early 2020s, it seemed as though many cultural forms—books, TV shows, movies, music, and visual art—primarily existed to garner ephemeral attention and populate the endless app feeds. Nothing stuck in the way that a masterpiece that will be revisited decades hence sticks. For me, a major signal came from the style of painting that became popular in the art world, with young artists netting huge prices from galleries and auctions. In 2014, the art critic and painter Walter Robinson coined the term "zombie formalism" to describe it. Zombie formalism was abstract expressionism shorn of its emotion and grandeur, with canvases of mushy brushstrokes or cold monochromes from the likes of Oscar Murillo and Jacob Kassay. The critic Jerry Saltz echoed that it was "look-alike art." Their tendency toward the meaninglessly decorative led the way to a slew of painters depicting glossy surrealist scenes, like Emily Mae Smith's paintings of anthropomorphized broomsticks. (Dean Kissick labeled it "zombie figuration.")

These were paintings adapted for Instagram, which was also where collectors increasingly tended to discover and buy them (often without seeing the art in person), mediated yet again by algorithmic recommendations. They could resell it frictionlessly on the same platforms as easily as resharing a post. In 2014, the infamous appropriation artist Richard Prince shortcut the process and produced a series of "paintings" that were actually printed replicas of found Instagram posts, which sold for prices up to $100,000.

Part of the fear of algorithmically driven art is the obviation of the artist: If viable art can be created or curated by computer, what is the point of the humans producing it? An artist like Mike Winkelmann, known by his alias Beeple, built up over two million followers on Instagram with his slapdash CGI cartoons, but that success required posting every day and rarely rising above the intellectual level of a thirteen-year-old boy. (Early in the 2021 boom for nonfungible tokens, Beeple artwork sold at Christie's for $69 million, both a joke and an entirely serious demonstration of popularity.) It's easy to worry about your own looming obsolescence as a creator. But consumers are equally affected.

In a 2022 essay, Jeremy Larson, an editor at the music magazine *Pitchfork*, complained that the algorithmic experience of listening to music on Spotify was getting in the way of the music itself. "Even though it has all the music I've ever wanted, none of it feels necessarily rewarding, emotional, or personal," Larson wrote. Though the artists' intentions may not have changed, "music becomes an advertisement for the streaming service, and the more time and attention you give it, the more it benefits the tech company." The platform becomes a filter, and sometimes a barrier, for the listener's relationship to the artist and their work. And not every artist allows the streaming service to broadcast their music in the first place. Musicians like Neil Young and Joni Mitchell have removed their catalogs from Spotify to protest some of the company's decisions, including funding podcasts that promulgate political and cultural conspiracy theories. It took years to negotiate digital rights for Aaliyah's catalog of music; it wasn't available on Spotify until 2021. The musicians' absence makes them harder to access and perhaps easier for a Spotify subscriber to forget about—or never discover in the first place—since the service encompasses so much of its users' listening habits. Its recommendation algorithms would fail to promote Aaliyah, Young, or Mitchell even if a listener might like them because Spotify can't profit from the listen. It passively limits how we perceive music. Larson described it as "a fabricated reality meant to replace the random contours of life outside the app."

In an evocative metaphor for our collective algorithmic consumption, Larson wrote that "millions of users now sit side by side at the ledge of one great big trough of recorded music for the monthly price of a Chipotle burrito." It's a symbolic and literal devaluing of the medium; as low as that subscription price is, Spotify passes on little of it to actual artists. Before the advent of buffet-style streaming services and infinite feeds, the scarcity of a single vinyl record, cassette tape, or CD provided an incentive for a listener to get to know an artist's work, because otherwise the monetary investment in the music might not feel worth it. The promise of an algorithmic feed is that if the music becomes at all boring or tiresome, you can flip to the next song. That next recommendation will probably stick to the limits of your predetermined taste, and you won't have paid anything more for it.

I get the same feeling that Larson describes when I watch Netflix shows, especially when bingeing multiple episodes of a series at once. Sure, the shows are enjoyable—so enjoyable that I can't stop watching them. But I can't name many Netflix-produced shows that have stuck with me. My personal streaming addiction is to food documentaries. I'll watch anything within that category: travel shows highlighting street food from different continents or a biopic that follows a Michelin-starred chef with copious B-roll of steaks hitting the grill. Given that few of these productions have charismatic individual hosts—their required presence would make it more difficult to manufacture episodes in high volume—they all blur together in my memory like one long screen saver. These shows are the equivalent of monotonous Instagram posts from tourist destinations—fodder for empty likes and thoughtless engagement, the endless reproduction of content.

It's not that such content can't be artful; the innovation of productions that Netflix acquired like *Jiro Dreams of Sushi* and the follow-up series *Chef's Table* was to focus on visual beauty above all, with soft-focus cameras trained on food close-ups. They translated the food porn of Instagram photos into television. Yet the artfulness was yoked to the need to be placid, undisruptive, and ambient—developing the audiovisual equivalent of perfect linen bedsheets. The productions inspire no thoughts, only sensory pleasure. Unlike the curation required in an art-house cinema or an independent video rental store to ensure that each offering stands on its own, the shows didn't have to provide meaningful one-off experiences; they could simply exist in bulk as a numbing narcotic.

Contrast the empty calories of ambient food documentaries with the rise of the Food Network cable channel in the 1990s and 2000s, which prompted the evolution of chef-celebrities and caused a sea change in the culture of home cooking. On streaming services, actual cooking shows are notably absent, as if they might encourage too much physical activity that would take away from time spent looking at a screen. What remains is pure, unproductive, hypnotic entertainment, because the core purpose is simply to have the viewers leave the service on as "active users." Netflix has gone so far as to produce replicas of its shows, set in different countries and using different languages. *Home for Christmas* began as a Norwegian miniseries about a single woman in the rural town of Røros trying to find a boyfriend before the holidays; it was remade almost shot by shot in the Italian *I Hate Christmas*, set in Chioggia—a cheap way to double your content. Once a formula works, it is repeatable, or scalable, across Netflix's vast global audience, who end up unknowingly consuming the same material. The replicated show can be served to any possibly interested viewer via algorithmic recommendation.

Earlier in the streaming era, Netflix was infamous for its autoplay feature, which was introduced in its first form in 2016. When a TV episode or movie ended, a timer counted down ten seconds and then another show or film started, either the subsequent episode in the series or an algorithmically recommended alternative. In a 2019 post on the forum Hacker News, one Netflix engineer recalled that the original ten seconds caused "the biggest increase in hours watched"; five was too jarring and fifteen too slow. At the time, autoplay felt like a radical departure. Wasn't a TV episode simply supposed to stop? On cable, you'd usually have to wait a week for the next episode in a series. But since Netflix most often added entire television seasons at once, the feature all but mandated binge-watching. It also pushed users to coast along algorithmic lines of consumption, perhaps sticking to a given genre, like Jane Austen remakes or action movies featuring aliens, as it recommended one example after another. (Variety is a difficult concept for recommendation algorithms.)

After Netflix played three episodes in a row without the user stopping the autoplay function, or after ninety minutes of continuous watching, the app even stopped itself and a fateful message appeared on screen asking, "Are you still watching?" This feature persists today. In part, it was a safeguard against the service remaining on after the user fell asleep in front of the TV. The times that I encountered it, in the dim illumination of the living room at night or emanating from my laptop screen, I felt a tinge of embarrassment. It wasn't that I was asleep, it was just that I was watching way more TV than I usually did, one episode sliding implacably into the next before I had the willpower to stop it. Bingeing was something that the platform itself encouraged me to do, and yet the warning message implied that it was negative. By the 2020s, however, autoplay had become the norm via YouTube and TikTok: you would never expect a feed to end. All culture is now content, and the platforms we use to access it encourage us to treat it as interchangeable.

In 2007, Amazon launched Kindle Direct Publishing, a marketplace for eBooks, which were consumed on its new Kindle e-reader. Over time, KDP became a hub for self-published authors who circumvented the traditional hierarchy of agents, editors, and bookstores by going online, where new books were automatically recommended to readers using the same mechanisms as blouses or blenders in the Amazon store. The content that succeeded on KDP was a departure from what succeeded in the established literary world, too. It was a space for literature-as-content, where subject specificity and word volume far outweighed the opinions of critics. The more books an author produced, the better. According to one estimate, KDP offered over twelve million e-books in 2022. Amazon wasn't just controlling e-books; in 2019, its larger digital storefront made up three-quarters of online sales of new books for adults and almost half of all new book sales overall. In other words, much of literature is forced to move through Amazon's platform to reach consumers, which pressures books into particular forms—high-volume series confined to specific genre categories and released consistently over time in a drip of content—the same way a tweet has to be written to succeed in the Twitter feed.

The Stanford University professor Mark McGurl has studied how modernist literature evolved through the twentieth century, including tracking how the development of fiction MFA programs influenced mid-century novels. Novelists-turned-professors, taking jobs to support their writing practice, tutored their students at institutions like the Iowa Writers' Workshop, often pushing them toward a style of self-conscious literary realism from a personal perspective. Wendell Berry, Richard Ford, Michael Chabon, Rick Moody, and Tama Janowitz were some of the successes of the MFA-program model. Today, MFA programs still act as gatekeepers, helping publishers identify new talent and ushering novelists into the professionalized industry. The handpicked nature of such programs, and the insular, handshake nature of the publishing industry, maintain the ability to promote a singular or challenging artist—an act of tastemaking—though they are by nature somewhat elitist.

McGurl identified the looming homogeneity of MFA style. But algorithmic gatekeepers can come first. Young writers often find ways to cultivate public presences online even before they enter

MFA programs, on Twitter, Instagram, or TikTok. They subject their voices to the force of social media flattening. These pre-prepared personae might even help in competitive grad school applications. At each step of the process, a literary idea is tested for its ability to draw online engagement in a marketplace of attention.

McGurl now sees us entering into an Amazon era of literature, in which the company is an aesthetic as well as a commercial arbiter. It is "offering itself as the new platform of literary life," McGurl wrote in his 2021 book *Everything and Less: The Novel in the Age of Amazon.* The platform's measure of quality is quantity, the same ruthless metric of engagement as other algorithmic feeds. More purchases, and more pages read, meant that a book was better than its peers. Not only did a book cover have to be designed to be legible on a small screen, but the writing also had to be optimized for page turning, as it were—grabbing the reader's attention with each successive line. (This is a quality that good writing often has, of course, but not always.)

On one hand, this is a kind of democratization: Anyone can publish a book and give it a chance to be sold through the exact same channels, presented in the same way. There is no obstacle of a store's book buyer or the curation of a front table; just the math of the algorithm. The hyper-bestselling author Colleen Hoover provides an example of the opportunities. Hoover began by self-publishing her novels, which often fall into romance, thriller, and young-adult categories, on Amazon. The success of her first two led a mainstream publisher, Atria Books, to republish them in 2012, and her novels began to consistently hit bestseller lists. (Hoover stuck with self-publishing for her third novel, despite other offers.) During the pandemic, Hoover made eBooks of her backlist free—another strategy to boost digital engagement—and sparked a wave of fans on TikTok, where the nascent book community made tearful testaments to her writing's impact. Sales of her more than twenty books are estimated above twenty million copies, "more books than James Patterson and John Grisham combined," as *The New York Times* reported. The flywheel has accelerated even outside of Hoover's control: "I read other people's books, and I'm so envious. I'm thinking, Oh my God, these are so much better, why are mine selling the way they are?" she told the *Times* in 2022.

On the other hand, the requirement of mass engagement is a departure from the history of literature, in which the opinions of editors and academics have mattered far more than how many copies of a book initially sells. The literary canon, McGurl wrote, is "a thing Amazon has no particular relation to at all except as a list of books that students tend to purchase." As filtered by the platform, "all fiction is genre fiction," he wrote, whether an experimental novel that took a decade to write or the fifth volume in an endless series of erotica eBooks. McGurl identified certain genres that found a successful home in Amazon's KDP marketplace. Romance books played well, including niche subgenres like "alpha billionaire romance," *Fifty Shades of Grey* being the most famous example, and "threesome MMF military." (It's not a coincidence the genre names themselves resemble search-engine optimization language.) Epics were another hit, including sprawling fantasy series.

At its most observable, the phenomenon of Amazon Literature is confined to a relatively small space: the digital storefront and the Kindle reader. Both are relegated to specific situations and might be particularly amenable to activities like reading guilty pleasures—on Kindle, no one can see the title of the book you're reading. It's easy enough to avoid the algorithmic influence and go to a physical bookstore, where a clerk might make a personal recommendation. Yet McGurl also linked the consumption habits that Amazon conditioned readers into with the rise of high-literary genres like 2010s autofiction—echelons of the publishing industry that were not seen as so algorithmic nor market-driven.

Autofiction is a genre "centering on a barely fictionalized writer-protagonist," McGurl wrote. Though it originated in France in the 1970s, coined by the theorist Serge Doubrosky, it came into vogue more recently with the success of novelists including Sheila Heti, Ben Lerner, Rachel Cusk, and Karl Ove Knausgaard. Their work is connected by a close but ambiguous relationship between author and narrator: Is the "I" of Cusk's *Outline* trilogy of novels beginning in 2014 really Cusk herself, like a memoir, or are the narrator and the events within pure fiction? The appeal comes from the voyeuristic tension of guessing which is which. Of course, readers are intimately familiar with this dynamic from social media, where other people present their lives and selves with varying degrees of truthfulness, whether in tweets or photos. Autofiction is a bit like an influencer's Instagram account: fragmented, non-narrative, and often deceptive.

Per McGurl's analysis, both Karl Ove Knausgaard and Rachel Cusk's autofiction novels came in series, offering readers a high volume of content, and presented a vicarious, almost consumerist view of the life of a successful writer. At times the books shade into a form of wish fulfillment, at least for their cultural-elite target audience. One buys the book as if one is buying the lifestyle of far-flung residencies and author panels, reading it as if watching a reality TV show. "I need the next volume like crack," Zadie Smith once wrote of *My Struggle,* the same thing you might say of a season of *Real Housewives.* I think Cusk and Knausgaard are two of the more interesting novelists of the twenty-first century, but I might unwittingly overlook the degree to which the seemingly avant-garde literary style masks their books' much more banal and mainstream content. Upon a recent reread, I was reminded of just how much of Cusk's *Transit,* the second in her *Outline* trilogy, consists of anecdotes about salon haircuts and home renovation. Is Cusk radically overhauling my relationship to narrative, or do I just wish I had a London flat to rebuild in a desirable neighborhood?

The point here is not that Knausgaard was paying attention to Instagram likes when he wrote about his youth in rural Norway. It's that algorithms have shaped the overall cultural landscape, conditioning our tastes. Everything exists within the algorithmic context of passive, frictionless consumption. No matter that a book or other piece of content seems to exist outside of the algorithmic ecosystem; it is still informed by the dominant aesthetics and trends that algorithmic feeds have given rise to. The end point of algorithmic culture is a constant flow of similar-yet-different content, varied enough so as not to be utterly boring but never disruptive enough to be alienating. Reaching toward an ambitious artistic ideal may have faded in favor of refinement toward the goal of likes and engagement above all.

Many popular cultural forms in the early twenty-first century seem to have been reduced to either narcotic mood enhancements or simplistic puzzles left for the viewer to solve and then move on to the next. This extends to even our largest productions. A film like the 2019 *Avengers: Endgame* was supposed to provide a capstone to many years of Marvel superhero films, the way that the original *Star Wars* ending once occupied the public imagination. Across its three-hour run time, much longer than the usual blockbuster, *Endgame* prioritized special effects and checking the boxes of fan trivia—you can spot your favorite superhero as they all return to fight the villain for the last time—over satisfying storytelling. Marvel devotees may have been pleased—*fanservice* is the term of art for content that overtly caters to hardcore fans' desires—but the end result is close to meaningless in terms of emotional impact or creative expression.

Rather than encouraging original artistic achievement, algorithmic feeds create the need for content that exists to generate more content: films that provide ready-made GIFs of climactic scenes to share on Twitter or TikTok and quippy lines that will inspire memes to serve as marketing. The need for engagement can encourage a capitulation to fanservice, or at least an attempt to do so.

The original *Game of Thrones* TV series fell prey to the same problem when it ended in 2019. Twenty million people watched the finale—one of the most-watched TV episodes ever. And yet it left many viewers cold. After many seasons of carefully developed character arcs, the final episodes seemed to throw established personalities out the window as Daenerys Targaryen turned evil and murderous. The royal maneuvering that the show recounted devolved into fantastical battles and dragons burning down CGI cities, spectacle surpassing plot. It may have looked good in clips shared on Twitter but it was nonsensical to watch. It's telling that the showrunners David Benioff and D. B. Weiss had to plot the finale themselves, since the novelist George R. R. Martin didn't finish the book series in time—perhaps another triumph of digital streaming over literature. Lacking an internal vision, they chased what might play well online and provided tidy answers to the sprawling puzzle. Optimization didn't work for a narrative so individual as Martin's; despite the great expense that went into it, the final season became ephemeral content and faded out of viewers' minds seemingly overnight.

The first three novels by the Irish author Sally Rooney, currently upheld as a peak of Western millennial fiction, are a trilogy of romances that dramatize coming-of-age in moody Irish and continental European landscapes. They are atmospheric books, absorbing in their wealth of local detail and soothingly written in Rooney's simple, elegant, and yet somewhat cold prose. The novels witness their characters falling into and out of love, love that happens best in rare moments when it pierces the narcissism of the young self. They also heavily feature instant-message and email transcripts, the native communication medium of Rooney's characters. Reflecting our digital social lives so accurately is a strength of her novels. Alongside their vicarious entertainment value, they depict various social problems that became tentpoles of Twitter discourse when the books debuted, with pundits taking various sides of the topic at hand in their think pieces (in fact, Rooney was a debate-club star as a student herself). In *Conversations with Friends*, it was polyamory and self-harm. In *Normal People*, it was masochistic sexuality. In *Beautiful World, Where Are You*, it was economic class differences and literary fame itself, moving toward autofiction.

All three novels inspired debate over how physically attractive the characters were or should be, a fact that has to do with Rooney's gendered position as a female novelist but also the stories' fundamental basis in aesthetic pleasure: beauty often drives the narrative. Rooney's first two novels have also been transformed into literal streaming content in two television series coproduced by the BBC. The 2020 TV iteration of *Normal People* might be best interpreted as a series of softcore-pornographic GIF sets that would have been extremely popular on Tumblr had the platform not banned adult material in 2018. Rooney was on Twitter herself, as many millennial literati were, and was accustomed to the flow of discourse. She left the platform after she became too much of a public figure; she didn't want so many followers. Still, her novels are inextricable from their parallel existence online.

The cultural ecosystem of Filterworld puts the cart before the horse: The needs of promotion and marketing supersede the object that is meant to be promoted. Not only does culture have to be designed to generate external content to serve as marketing on digital platforms; the platforms also profit from the increased engagement driven by new content. It can be seen as either a symbiotic relationship or a vicious cycle, reinforcing the need to cater to the aesthetic requirements of the platform. Optimizing for this equation—second-guessing a creative process in advance—is much easier than finding an alternative to it. At this point, many pieces of contemporary culture have come to resemble or glorify the social platforms themselves—all the better to be distributed through them.

## THE RISE OF INFLUENCERS

One streaming television show epitomized the flattening of culture in the algorithmic platform era. It debuted on Netflix in October of 2020, during a pandemic that still had most people the world over stuck in their homes with no other choice but to watch TV. Still, it was surprising how quickly the show came to dominate conversation (online, at least, where all nondomestic discussion was happening). *Emily in Paris* was the creation of Darren Star, the director and producer best known for the *Sex and the City* series, an intermittently glossy and gritty portrayal of Manhattan life in the late 1990s. *Emily in Paris* was originally meant for cable television but eventually landed at the streaming service, where the entire first season was available immediately to binge-watch.

A show both of and about social media, the titular Emily Cooper—played saccharine in the extreme by Lily Collins—is a woman in her early twenties from Chicago. She might be called "basic" for her job at a marketing firm, her long ponytail, and her habit of jogging around cities in athleisure. Emily heads to Paris to bring her American expertise to Savoir, a fictional agency that specializes in marketing luxury fashion brands. Specifically, it is Emily's job to train the staff on creating content for the Internet. Like a well-meaning missionary, she disrupts the relative peace of French tradition—long lunches, print magazine ads, runway shows—and tries to convert the locals to Instagram posts instead.

In Star's *Sex and the City,* Carrie Bradshaw was a newspaper columnist who wrote about her dating exploits, shopping habits, and deep friendships—articles that were only hinted at in maudlin draft lines that appeared as she sat at her laptop. Bradshaw's role as a writer made her a productive part of culture: she was constructing a particular personal philosophy of life and love. Emily, by contrast, is simply a professional consumer. Her version of Carrie's writing is taking photos with her phone, which is a constant presence in the show.

In the first episode, she pulls it out and takes a selfie with the view from her *chambre de bonne.* Then a symbolic representation of her phone screen pops up within the camera's real-life frame. Emily posts the photo to an unnamed Instagram equivalent (to avoid copyright infringement), and her number of followers on the generic platform appears on screen. She changes her username from @emilycooper to @emilyinparis. Later in the same episode, she takes another Parisian selfie—her follower count has quadrupled, and then it jumps up again when she posts the image. She reacts to the number with bemused satisfaction. In the second episode, her followers have gone up by a factor of ten as she posts snapshots of a market. The number of likes and comments on her images spin upward like the wheels on a slot machine: she has hit the social media jackpot, acquiring strangers as intimate fans of her personal life.

This visual gimmick persists throughout the show as Emily takes yet more selfies, documents parties, and shows off outfits. Nothing new is created and no insight is imparted; the posts just rack up while the character progresses through her bildungsroman of accruing followers. Unlike, say, an art photographer laboriously framing a composition before pressing the shutter, the act of taking a photo for Instagram appears to be instantaneous and thoughtless for Emily. She just acts on instinct, already conditioned by her consumption of social media, transforming her life into optimized content in real time.

When I first watched the series, the way it visualized and valorized social media struck me as dystopian even as it was completely realistic. The specter of our online presences haunts every moment, causing us to constantly judge which scenes in our lives are worth broadcasting to our personal audiences, offering them up to the feed. Worse still, *Emily in Paris* glamorized the transformation of life into content, casting it as evidence of the protagonist's character development. Emily succeeds at Savoir because she is so expert at social media; there is no line between her professional labor, creating content for fashion brands, and her own sense of self, which is constructed through the same medium. She is a commercial brand of one, and happy because of it.

Beneath the show's smoothed-out surface are a range of buried assumptions. Emily's inherent privilege goes unremarked upon, as if it were simply a fact of life. She is white, extraordinarily thin, conventionally attractive, and always wearing heavy makeup. Considered out of context, she is a bizarre "hallucination of the normal," as the architect Rem Koolhaas wrote. Emily wears elaborate, expensive outfits—made more for photographing than walking around in—every day, without the show giving any hint of where the luxury clothing or the money to buy them came from. (It's as if Emily is a whimsical aristocrat, free to do whatever she pleases, which turns out to be posting online.) The rest of the cast is very white, too, from Emily's primary love interest to her boss and most of her colleagues. It's a poor depiction of an international city. But then, real Paris mostly functions as a backdrop for Emily's selfies.

During the first season, Emily becomes an influencer—the term for a person known not for any great creative feat but for the number of their followers and their ability to inspire likes online. The character eventually gets included in deals to promote Savoir's clients, a victory presented as worth celebrating the way that a band signing to a record label or an author getting a book deal once was. Marketing has taken the place of creation in the same way that conforming to the algorithmic feed has taken the place of creative self-expression—neither is particularly concerned with originality. *Emily in Paris* is cognizant of how life has been taken over by social media feeds and the need for any piece of culture—fashion line, retail store, public art installation—to spark content creation. The show documents our flattened culture without critiquing it; rather, it accelerates the flattening. By season three, every major plot point seemed to resolve in an Instagram post, and several episodes had blatant product placement from real-life brands, including McDonald's, McLaren, and AMI Paris: the show's fictional marketing became literal marketing.

That the show celebrated being an influencer made a kind of sense; in 2022, a United States survey found that 54 percent of the respondents, ages thirteen to thirty-eight, would become influencers if given the opportunity. Another survey of three thousand children in 2019 found that 30 percent of them would choose to be a YouTuber—another kind of influencer—over other careers like professional athlete, musician, and astronaut. In the 2010s, the figure of the influencer was both invented and metastasized, becoming perhaps the single dominant protagonist of the cultural landscape. After all, if the bulk of culture now takes place on social media, what more powerful role could there be than controlling the flow of attention and being able to direct an audience in particular ways? (Influencers are the cowboys of algorithms.)

The superficiality of the word itself is indicative: "influence" is never the end point, only a means of communicating a particular message. An influencer is easiest to define by how they make money. Like a media company producing magazines or podcasts, they sell advertising shown to the audiences that they have gathered. But the content that draws the audiences in in the first place is most often the influencer's personal life, their aesthetically appealing surroundings (as well as aesthetically appealing selves) and entertaining activities. The material of their lives—in varying degrees of organic and staged—is copiously documented on social media platforms like Instagram, where they also publish sponsored posts for brands. Another difference is that unlike a free newspaper distributed on the street or a radio station sending out a signal, influencers don't own the infrastructure of their medium. They piggyback on the digital platforms' ability to distribute content, both through widely installed smartphone apps and through in-app feeds.

Fascination with a person, particularly their appearance or personal life, smoothing the way to self-promotion began long before the Internet era. Historically it shows up most often in the confines of a royal court or an urban intelligentsia, where members in geographical proximity observed each other with as much daily scrutiny as we post on Instagram today. Ninon de L'Enclos was born into a wealthy family in Paris in 1620; after her father was exiled and her mother died, she was left to make a life on her own, and she committed to never marrying. She became a courtesan with a succession of noble lovers, as well as an author and anti-religious philosopher. In one particularly dramatic episode, she broke up with a long-term lover in the countryside and moved back to Paris. Her ex, the Marquis de Villarceaux, promptly moved into a house across the street to spy on her, watching for new visitors. To mollify him, she chopped off a length of her hair to send to him as a parting gift. It worked, but also launched a mania for copycat bob haircuts, called "cheveux à la Ninon," as Betsy Prioleau recounts in her book *Seductress*. It was a hairdressing meme from a consummate influencer.

Later, in 1882, the British socialite and actor Lillie Langtry became the first celebrity to endorse a product when she became the face of Pears Soaps, her portrait reproduced on advertising. Langtry was known for her bright white complexion, likely more hereditary than an effect of the soap, but her personal image lent authority to the ads. In fact, Langtry had become famous through the reproduction of her image, first by prominent British painters and then in sketches printed on postcards. When reproduction was so scarce, its very fact could stand in for approval—the proliferation of an image the equivalent of a like.

Consumers have always cared about the lifestyle decisions of celebrities famous for something else: the actor's diet regimen, the tycoon's racehorses, the painter's affairs. Fame—which could also be defined as attention—casts its own aura, making just about anything interesting. In the 1960s, Andy Warhol took the banality of fame to its end point with his group of "Superstars." For Warhol's "Screen Test" series in the early 1960s, a set of countercultural characters, not well known outside of their milieu, posed in front of a video camera for extended durations, the lens simply observing their faces, like an audition for a nonexistent film. (Today, they bring to mind rehearsals for selfies or the moments before a front-facing video is recorded for TikTok.) The videos demonstrate that we need do nothing more than gaze at someone to feel as though they are important—the framing of the camera lens and the projector casts a spell.

The computer or phone screen accomplishes the same feat: anyone within a TikTok feed appears just as famous as everyone else, another form of flattening. Warhol once said, "In the future everyone will be world-famous for 15 minutes." In 1991, the musician and online blogging pioneer Momus presciently updated the prediction to "In the future everyone will be famous for 15 people." On social media, that has simply become fact. Every user is famous to their followers.

The influencer is something of a successor to the blogger, the star of the nascent mainstream Internet in the 2000s. Bloggers similarly used digital tools to self-publish and dramatize their personal lives in running textual dispatches—the wave of "mommy bloggers" starting around 2002 foremost among them. Bloggers sold advertising, too, in the form of sponsored posts and banner ads that appeared on the borders of their websites. According to Google's trend tracker, which documents the popularity of search terms, "blogger" has been on a slow slide downward since 2011, while "influencer" emerged in strength around the beginning of 2016. That was also when Instagram passed five hundred million users and social-network feeds were generally becoming more algorithmic. Instagram offered a perfect venue for the influencer: no voluminous writing or emotional disclosure of the self were required. Glossy images alone were enough to attract a following that could later be monetized. Where the term *blogger* described a literal activity of writing, "influencing" is closer to the financial side of what's going on. It's a sales job, convincing audiences to buy something, first a vision of aspirational lifestyle and then the products that make it up.

Patrick Janelle is something of a real-life version of Netflix's Emily Cooper, though his career as an influencer started long before hers. In the early to mid-2010s, he turned his life into content and gradually built a career, and then businesses, from it. Though it's no longer his primary focus, his Instagram account today still has over four hundred thousand followers and over six thousand images from a decade of use under the approachable account name @aguynamedpatrick. His posts resemble photo shoots from a men's magazine like *GQ:* palatial hotel rooms, airy coffee shops, the art-bedecked walls of his well-furnished Manhattan apartment, all starring the ruggedly handsome Janelle as the main character. Crisp, clear, and geometrically composed, all the photos are taken by Janelle himself with an iPhone, sometimes with the help of a remote trigger. His life wasn't always so manicured, however, particularly when he got on Instagram in 2012.

I first met Janelle years ago at The Dutch, a restaurant he suggested on a corner in SoHo near his apartment. It was outfitted with the requisite orb pendant lamps and open shelving. The restaurant was something of a headquarters for Janelle, who even featured it on his website. In 2011, he had just turned thirty, moved to New York, and taken a freelance gig as a designer at the food magazine *Bon Appétit.* Instagram became a way to share his life with friends, both from his travels abroad and back where he grew up in Colorado. "The medium was built for documenting your life," he told me. He had the placid confidence of a professional model. Frequenting Manhattan cafés before magazine work, Janelle started an Instagram hashtag, #dailycortado, referring to the short cappuccino that was a favorite of coffee aficionados at the time. Every day, he would take a photo of his latte-art-topped coffee resting on a marble or wood table—artisanal surfaces that also happened to contrast nicely with a smooth porcelain coffee cup—and post it on Instagram. The materials were signs of expense and quality; their naturalness and texture created a compelling contrast with the slick flatness of the smartphone screen, though the photographs were so much digital fodder, too.

Janelle was one of the pioneers of this aesthetic on Instagram, helping to firmly embed it as the signal of tasteful generic café design. He also popularized that hashtag for other people to use, inviting participation as any good meme does. A decade later, #dailycortado is still active, part of the bedrock of the platform. Now, it's included in lists of hashtags that users pile into captions so that more people can discover their accounts, goosing the algorithm to recommend the photo to coffee fans.

If we look back at the photos, they have a paradoxical quality. Janelle was capturing a moment of slowing down and paying attention: when you set down your coffee cup, sit down, and appreciate it for a split second before drinking. It's a restful moment in bustling city life; you stay still while everyone else on the street careens by. And yet each Instagram post feeds the beast of the feed, which sends as much content as possible by your eyes as fast as possible—the opposite of slowing down. Instead, the photo is a vector for acceleration, both for content consumption and the expansion of Janelle's online footprint, the audience that makes him money as an influencer. Janelle can slow down, but only to take the perfectly composed photo, and his viewers can perhaps vicariously slow down for a moment before the feed sweeps their attention on to yet more stimulation.

"In the beginning it was just coffee, and images I would see that were just visually pleasing; it was about being in the city," Janelle said of his early Instagram use. His posts were drawn from the vocabulary of street photography: fire escapes, building facades, milling crowds. But over time, and with the booming popularity of Instagram and influencers, his aspirational photos of city living became a way to achieve that same lifestyle. Images of luxury led him into luxury situations. "Lifestyle begot lifestyle," he told me. "As I continued to post, I was able to become more in demand as a participant in things, having more access to opportunities, building out a brand financially." His personal fashion sense, shown off in selfies, led to a promotional deal with Ralph Lauren. A vacation that he posted led to offers of free hotel rooms.

Influencing became a career, though Janelle dislikes words like "tastemaker." "I don't think I'm creating it, making the taste, but I am selecting the things I think are new and exciting, documenting them," he said. In 2014, the Council of Fashion Designers of America named Janelle its first "Instagrammer of the Year." I found Janelle one day in 2015 on my Instagram Explore page, which collected algorithmic recommendations of posts to like or accounts to follow. My guess is that I was following enough New York City restaurants and interior design inspiration accounts, filled with downtown lofts and mid-century furniture, that Janelle's account slotted squarely into my perceived taste, at least according to the algorithm.

I was also entering my late twenties as a Brooklyn resident and looking for some definition of what adult life should look like—in essence, how and where to spend the little extra money I had. Janelle's composed and curated photos gave a hint of that, though his evolving persona as a luxury-focused gadabout was less relatable than his street-scene snapshots. Instagram also lent a veneer of authenticity to such lifestyle content that a print magazine produced by a media corporation wouldn't have had for me—though his posts were corporate in a different way, since they were filtered through Instagram as a tech company. "I understand that I'm an aspirational figure," Janelle told me. "By me putting up an image and giving it some exposure to an audience, I'm implicitly saying, 'I endorse this.' I want to sort of jump-start people into creating for themselves the best life possible."

There's a persistent issue of class throughout Janelle's path: He enacts upper-class consumerist tropes and in doing so achieves them, reinforcing their status signaling, as many influencers do. (Influencing runs on jealousy.) White, traditionally attractive, and thin, Janelle was able to easily inhabit the luxurious imagery he made for himself. In a way, he was primed for algorithmic exposure because his appearance was so acceptable, fitting within the established visual vocabulary of urban wealth. Even as Janelle was gaining followers, others found their accounts throttled by the recommendation algorithm or blocked by aggressive censorship: activists posting political agitation memes, sex workers promoting themselves, and women who wanted to be as topless on Instagram as Janelle often was (a discrepancy that inspired the Free the Nipple campaign).

Over the years, Janelle has become something of a historical figure as the march of social media has passed him on. His Instagram following peaked in the 2010s, which is when his aesthetic feels frozen: it was the era of faux-industrial restaurants with ampersands in the name, arduously mixed craft cocktails, and preppily neat men's fashion (everyone looked like a lumberjack attending a wedding). In fact, Janelle cites a retrospective turning point in his relationship with Instagram, though he is still quite active there: 2016, when its feed changed from chronological to algorithmic.

"For me, personally, in the way that I grew through social media, the change of the platform to give power to the algorithm was worst possible thing," he told me. Originally, he could post several times a day and know that his posts would reach his followers in real time, in a chronological order that made sense for his storytelling. Now he can't tell when or in what order his images will show up. It's frustrating on the consumption side as well as creation: "No one is really given that choice to make that decision for themselves, to curate what they're seeing in a way that feels great to them. It's all being dictated by the algorithm."

Instagram shifted formats over the years, too, moving away from a feed of still images and adding stories, for ephemeral posts that mimicked Snapchat; Instagram TV, for longer videos; and eventually Reels, for short videos to copy TikTok. The app gradually lost its identity as a relatively austere space for expressing your own taste. "At no point were these decisions made to make the platform a better place for the people creating the content," Janelle said. "They were purely decisions made by the growth team and by the business team to figure out how they could expand."

The ever-shifting nature of Instagram's design means it is almost impossible to experience Janelle's work in the context in which it originally existed. You can't rewind time and see how the account was presented in 2015, for example, on the grid or in the timeline. Digital platforms lack the kind of stability that is vital for the longevity of culture, the way you might see a photographer's decades-old film negatives displayed in a museum. Context is swept away as the companies change priorities. "Not only are things changing in the moment, but because all of this is digital, it could be changed retroactively, because we don't own the thing. We have no control over how it's presented or used at all," Janelle said. The Instagram feed changed from solely square images to any size, and then began including videos that clashed with still photographs, all in the name of competing to deliver more compelling content, faster and more personalized.

Janelle became disaffected with Instagram but also didn't want to switch to newer alternatives like TikTok—a game of hopscotch that is often required to survive in the current influencer economy. He knew TikTok might offer better business opportunities, but it also would have taken up too much of his creative energy. (Still, the gravity of the latest feed might be irresistible: months after we spoke, he began tentatively posting TikTok videos and accruing followers there, too.) The constant need to figure out the next big social media platform is reminiscent of early silent-film stars trying to make the switch to talkies in the early twentieth century, or theater actors moving to television: not everyone made it, and not everyone's artistic approach functioned in the new medium.

The need to pivot now happens every few years (if not annually) instead of decades and requires a stronger sensitivity to technological bullshit. You must know when to avoid the total duds, like the short-lived mobile video streaming service Quibi (short for "quick bites"), which drew few users despite its high-budget content and shut down after less than a year. Much of the hype doesn't pan out, and any effort an influencer invests in a failed platform is lost.

Janelle is a savvy entrepreneur. Fads shift quickly in Filterworld, so rather than continually adapting his own content to whichever formats feeds favored, he built a company called Untitled Secret that represents a dozen other influencers and coordinates marketing deals with corporate clients, helped by a growing staff. He influences the influencers.

While the overall industrial-chic vibe of the 2010s that Janelle espoused is still very prevalent, cutting-edge taste has moved on to the messier and more chaotic, even the aggressively inauthentic. Influencers now regularly have millions of followers, a scale at which personal connection is barely possible, replicating the remove of traditional celebrity. Kardashian-style reality television ushered in a new class of influencer who moved smoothly between the small screen and the even smaller one of phones: You could watch Kim on TV and then follow her on Instagram, where she now has 349 million followers, the population of a dispersed nation of fans. Unlike Janelle's case, Instagram wasn't the source of Kardashian fame so much as just another container for it. Preexisting fame is the best way to kick-start algorithmic promotion, which further enhances it.

While the early promise of social media was to connect users to their actual friends, over time inauthenticity became something to embrace. In 2016, Trevor McFedries and Sara DeCou, cofounders of a technology company called Brud, created an Instagram account named @lilmiquela (Little Miquela). The account's bio described a Brazilian American nineteen-year-old, and its images were the standard Instagram fare: casual selfies, snapshots with friends, and posed portraits in front of city walls. Miquela's aesthetic was generic influencer, the average of successful accounts before her. She was generic, too: not a human but a computer rendering.

Her skin was waxy and inhumanly smooth, glowing from within. Her eyes were strangely blank. Nevertheless, she appeared next to real people, dressed in real clothes, in real places. The essence of the account is a virtual three-dimensional model, a nigh-photorealistic digital doll that can be posed any conceivable way. The glossy imagery, only slightly faker than most fashion shoots, proved successful: she made headlines as the first famous "virtual influencer" and signed up with the talent agency WME (or, at least, her creators did). Miquela currently has nearly three million Instagram followers and, like any successful influencer, does promotional deals with luxury fashion brands like Calvin Klein and Prada.

That she doesn't exist makes her influence more salable, because there is no human being with an independent personality to stand in the way of the advertising. Miquela won't feel alienated by changes in the feed, as Patrick Janelle did, or fail to adapt to the next big multimedia format. She will also stay nineteen forever—until it becomes more profitable for her to suddenly age into a new demographic. And when the account has outlived its relevance, it can simply shut down and develop a new persona. This is another consequence of content's interchangeability as the feeds grow larger and faster: we don't necessarily notice when one source of content is swapped out for another. The aura of intimacy that once drove social media users to people like Patrick Janelle is now cultivated for entirely imaginary characters. If influencers' lives were already tinged with fiction—glitzed up with sponsored travel and gifted outfits, the deals undisclosed as if they happened naturally—then the influencers have since become fictional themselves, like the cartoon mascots of cereal brands.

The influencer identity has been both professionalized and dispersed. There is a viable career path in catering to the feed, accruing followers, and selling access to your personal audience. Charli D'Amelio, a relatively unremarkable teenage dancer living in suburban Connecticut, joined TikTok in May 2019, when the social network was mostly oriented around lip-synching and dancing videos. By jumping on trends and participating in choreography memes, D'Amelio now has over 150 million followers, perhaps the fastest rise of a once-obscure social media account ever, thanks to TikTok's algorithmic feed. Over just a few years, D'Amelio went from minor social media star to fully mainstream celebrity, even dating a tertiary member of the Kardashian clan in a crossover worthy of cable sitcoms.

Individual influencers are less remarkable in this decade also because so many users of digital platforms are pressured to act like influencers themselves, constantly creating content, accruing an audience, and figuring out ways to monetize it—either immediately through literal advertising or more gradually through the attention of their peers. We are all influencers: the visual artist trying to get the attention of galleries or curators on Instagram; the novelist documenting their writing process with a litany of tweets; the amateur baker making bread TikTok videos and replying to comments as they try to build a business out of their apartment. There are dating influencers and personal finance influencers. For so many career paths in Filterworld, following the demands of various feeds has become an almost unavoidable commandment. The pressure is so great that the promotional content has a way of superseding the actual craft.

## CONTENT CAPITAL

In Filterworld, culture has become increasingly iterative. It's harder for a creator to go straight to making a movie or publishing a book; she needs to first publish her sample material, describe her vision, and gather an audience online who are engaged fans of her work. A book, for example, must first make for good tweets and then provide the material for good essays prompting public dialogue, perhaps inspiring a follow-up or an op-ed. Readers must retweet her thoughts and share pull quotes on their Instagram stories. An agent must notice the burgeoning momentum and sign the nascent author. Then finally, perhaps, a publisher will consider her manuscript—if she has accrued enough of a "platform," that is, high enough numbers of social media followers and an ability to influence the content stream. (The choice of word is telling: people are platforms, too.) Once the book sells to a publisher and debuts on bookstore shelves, the author leverages that platform, tweeting to her fans, posting images of the cover, holding it up in a TikTok video—driving attention to its launch in as many spaces as possible. (The same will be true for this book by the time you are holding it, at least if I'm effective at it.)

This need to corral an audience in advance by succeeding on social media can be explained by the useful phrase "content capital." Established by the scholar Kate Eichhorn in her 2022 monograph *Content*, it describes the Internet-era state in which "one's ability to engage in work as an artist or a writer is increasingly contingent on one's content capital; that is, on one's ability to produce content not about one's work but about one's status as an artist, writer, or performer." In other words, the emphasis is not on the thing itself but the aura that surrounds it, the ancillary material that one produces because of living the lifestyle of a creator. That ancillary content might be Instagram selfies, photos of a painting studio, evidence of travel, tossed-off observations on Twitter, or a monologue on TikTok. It all builds an audience for the person, who remains a separate entity from the things that they make. If Roland Barthes's 1967 essay predicted "the death of the author," the author's personal brand is now all that matters; it's the work itself that is dead.

Eichhorn responds to the sociologist Pierre Bourdieu's 1970s concept of "cultural capital": the fluency in forms of high culture that could bestow social status and help members of elite classes to identify one another. Cultural capital is knowing that cashmere is a more aspirational fabric than cotton or that a Jackson Pollock painting is much more than a mess of drips that a child could replicate. (Bourdieu points out that, in the West, being open to radical aesthetic experimentation and abstraction are markers of the elite class.) Not only is it an understanding of art; it is an understanding of what art means in a social context, and what different pieces or artists symbolize. Content capital, then, is fluency in digital content: the knowledge of what kinds of content to produce, how the feeds of various platforms work, what they prioritize, and how audiences might react to a given creation. Those who have more content capital gain more followers, and thus more power in the cultural ecosystem of Filterworld.

The rule is a mundane fact of online life, so pervasive that it's easy to forget it exists: more followers and more engagement are always posed as better. (One is no longer supposed to be satisfied with mere hundreds of followers, though that might be the limit of people you know in the physical world.) The primary incentive is to make the numbers go up. "One builds up one's content capital simply by hanging out online and, more precisely, by posting content that garners a response and, in turn, leads to more followers and more content," Eichhorn wrote. That content capital can be used or transformed into other forms of capital: making money by selling sponsorships or selling products directly to followers, whether a T-shirt emblazoned with an influencer's account or a hardcover book with an author's name. The two are not so different as physical symbols of fandom for a particular person, also known as swag.

This equation holds for any cultural production or field: The more followers, the more money you make. Social media has quantified culture into a banal set of metrics measuring views, click-throughs, and, ultimately, purchase rates. The net effect is homogenization as creators all chase the same incentives to attract more attention, copying whichever formula works best in a given moment. "As time goes on, the distinctions between mediums (e.g., film, video, audio recording, printed book) and between genres (e.g., nonfiction versus fiction or television drama versus sitcom) seem to matter less," Eichhorn wrote. She described that endless race: "Increasingly, what matters is simply that one is producing content and doing so at an increasingly high frequency and volume." Elsewhere in the book, Eichhorn puts it more simply and brutally: "Content begets content."

That is not to say that content begets *art*. In fact, the excess content demanded by algorithmic feeds more often gets in the way of art, because it sucks up an increasingly high percentage of a creator's time. "Cultural producers who, in the past, may have focused on writing books or producing films or making art must now also spend considerable time producing (or paying someone else to produce) content about themselves and their work," Eichhorn wrote. As anyone who has tried to get an undertaking off the ground online—a bake sale, a party, an art installation—knows, ancillary content quickly becomes a distraction. The author (me) is too busy Instagramming his artfully cluttered desk, broadcasting his writerly identity, and checking for subsequent likes to actually write his book.

We all have to worry over our content capital online, even if we're only communicating with our friends. Certain restaurant meals or vacation destinations have more content capital than others, resulting in better Instagram posts, just as certain life milestones make more of a splash in Facebook feeds. One might take advantage of a birthday or wedding to get some extra promotion. But the exposure is not always personally affirming.

On TikTok, even when a video might show a person recounting a personal trauma or displaying a new artistic creation, the comments are full of rabid questions about which brands of clothing the creator is wearing or the furniture that they have in their home, as if those recommendations would be their most compelling cultural contribution. I recall one woman on TikTok discussing an incident of harassment at work, facing the camera of her iPhone. Commenters badgered her for where her halter top was from; the brand was Zara, but that certainly wasn't the point of the video. Even the expression of personal vulnerability was lowered to the level of visual content.

One food-focused creator I observed took to discussing her experiences of racism on top of placid videos of her cooking processes, chopping and sautéing vegetables to make a soup. The visual ambience was used to mask the personal content, perhaps making it more likely to reach the distracted viewer within the algorithmic feed.

Building content capital is a distraction, albeit a necessary one to reach consumers. And in Filterworld, making art without the goal of it being consumed is almost unimaginable. It's the opposite of the way a painter like Carmen Herrera, who didn't achieve fame until her nineties and passed away in 2022, toiled in obscurity on her minimalist canvases for the better part of a century. Today, it can often feel like there is no creativity without attention, and no attention without the accelerant of algorithmic recommendations.

My personal content capital is only middling. Through more than a decade of working as a professional journalist and being on Twitter since its early days in 2008, I "only" have around twenty-six thousand followers on the platform. On Instagram, I have just over four thousand—a number I can't quite explain, since I don't post much more than mundane evidence of my IRL existence: dinners I cook, photos of my dog, aggressively static and normal scenes that sometimes mimic Stephen Shore, one of my favorite art photographers. The images I post are largely for my own consumption, building a personal archive barely directed at a wider audience. As such, they don't command much engagement.

I decided long ago against fully adapting my voice to the algorithmic feed—or perhaps not decided so much as felt incapable of doing it. I wasn't cool enough, funny enough, attractive enough, or Machiavellian enough to know exactly which variables to manipulate. My tweets rarely went viral, and I certainly didn't have enough lifestyle material to fill an Instagram feed. I could never be that kind of influencer. Yet over the years, I realized that even though I wasn't an Instagram star with hundreds of thousands of followers, I was influential to a set group of people who were watching what I was posting, and eventually their attention did influence what I posted.

I found that there were certain ways I could present the things I was doing to maximize my possible content capital. I labored over tweets to share my latest articles, trying to figure out what would get shared the most: a curiosity-gap headline that left a question open, perhaps, or highlighting the most dramatic quote in a story. I catered to my online audience, hitting the subjects that people knew me for: niche design criticism, complaints about Silicon Valley culture, art-historical references. Evidence of my personal life, like a complaint about a coffee shop I was working in, always did well. The problem was that I began to confuse the subjects rewarded by the feed with my personal taste—I wrote what Twitter wanted to see, which began to occlude my awareness of what I would have written or been interested in on my own.

The instantaneous wave of likes in response to a post helps the recommendation algorithm evaluate which pieces of content should be promoted, but it also gives the creator an unprecedented real-time measure of what resonates with their audiences, as if every thought was gauged by a Nielsen rating viewable on a smartphone. Cultural flattening is one consequence. But the same mechanism is also what makes our public political discourse more and more extreme, because conflict and controversy light up the feed and attract likes in a way that subtlety and ambiguity never will.

## INSTA-POETRY

The kinds of culture rewarded by digital platforms and algorithmic feeds are markedly different from what was successful in the traditional model of human tastemakers, both in form and content. Poetry offers one of the most blatant examples of algorithmic feeds altering both an art form and its public reception. Over the past decade, a generation of "Insta-poets" have emerged on Instagram and sold millions of books to their followers by shaping their work to the structure and demands of the platform. Rupi Kaur is the most famous: a Canadian woman born in India in 1992, she has amassed 4.5 million followers by posting brief poems, broken into short lines, fit into the Instagram image square along with her own simple line drawings. The poems are written in a standard serif font and all lowercase, as if dashed off on a phone keyboard—though also in reference to the Punjabi language, which doesn't have different cases. One reads, in part, "they did not tell me it would hurt like this / no one warned me / about the heartbreak we experience with friends." The poem-images are signed "- rupi kaur," a gesture that reinforces personal authorship—a name brand—but also serves as a kind of authorial watermark, should the image, as is very likely, become divorced from its original digital context or get reposted elsewhere in the feed. The viewer always knows who wrote it.

Other Insta-poets are men espousing a self-consciously vulnerable form of stereotypical masculinity. One goes by the name Atticus, a pseudonymous poet with 1.6 million Instagram followers and multiple bestselling books. Atticus's poems are often splashed across stock photos of wine bottles or people on vacation, focusing on themes of love, beauty, and getting drunk: "My darling / let's you and I ramble on this life a while" is one post in its entirety. Then there's R. M. Drake, 2.8 million followers, who prefers prose-poem paragraphs that echo rote self-help mantras: "It is not a loss if you lost someone who didn't give a fuck about you," one brief poem begins. R. M. Drake, too, appends his name to every Instagram frame, appearing as a bro version of Kaur. Together they have developed the generic style of Insta-poetry, with the same homogeneity as the international minimalist coffee shops. The style follows the principles that I've been outlining as characteristic of Filterworld: The poems have to function as images as much as text and travel seamlessly through various digital platforms, whether Instagram feed, Facebook post, or TikTok slide. The content of the poems themselves has to be relatable and sharable, speaking less to an individualized experience or perspective and more to universal, recognizable themes.

Somewhat unfairly, Kaur has been made both the face and the scapegoat of the movement, when the platform itself may be more to blame for Insta-poetry's vapid aesthetics. Kaur first performed spoken-word poetry as a teenager, then moved to posting on Tumblr, and then Instagram in 2013. In 2014, she also self-published her first collection, *Milk and Honey.* As her online fame grew, the volume was re-rereleased by a professional publisher in 2015 and went on to sell over two million copies and hit number one on the *New York Times* bestseller list. Critics—long the sole arbiters of the niche art form of poetry—largely hated Kaur's work, however. They likened it to greeting card copy and bemoaned its literalness. It didn't bear thinking about for any length of time.

Some of the reviews perhaps inadvertently reflected how much her poems answered the demands of Instagram for distribution: "Kaur's poetry states obvious, mildly interesting stream-of-consciousness shower thoughts in visually appealing ways," one critic, Fareah Fysudeen, wrote. "Her poems are expected, obvious, and vacuous, painting an illusion of depth where there is none." On Instagram, everything must be visual: hence the graphic clarity of Kaur's plentiful line breaks and the added interest of the drawings. Superficiality is not such a flaw when a post is designed to emerge in the feed once, attract the eyes for a few seconds, and then scroll by without offense, never to be seen again. "Kaur's achievement as an artist is the extent to which her work embodies, formally, the technology that defines contemporary life: smartphones and the internet," the novelist Rumaan Alam wrote in a 2019 essay for *The New Republic,* a bastion of traditional literary criticism, titled "Rupi Kaur Is the Writer of the Decade."

I called Alam in 2023 to see how he felt about his judgment at that time, which had prompted some backlash from other critics. "I feel vindicated," he said. "Text that can fit comfortably inside a glance, where you don't have to move your phone screen at all, is much more appealing." He cited the example of the 2016 poem "Good Bones" by Maggie Smith, which can be compressed into a single screenshot and is often shared as a meme, on Twitter or in Instagram stories. "Life is short, though I keep this from my children. / Life is short, and I've shortened mine," it begins, like an incantation, before ending fifteen short lines later. Rupi Kaur, Alam said, "is not really a great poet, but that doesn't mean that she's not hugely influential. She identified something about a change in how taste is made and a change in how stuff is disseminated." "Art will adjust to meet the attention span of contemporary life," he continued.

It doesn't hurt that Kaur herself is visually striking: her long face, sharp jawline, and wide, dramatic eyes star in the copious selfies that also fill her Instagram account. In recent years, she has settled into a pattern of alternating between poem-images and self-portraits, most fully posed (rather than the standard casual snapshots), costumed in elaborate high-fashion outfits and makeup. She poses her physical presentation as equal to her art, a conflation that not every creator is capable of or desires to make. (We are all unequal in the very human evaluation of beauty, which is a different kind of algorithm.) Does one have to be attractive to be a successful artist? Of course not, but it helps, particularly in the Instagram era.

Kaur and her poetry possess a maximum of content capital. She is an influencer as much as a poet, two identities that in her case don't cancel each other out but are mutually reinforcing: she is a popular influencer in part because of her poetry, and her poetry is popular in part because of her established online platform. The same dynamic is true for Patrick Janelle as a photographer—we overlook his artistry in favor of his lifestyle porn—and perhaps a novelist like Sean Thor Conroe, whose 2022 *Fuccboi* adopted the language of social media and text messages, with clipped aphoristic lines and digital slang. Conroe's personal Instagram account is filled with moody cigarette-smoking selfies that resemble his novel's eventual cover, documenting and dramatizing the life of the writer in the mold of a bad-boy novelist. Being a working artist has always meant being something of a public figure, but in Filterworld the perfected image is a prerequisite to the art.

Kaur is aware of how Instagram exerts aesthetic pressure on her work, rewarding some subjects with more attention than others. In a 2017 interview with *Entertainment Weekly*, she said, "I get the most love online for love poems and heartache." Poems about sexual violence, for example, got fewer likes. At one point, she switched to only posting about those basic subjects for a month, and her engagement numbers went up. But it also didn't feel genuine, she said. The artist must work actively against the incentives of social media, the constant temptation to just give audiences more of what they click the most (keeping in mind the fact that audiences are equally manipulated by the feed in their own decisions). "When you dive too deep, you let people's ideas change what you want to create and what you want to write," Kaur said. The constant passive consumption of social media has led to a lack of deep self-awareness, which Kaur acknowledges even as her work takes advantage of it to dress platitudes up as singular insight: "We're so plugged in that we're almost not plugged into ourselves," she said. According to some interviews, Kaur doesn't have social media on her phone and, like many celebrities, has a team of staff to manage her actual accounts, separating herself from her online presence even while benefiting from its suggestion of intimacy.

There is an element of elitism at play in any evaluation that casts social media as the opposite of art. Not everyone has access to the traditional, more acceptable routes of art making: Ivy League universities, literary magazines, Chelsea galleries. Leveraging a compelling image or Internet presence can be a way to cultivate an initial audience, prove a level of established interest that some artists don't have to demonstrate, and break into the closed ecosystem. Readers can be attracted to the accessibility of the figure of the artist online, the artist-as-influencer. Millions of people value Kaur's work, for example, enough that they buy her books and follow her on Instagram, and her poem-images each rack up hundreds of thousands of likes. In fact, poetry consumption overall has increased in recent years, with traffic to Poets.org up 25 percent from 2020 to 2021 and higher sales numbers for poetry books—in the United Kingdom, poetry sales increased 12 percent from 2018 to 2019. It might be due in part to how the Internet has encouraged the consumption of fragments of text, though it could equally be the chaos of the last several years inciting a desire for spiritual contemplation. Literary poetry—or poetry that is accepted by the establishment of elite institutions—is still easy to find, too, coexisting with Insta-poetry, though usually with much lower sales figures.

In literary context, I appreciate the poetry of Myung Mi Kim, a Korean American poet born in 1957. Some of Kim's poems might equally fit in an Instagram image, but they are far less immediately scrutable. Her poem "[accumulation of land]" is a grid of phrases in three columns—"counting herds possessions," "production heirs number," "bearing child rearing"—that are meant to be read dynamically in any order. The phrases evoke, but do not pin down, a feeling of antiquity and human prehistory. The aggressive fragmentation of her poetry speaks to the very fragmentation of language in our own era. In another short (though perhaps infinite) poem "[Exordium: 'In what way names'],", she suggested a vast deconstruction in a few lines: "In what way names were applied to things. Filtration. Not every word that has been applied, still exists." (The past tense of the first sentence is at first subtle and then heartbreaking.)

Blatant clarity and simple, literal takeaways versus linguistic difficulty and the need to accept irresolution: one aesthetic approach is not better or worse than the other; they are simply different sets of choices. Yet in Filterworld, we face a cultural environment that inevitably prioritizes the former over the latter because it travels more effectively through algorithmic feeds, and there are fewer and fewer outlets outside of those feeds available for creators to access the audiences they need to survive in such a capitalistic environment. Whether Twitter, Instagram, TikTok, or Amazon, the artist contends with the invisible force. They can devoutly follow a personal vision, perhaps to the detriment of their engagement numbers and future potential to make a living, or they can cater to both feeds and audiences—creating the equivalent of only love and heartbreak poems—in the hope of surviving as an influencer, with the backup of selling sponsorships or swag if the art itself doesn't profit. Ultimately, the algorithmic feed may not be the death of art, but it often presents an impediment to it.

## BOOKSTAGRAM AND BOOKTOK

Social media influencers are forces of marketing: They can popularize almost anything, whether a new product from a fashion brand or a damaging political ideology. If you want something to be popular in Filterworld, the fastest way is to get the influencers on your side. Entire industries have been reshaped around their gravity. When Hannah Oliver Depp decided to open a new bookstore company called Loyalty Books in her hometown of Washington, D.C., a process she began in 2018, she decided to design it around the burgeoning group of influencers that made up "Bookstagram." Rather than fashion or travel, these influencers gained their audiences by recommending books, and their power and authority in the staid publishing industry was growing. "There was an opportunity for me to create a beautiful space that I would want to be in, knowing that was the kind of space Instagram needed for content," Depp told me. She launched pop-up bookshops with a picturesque poofy armchair that visitors could pose for photos in. Later, she adapted her stores to the literary-influencer side of TikTok, called Booktok, too, making space for shooting videos instead of still images.

I first met Depp through a mutual novelist friend; she was coming through the city for her book tour, and she asked me to host her event at Depp's D.C. shop. Given the endless and unpredictable surges of the pandemic, the novelist and I were together in person, but our conversation was beamed out over Zoom to a physically absent audience. The upside to the surreal moment was that after the event Depp, the novelist, and I headed to Depp's favorite bar, Red Derby. It's a rambling, ramshackle place with cluttered walls and a wide rooftop bar that offers plentiful whiskey gingers. Red Derby is the kind of bar that is proudly of and for its geographical place and community: It doesn't try to cater to Instagram or cultivate positive Yelp reviews. The bar and its owner are known as a great employer for the local creative set, building a sense of hospitality that was also an inspiration for Depp in growing her own business.

Over various drinks at Red Derby, Depp and I discussed the impact of the Internet on books: writing them, selling them, finding them, and reading them. Depp is a naturally authoritative presence; as a Black, queer woman in the very white, homogenous, and staid world of book publishing and selling, she has had to chart her own path and build a new kind of institution. She originally studied art history, which gave her a taste for visual culture, and worked in established bookstores like D.C.'s Politics and Prose. Discovering a community of other people of color talking about books first on Twitter and then on Instagram gave her more confidence to venture out on her own. (Algorithmic feeds can also help people find each other and build communities.) Loyalty began without a fixed location, but Depp was careful to arrange her temporary storefront installations with a sense of permanence. She copied the aesthetic of her own home living room: "Antiques store meets IKEA," she said.

She had noticed that Washington had a high concentration of bookstagrammers, in part due to the city's primary industries, which employ well-educated bureaucrats with the free time on their hands needed to maintain social media accounts. Bookstagrammers also felt isolated from the literary establishment. They were ignored in favor of traditional critics at print publications; publishers started working directly with influencers only in the last few years, handing out hard-to-get galleys. Bookstagrammers "tend to be female or queer," Depp said. "They wanted a bookstore that wouldn't be like, 'Why are you taking pictures?' or treat their reading taste as inherently lesser." The kinds of books that become famous via social media were often romances and fantasy novels, like Casey McQuiston's *Red, White & Royal Blue*, a gay love story about an American and the Prince of Wales, and V. E. Schwab's *The Invisible Life of Addie LaRue*, about time travel and a curse of immortality.

So when Depp moved into her long-term locations, the spaces had to be full of moments of interest that could provide good photo backdrops. "It's the visual part that sells. What would make someone come in and say, 'Oh my god I have to post this'?" Depp said. "Everything is arranged in a way that if you take a snapshot of it, it will look good. I'm imagining every inch of the store not just in three-dimensional, real-life space, but also if it's in a square, or a long video, does it capture your eye?" It's optimized for online content creation, because the store as well as the books must be distributed through algorithmic feeds just as much as function in physical space: for the online passerby as well as someone walking in from the sidewalk.

What Depp has less of a grasp on is which books become popular on Bookstagram or Booktok. Instagram was slower and more localized; the bookseller could keep an eye on what was trending for her customer base and be sure to stock the set of books that drew buyers in. (Many bookstores began setting out tables of "Books You Saw on Instagram.") But TikTok was more instantaneous and reached a much wider, global audience. "It gets out of your control in a much faster way," Depp said. "It's simply a more powerful trend algorithm." Publishers are often caught by surprise by which books go viral, and they struggle to print enough books and ship them to the right locations, which means that stores like Loyalty can't stock enough copies to sell to customers. That sometimes leads customers back to the algorithmic villain of Amazon, which can receive and hold on to many more copies—in part because publishers prioritize supplying the much larger company.

There's a homogeneity to the kind of literature that influencers promote, too, narrowing down to the kinds of books that can accelerate through feeds. "The top-selling folks are straight white women writing somehow emotional books: self-help-oriented books, romance, or romance-adjacent," Depp explained. The Booktok star Colleen Hoover might fall into the latter category, while Madeline Miller's two retellings of Greek mythology, *Song of Achilles* and *Circe,* which have both passed a million copies after being taken up by Booktok, mingle the grandeur of ancient archetypes with a very millennial sensibility of love and relationships (Ulysses as marooned fuckboy).

TikTok-era popularity tends to be all or nothing, and when one book or topic becomes popular, it drives copycats who want to get in on the traffic. "The problems of homogeneity are not just that it is boring; the most or least offensive stuff rises to the top, because that gets clicks," Depp said. "This is the issue about whoever is succeeding on TikTok this week: People who have never read the book are going to make a video about it, because that's the trending topic. Things start out with genuine interest, but by the thousandth video about it, it has nothing to do with the thing itself." The algorithmic feed alienates the superficial symbol of the book from its actual value as literature.

Algorithmic curation can alienate consumers, too. Eleanor Stern, a writer and recent grad student, is a part of Booktok but also skeptical of it. She joined the platform in 2020, during the pandemic, and began making videos in early 2021. I think of her as the TikTok-native version of a critic. She delivers spoken essays to the camera on everything from obscure linguistics to new books and magazine articles. She has over seventy thousand followers, a high number for her subject matter. When it comes to literary culture, TikTok's algorithmic feed "does drive it all toward sameness," Stern said. Which is a problem because the "For You" feed, your personalized algorithm, is also seen as an "externalized version of your subconscious." Stern has observed how TikTok encourages users to slot themselves into particular categories or genres of identity, just as it brackets genres of culture. "Whatever it is that you're consuming just becomes an expression of your self; it exists only insofar as it can describe you," she said. On the platform, books are popularized less as texts to read than as purchasable lifestyle accessories, visual symbols of an identity. Such is the narcissism encouraged by Filterworld.

Depp finds that some people coming into her stores are surprised when she doesn't have the latest hyperpopular TikTok book displayed front and center, or perhaps even in the store at all. They expect her space to follow the logic of the feeds, but it doesn't. That's because Depp selects everything in the store herself: an algorithm of one. "They don't realize the curation isn't being done by some third party on the Internet, because the way they see all information is something that's been curated by an invisible hand on the Internet," she said. The line between catering to algorithmic feeds enough and relying on them too much is a hard one to walk. The temptation to court the extreme attention, and thus profit, is always there, but the cumulative effect of so much reliance on automated feeds is a kind of desensitization. We end up not being able to imagine culture operating any other way than algorithmically.

## ALGORITHMIC PRESSURE ON CREATIVITY

I first met my friend Hallie Bateman in the early 2010s when we were both living in Brooklyn. She had moved from the Bay Area and was working as a barista while pursuing her artistic practice of drawing and editorial illustration. We met through a mutual friend who ran a blog where Hallie—it feels too formal to use her last name—contributed comics and I wrote posts. But really it was Twitter and Instagram where we followed each other's work on a daily basis. I cheered her on when she published art and writing at publications like *The Awl*, an influential New York blog that shut down in 2018, and eventually the website of *The New Yorker*.

What always struck me was the quirkiness and personality of Hallie's artwork. The 2010s was the era of clean, flat design, with smooth, pastel-colored graphics that looked like they had been run through an ironing press. (One Twitter account, called Humans of

Flat, collected examples of the generic style of start-up illustration that was primed to be promoted across social media.) Hallie instead drew resolutely on paper, with scribbly, wavering lines that were reminiscent of comic artists like Lynda Barry and Roz Chast. Clean perfection was never the point; instead, it seemed to be how much feeling she could pack into every doodle, whether it was a quick sketch of her dog or a narrative scene depicting the chaotic nature of life itself. One of her best-known images is a white square that she posted on Instagram, occupied by a handful of tiny human figures walking across it, each trailing their own primary-colored line. None of them seem like they're going to intersect. In the center of the drawing, Hallie wrote, "It's a miracle we ever met." It's a bittersweet piece: our lives really overlap with so few other people in the world, and yet the fact that they do at all is worth celebrating. The piece is so popular, and has spread so far beyond Hallie's account, that many people have gotten it tattooed on their bodies without even knowing its origin. In Filterworld, it was forcibly decontextualized.

I remember evenings sprawled around the low coffee table in the living room of Hallie's Brooklyn apartment; her roommates were academics, writers, and other artists. The atmosphere was such that anyone could be creative: You didn't need to consider yourself an artist to make a drawing, play an instrument, or write a poem. Nor did anyone else, no matter their level of expertise, have the authority to judge whatever you made as artistically unworthy. (The opposite of the Internet, where everyone feels entitled to critique or comment.) Hallie also exuded that spirit through her online presence—which is why I was eventually surprised when she began posting that she couldn't stand Instagram anymore, though she had gathered over a hundred thousand followers there and used her platform to sell prints of her work and, eventually, books with major publishers.

The arc of Hallie's career and artistic practice online sketch out a history of creativity on the Internet over the late 2000s and 2010s, as user-made, small-scale websites gave way to massive social platforms where the algorithmic feed dictated what audiences saw. It also shows how the sheer scale and automation of those feeds have become alienating to the creators who made them appealing to audiences in the first place.

I called Hallie in Los Angeles, where she lived at the time and kept a studio space in her apartment covered with drawings— drawings that she doesn't publish online so often anymore. High on one wall above the mirrored closet, she taped pieces of paper with a simple message written on them in tall capital letters: I BELIEVE IN YOU. She started her Twitter account in 2007 while attending U.C. Santa Cruz; since it felt like a private and personal space, she used a nonsense version of her name, "hallithbates," that has since stuck for all of her social media. The first place she shared her art online was a Blogspot site. She got on Instagram only after college, when she was traveling alone in Paris and Barcelona: "It came out of this feeling of being lonely," Hallie told me.

When a full-time illustration job for a technology website fell through, she moved to Brooklyn and took barista shifts. Twitter and Instagram became a way to share her work and connect with other artists, listening in as the people she wanted to have as peers and colleagues swapped notes on different pens and paper types. Social media provided an artistic community, which bled into the physical world as she met people she first got in touch with on Twitter.

"I was not making things to post on Instagram at that point; I would just take pictures of my sketchbook. It was incredibly casual," she said. The likes she got provided encouragement early in her professional career: people were watching and were fans of what she was doing, even though she didn't have any art-school credentials or institutional affiliations. "It felt like I was getting a lot of thumbs-up from the universe to keep doing what I was doing." When Hallie moved to New York, she had a thousand Instagram followers; by 2015 she had accrued twenty thousand. She began scanning her drawings, editing her images more, and being as thoughtful about Instagram posts as her comics for publications. The platform became an end in itself.

Hallie also realized that the Instagram feed rewarded specific qualities. She had always combined visual art and writing, but posts with clear written messages got the most engagement. "If I posted something pretty to look at, it didn't get as much of a response," she said. This effect isn't solely a consequence of the algorithmic feed; consumers have tastes that don't always mesh with an artist's own vision. But the acceleration of the feed and the instantaneousness of the feedback begets an intensified self-consciousness on the part of the artist. Hallie saw the biggest growth of her Instagram account, going from thirty thousand followers up to more than sixty thousand, when she began posting her "Directions" series. For that series, she wrote aphoristic lines of life advice—"Do not mistake sadness for depth," "Articulate what you love about the ones you love"—in bold strokes of ink on colorful construction paper.

"It's a format; it's identifiable; you can repeat it. I would draw them in big batches and then go through them and post," Hallie explained. It was a meme-like assembly-line process perfectly suited for Instagram: the bright colors and simple text added a little spice to her followers' feeds along with simple moral messages. Followers came to rely on her account for those pieces alone. "People follow you and continue to expect that," she said. Each "Directions" image would get thousands of likes. The series counted as an unmitigated success purely in terms of engagement, but Hallie was ambivalent about it. Her style had always varied from piece to piece. "I was starting to resent and get confused by the popularity of it. I had to tell myself, 'Don't be affected by this, just keep going.' It all starts to feel like a commentary on your other work, too," she said. Did the fact that all her other drawings got fewer likes mean that those pieces were worse? Should she just keep making her "Directions" forever? The pressure that Hallie felt to make the rest of her artwork similarly bright, clear, and simple is much like the pressure that a musician feels to frontload the hook of a song so it succeeds on TikTok or a writer feels to have a take so hot it lights up the Twitter feed.

At the same time, Instagram was changing, too. Hallie felt a marked difference in the algorithmic feed around 2017, just as Patrick Janelle and others did. "I started to actually feel the psychological shift from fun and encouraging to being a little tired of it and overwhelmed by it. Instagram was becoming much more volatile," she said. Instagram recommendations pushed her work to audiences that didn't understand its context; when her art or captions addressed political issues, she began to receive hateful comments.

Hence Hallie's decision to move off social media. She still makes plenty of other art, but she doesn't post it. Before, her creative process was inexorably shaped by what played well online, with the help of the constant feedback loop. Now, it's different. "I have transitioned from being a test-balloon-style artist to being the 'I'm working on a ton of stuff that I'm not telling anyone about except my friends' type of artist," she said. "If I'm not making art for this platform, I'm making it just for myself, or humanity."

That kind of internal creative process, or even the process of thinking on one's own, is something that feels lacking in the Filterworld era, when any idea or thought can be made instantly public and tested for engagement. The artist-as-influencer isn't introspective; she exists on the ephemeral surface of things, iterating and adapting according to reactions. Hallie's comments made me feel a kind of personal grief: Have I been left incapable of truly thinking for myself, or unwilling to do that creative work without the motivation of an invisible audience? The philosopher Byung-Chul Han has described how people living in post-Internet society may "no longer have an unconscious."

The way that art is made and distributed now is not how it was for the past few centuries. There was no constant heckling from an audience in a quiet studio or workshop or at a writing desk. Innovation came not from adaptation to a metric of constant engagement but in creative leaps that might have been shocking at first glance. When you conform to expectations too much in advance or rearrange your imagination to fit a particular set of variables, it can mean that that leap is denatured or cut short. That's bad for both artists and consumers. "Sometimes people don't know what they want until you show it to them. There is some part of me that resists just giving people exactly what they ask for," Hallie said.

I asked Hallie if she was worried about not chasing more followers hurting her ability to make a living. She explained that not relying on algorithmic feedback and the numbers continually going up actually made her feel like she was creating a more stable base for her creative practice. Trends and platforms always change, but she could be sure she knew where her work was going: "If I adapt to every trend, if I hop on every new platform and try to build a following there, I'm going to be building sandcastle after sandcastle. If the algorithm is failing us now, that means it was never stable. It was like a fair-weather friend."

The sandcastle metaphor felt apt. The followings, likes, and engagement, the real-time recommendations that presented a too-conveniently siloed version of my interests—they were temporary and contingent on the platforms themselves, which inevitably change and fade with time. The recent history of the 2010s, with the rise and then growing irrelevance of Facebook, has shown that no social network is too big to fail or get supplanted by a competitor that chooses to play by a new set of rules, social or technological. When that happens, users are left to fend for themselves, as our digital lives are dictated more by business concerns than our best interests.

. . .

# CHAPTER 5

# Regulating Filterworld

## MOLLY RUSSELL

Right now, we users are at the mercy of algorithmic recommendations and feeds. They are a Frankensteinian phenomenon, invented and given power by humans but far surpassing their expected role. We cannot control or influence them. We cannot wholly opt out while still using the digital platforms that have become necessary parts of modern adult life. Like the post office, the sewer system, or power lines, they are essential, and yet, unlike such public infrastructure, they aren't subject to government oversight or regulation, or the decisions of voters. Recommender systems run rampant. Perhaps we tend to overlook their capriciousness within the cultural sphere because the material that they influence seems less important than, say, running water. If Spotify begins recommending a litany of metal music after a user listens to a Metallica album, then the algorithmic monotony can be laughed off or ignored as a glitch. It may not seem particularly dangerous, since the biggest risk is boredom. Yet the algorithmic acceleration of content can be a life-or-death problem.

In November 2017, a fourteen-year-old student from northwest London named Molly Russell died by suicide. Russell wasn't wholly responsible for her actions, however. In 2022, Andrew Walker, the senior coroner for North London, described her death in a different way: "She died from an act of self-harm while suffering from depression and the negative effects of online content." In a pioneering moment, Walker formally cited social media as potentially lethal, a medical danger. Russell's background tells a familiar story of youth in the age of social media, when life is lived as much online as it is off. Like any teenager, Russell spent a lot of her time using digital platforms. In the six months before her death, she was exposed to more than sixteen thousand pieces of content on Instagram. Twenty-one hundred of those, or 13 percent, were related to suicide, self-harm, and depression, according to the government inquiry into her death. Russell had also assembled a Pinterest board of 469 images around the same themes. Social media feeds can play host to friendships and romantic relationships or deliver content based on any interest. Yet the same social and technological forces that propel Marvel movie fandom or make a song go viral can influence or exacerbate mental illness.

Algorithmic recommendations played a major role in delivering Russell so much mental-illness-related content. *Wired* reported that Russell had received one email titled "Depression Pins you may like" that included a picture of a bloody razor as a suggestion for her board—treating such negative imagery the same as the home-decor inspiration that occupies so much of Pinterest. Later, Facebook revealed that Russell was recommended thirty different accounts that "referred to sad or depressing themes" in their names, providing even more avenues for receiving content that may have worsened her mental health. On her own secret Twitter account, Russell retweeted accounts with names like "depression quotes," shared images that glorified suicide, and reached out to influencers who spoke about depression. The social-network feeds drove what the coroner called "binge periods," when Russell would consume content that was automatically delivered to her.

Russell's death was part of the human toll of algorithmic overreach, when content moves too quickly at too vast a scale to be moderated by hand. No magazine's editor would have published a flood of such depression content, nor would a television channel broadcast it. But the algorithmic feed could assemble an instant, on-demand collection, delivering what Russell may have found most engaging even though it was harmful for her. The tragedy of Russell's case demonstrates how the problems of Filterworld are most often structural, baked into the ways that digital platforms function. Users changing their behavior can only go so far; we can't trust that the mechanisms will ever prioritize our well-being over sparking more engagement that drives advertising revenue. Users can exert only certain kinds of agency within digital platforms. They can pursue a specific theme of content, for example, but can't alter the equation of the recommendation algorithm. We don't have enough alternative options to navigate the Internet outside of algorithmic feeds, in part because the Internet is now so dominated by just a few companies.

## STRUCTURAL MONOPOLIZATION

Our experiences online today are heavily centralized. Consumers are herded into a handful of massive platforms—Twitter, Facebook, Instagram, TikTok, YouTube—and left to seek out whatever it is they want to discover within the platforms' confines. Because audiences are so concentrated on those platforms, creators must work within them, too, transforming their work into content and adapting it to platforms' feeds. If they don't, they will remain relatively invisible. Though so much of the content we see online is "user-generated"—uploaded freely, without either gatekeeping or support—it still has to fit into preestablished molds determined by corporations. Yet the Internet has gone through several cycles of centralization and decentralization over its decades of history, and earlier eras might provide a better model for user experience.

In 1969, there were just a handful of networked computers under the control of the Defense Advanced Research Projects Agency, or DARPA, part of the US Department of Defense. ARPANET was the first wide-area computer network. It was possible to map every computer that it included on a small diagram of the United States—not only was it centralized, but you could access it only through the government and universities. Gradually, it expanded. If ARPANET was like a subway system, only connecting specific points, then Usenet, created in 1980, was more like a roadway: anyone with the right equipment could get on it. Usenet was one of the earliest ways of distributing and consuming content over the Internet. It was a digital billboard system that eventually connected to ARPANET.

Anyone with a server could host a "newsgroup," which people could use to publish articles and posts. The newsgroups provided space for discussions of anything from recent political news to the best methods for home winemaking. Each one had its own themes and rules; no single newsgroup had control over the network. The curation and pace of these groups were entirely set by their participants.

Still, this online audience was a self-selecting group of power users who were fluent in the nascent technology. They were also likely to be educated and affluent. Most people accessed Usenet for the first time, as well as the Internet itself, at universities when they went to college, leading to a peculiar problem. Every September, a flood of new students would make their way into the newsgroups without knowing the rules or etiquette. It wasn't their fault; they had simply never been in an online community before. But they tended to wreak havoc, publishing off-topic comments, getting into fights ("flame wars"), and disrupting the established tone like a bulldozer rolling into a peaceful forest. Gradually the noobs—as my generation of Internet slang would put it—became overwhelming, annoying the veteran users. Corporations also began to offer access to Usenet over home dial-up connections. America Online (AOL) incorporated Usenet in 1993, and the sudden influx of noobs became known as "Eternal September." The implication of the phrase was that the wrong kind of user was suddenly dominant in these once-niche groups. The digital landscape, the early version of digital culture, seemed to be ruined, though of course it persisted.

AOL simplified the Internet into an easy menu of options, centralizing it for the peak of twenty-three million subscribers that it reached around the year 2000. Its omnipresent compact discs, which arrived in the mail every month regardless of whether you already had the service or not, loaded a series of banners on a simple web interface. Clicking into them allowed the user to enter into designated website areas for entertainment, sports, and personal finance, among other topics—like Usenet but more approachable and less user-generated. These themed channels were home to some of my own earliest Internet experiences in the 1990s. Of course, the one I spent the most time in was the "Kids Only" section, which hosted safe (theoretically, not in practice) chat rooms for kids, "homework help," and rudimentary computer games with online high-score charts.

I remember these early Internet spaces most clearly from when I would log on via the desktop at my grandparents' house during family trips. Perhaps it was because my parents paid less attention to me when we were there; I could sit at the small desk in the "computer room," a miscellaneous antechamber off the living room, on a swiveling mid-century chair and stare into the chunky white plastic monitor. There was a tower of CD jewel cases, now an utter anachronism, holding computer games and software, but it was a revelation to discover that you could find things to do entirely online, within AOL's software, which incorporated the Internet Explorer browser. I was drawn in by that sense of possibility. The AOL channels were my first version of social media and my first access to culture online. They gave me a sense that there were other people doing and thinking about things through their own screens.

But as soon as I could, I ventured out of that corporatized space and found a much wider Internet that was more decentralized again. People built their own HTML websites without oversight and often without much professionalism. The web was an amateur zone made up of handmade pages espousing some particular fandom (say, the TV show *Gilmore Girls*) or niche hobby (building canoes) that were easy to stumble upon with early Google searches. You could use a service like Geocities, which launched in 1994, to build and host a website using basic tools, but no two Geocities pages looked the same. They were quirky collisions of animated GIFs in messy frame layouts, as though a child had made them.

LiveJournal, which launched in 1999, offered a more straightforward diary-keeping experience where what set each user apart was the text they published. It was the predecessor to more popular forms of blogging, a service where users could have their own personal pages and design the presentation to match their personality or chosen theme. Forum architectures allowed people to design their own communal spaces, too—the names of those software tools, like vBulletin and phpBB, evoke for me visions of avatars and signature banners. I joined forums for communities of the massive multiplayer online role-playing games that I was obsessed with.

One of those websites was called Merchant Guild, a green-and-gold bulletin board where people discussed *Ragnarok Online,* a Korean MMORPG that occupied far too much of my early teen years. There I could interact with pseudonymous strangers who treated me as a peer, which gave me a sense of agency that I lacked in the rest of my life, dutifully paying attention in high school classes where computers existed to play *Number Munchers* and *Oregon Trail.* Instead of raising my hand in English class, I could debate how best to equip a knight character. I was learning a lot online; it just wasn't relevant to anything else in my life at that point. Other forums I participated in were focused on particular jam bands or sharing concert recordings. These were niches I had no way to access offline, because I lacked any physical proximity to the communities.

Generally, if a website existed, it was because people—one or many—had worked hard to get it there and keep it running. My first brush with publishing online came in high school, which I entered as a freshman in 2002, when a friend named Parker set up a blog on a website that she had built for herself as an art portfolio. After reading her posts week after week, I asked her to make the same thing for me, then spent endless hours tinkering with banner designs and typefaces. I ended up with something that evoked a café interior—I remember a heavily photoshopped photo of a steaming coffee cup in the site's banner—or a hushed library room, with a background palette of soft grays and browns. Even then, when the only café I frequented was a freestanding Starbucks with a drive-through window, where I mostly ordered tall paper cups of too-hot green tea, that atmosphere felt aspirational to me.

I published dozens of posts on that blog before I really knew what "publish" meant, though they were mostly complaints about school or my parents. I didn't even fully appreciate that other people were privy to these angsty screeds. Being on the Internet in the early aughts was still a nerdy enough pursuit that few people understood what it meant. It didn't incite teasing at school because other kids didn't know what a forum was, and digital life was quieter, too, because the public arenas of social media, where personal attacks are now rampant, did not yet exist. Armies of trolls or bots couldn't harass an individual user. Everything was smaller in scale, because it was less centralized. Parker was likely the only person who ever read my posts. Still, the blog made me understand what it meant to have a digital shadow self, a version of your life and personality that only existed online. At that time, it felt like a radical innovation, a refreshing novelty. I could control how I presented myself online. Still, I was less aware of who was paying attention on the other side of that screen, in part because our Internet presences were less tied to our physical lives—going by your full name online would have appeared bizarre. Before it took over the world, social media was once a niche itself, an obscure hobby. That sense of disconnection slowly changed and dissipated as the Internet became inextricable from "real life."

By 2004, I had a MySpace account, but only a few of my high school friends did, and the most popular activity to be had on it was rearranging lists of your favorite songs and best friends. Friendster, which predated MySpace and was popular with a crowd slightly older than mine, persisted, too. Facebook started out with the demographic of college students. As with Usenet, getting into school was the way you got on. The now-universal social network was initially used to connect with classmates and post party photos or relationship updates, but it quickly became a vacuum that sucked in other kinds of digital content, particularly as it opened up to non-college populations.

Friends' status updates became interspersed with group notifications, news articles, and advertisements, filtered by the algorithmic feed. The company pioneered this kind of collision of content, less because users demanded it and more because it served its own interests—like Walmart or Amazon, if Facebook could offer everything at once, then its users would have less reason to use a competing service. From total specialization in the form of hand-built HTML sites, the Internet was moving toward a one-size-fits-all approach. Facebook was a personal blog, a forum, a news feed, and a photo dump all at once. It was clear that Mark Zuckerberg didn't want it to be just a website, but the entirety of our digital lives. The Internet had begun to congeal into a small set of giant platforms.

Facebook did have competition in the early 2010s. Twitter, which launched two years after Facebook's debut, offered a real-time, chronological feed of information for news addicts who wanted to consume as much information in as small a space as possible, hence the appeal of the original 140-character limit. Tumblr offered a more image-heavy and intimate experience; like an update to Live-Journal, it tended to play host to private musings and collections of esoterica. Some of my favorite Tumblrs curated material like evocative anime screenshots or medieval manuscript illuminations. (Pornography, in varying degrees of artsiness, was also plentiful, setting Tumblr apart from other social networks.) But nothing really threatened Facebook's grip on online socializing until Instagram. I remember the app feeling like a breath of fresh air when I joined in 2011. Instagram did what Facebook so successfully achieved in the first place in positioning itself as the way you could see what your friends were up to. But it didn't have the same scale, chaotic combination of content, and messy interface that Facebook had accrued by trying to encompass so many formats at once. Instagram's feed was non-algorithmic and offered a single type of content. It was a minimalist tool for doing one thing: sharing smartphone photos in an environment that made them look good.

Zuckerberg quickly realized that the smaller company—Instagram had only thirteen employees and no revenue whatsoever—was a threat. In early 2012, he complained to Facebook's then chief financial officer about Instagram and other new social apps like Path and Foursquare, "If they grow to a large scale, they could be very disruptive to us." So, his solution was to buy the smaller companies, offering such a large amount of money that the founders couldn't refuse—he suggested $500 million or $1 billion. Buying the apps would "give us a year or more to integrate their dynamics before anyone can get close to their scale again," Zuckerberg said. In other words, Facebook would acquire the companies, merge them into the Facebook ecosystem, and then copy the features that made them fresh to neutralize the competition. "New products won't get much traction since we'll already have their mechanics deployed at scale," he said.

The company executed that plan. Zuckerberg offered to buy Instagram for $1 billion, and in April 2012, the CEO and cofounder of Instagram, Kevin Systrom, accepted it. He didn't think he had much of a choice. As Systrom told one Instagram investor, "I don't think we'll ever escape the wrath of Mark." Either Facebook would acquire the company, or it would make sure its growth slowed down by cutting off the start-up's access to Facebook's much larger platform, with its business software and social data. The strategy was "buy or bury."

For several years after the acquisition, Instagram remained more or less the same. But in 2015 the app incorporated advertising, in 2016 it switched to an algorithmic feed, and in 2017 it added Stories, the ephemeral posts that were its attempt to copy (and destroy) its competitor Snapchat. Instagram gradually became more and more like Facebook itself: a mishmash of different content types; personal and impersonal social connections; and a feed that gave you less what you wanted than whatever the company was emphasizing at the moment, like videos or shopping opportunities. The chaotic changes were frustrating for an app that had been devoted to aesthetic experiences. In late 2018, Systrom and his Instagram cofounder Mike Krieger left Facebook entirely. ("No one ever leaves a job because everything's awesome," Systrom said at the time, hinting at his dissatisfaction.)

Already, when Facebook bought Instagram, it felt as though the walls of the Internet were closing in a little tighter around us users. The broad expanse of possibility, of messiness, on a network like Geocities or the personal expression of Tumblr was shut down. Digital life became increasingly templated, a set of boxes to fill in rather than a canvas to cover in your own image. (You don't redesign how your Facebook profile looks; you just change your avatar.) I felt a certain sense of loss, but at first the trade-off of creativity for broadcast reach seemed worthwhile: You could talk to so many people at once on social media! But that exposure became enervating, too, and I missed the previous sense of intimacy, the Internet as a private place—a hideout from real life, rather than the determining force of real life. As the walls closed in, the algorithmic feeds took on more and more influence and authority.

Innovation slowed down. The various other tools and platforms that popped up were quickly crowded out by Facebook and Google. Twitter created the short-form video site Vine in 2013, but mismanagement shut it down in 2017. Google's own social network Google Plus was incomprehensible from its launch in 2011 until it quietly disappeared in 2019. Crowdfunding services, like Kickstarter and Patreon, offered hope for more niche cultural projects by allowing supporters to pay directly for what they wanted to see, but they didn't achieve the kind of momentum that Snapchat and TikTok—the only real competitors to Facebook's social dominance—later did.

Soon the next threat to Facebook emerged: instant messaging. The company was seeing new apps take advantage of smartphone owners' lists of contacts, supplanting SMS and iMessage as the way people communicated directly with each other (the messaging apps used Internet connection rather than phone signal). Facebook had its own messaging tool, an app called Messenger that first launched in 2011, but the company was rightly concerned that a messaging app could branch into larger-scale social networking and thus draw users away.

Messaging "is one of the most dangerous beach heads to morph into Facebook," one Facebook vice president wrote in early 2013. WhatsApp, a messaging app founded in 2009, proved their point, becoming increasingly prominent, particularly in Asia and Europe. By the end of that year, it had over four hundred million users, with revenue coming from download and subscription fees rather than ads. So Zuckerberg made another unrefusable offer. In early 2014, Facebook agreed to acquire WhatsApp for $19 billion—though WhatsApp had most recently been valued at $1.5 billion—an incredibly high price to pay for a start-up company. In turn, WhatsApp was denatured. In 2020, it incorporated advertising, but it never turned into a social network to rival Facebook, because Facebook managed the company's goals and ambitions. Zuckerberg could stop it from expanding its features—the acquisition neutralized the real threat to the parent company.

Instagram and WhatsApp are just two of Facebook's dozens of acquisitions. Google similarly acquired YouTube in 2006 and turned the video-uploading site into a media-consumption juggernaut, a replacement for cable television. Other social networks didn't survive. Tumblr, for example, once on par with Twitter and Facebook, was bought by Yahoo in 2013 for $1.1 billion. Yet it suffered through years of mismanagement and declining growth, barely changing its initial product. It finally sold again in 2019 to WordPress for just $3 million. Perhaps the same fate would have awaited an app like Instagram under different circumstances. But we did not have the chance to find out—it got sucked into Facebook's gravity. Facebook became too big—not just too big to fail, but perhaps illegally big. Many of these internal business details come from a lawsuit laid out by the US Federal Trade Commission in 2020 arguing that Facebook had become a monopoly in the space of social networking through its "anticompetitive conduct." Many state governments have joined the lawsuit or mounted similar ones, too.

There's a certain amount of whiplash that comes with experiencing these cycles of the Internet. We users think we're supposed to behave one way, and then the opposite becomes true, like the movement from pseudonyms to real names. We're asked to use tools to build our own spaces, to freely express ourselves, and then commanded to fit within a preset palette determined by a social network. Yet as soon as one standard becomes dominant, it seems to lose its grip. There is no teleological arc for digital platforms; they don't move in one direction toward perfection, the way hard drives have been able to store more and more data over time. Instead, it is cyclical, swinging between different strategies of centralization and decentralization like a pendulum.

Innovation starts at a small level, with a group of users or a new app enabling new forms of behavior, like publishing a new kind of content or creating new communities. For a time, digital culture feels organic and exciting, different from what came before it. But then those new behaviors and features are adopted by larger companies, by copying, by business pressure, or by mergers and acquisitions. Users jump on board with newfound excitement about their old apps, but the newness fades as the innovations are monetized to death. Any joy in the new forms of expression is ruthlessly exploited, most often in the form of increased advertising. There's something Sisyphean in the whole process. Authentic online cultures are always being ruined, as users inevitably complain, but also always emerging again. No platform is ever completely safe. The biggest incumbent could be threatened by a tiny newcomer, simply because of a slight technological evolution—like Snapchat's ephemeral posts or TikTok's wholly algorithmic feed—or the unavoidable fact that people simply get bored, and technology, like fashion, must constantly change to maintain its hold over its users' attention.

Still, the Internet in its current era has never looked more monolithic. Individual websites have been subsumed into ever-flowing feeds. All content has to fit into the same few molds. Content creators may have their choice of platform, but the platforms themselves increasingly resemble one another and function in similar ways. It feels like our options have narrowed to a choking point. The Internet incumbents are so large and powerful, with billions of users and market capitalizations in the hundreds of billions of dollars, that even innovative start-ups have a hard time thriving without being crushed in one way or another. Their advantage is too strong, and they don't have any incentive to change the extractive methods that are flattening our experiences. As the FTC's lawsuit against Facebook argued, "The result is less competition, less investment, less innovation, and fewer choices for users and advertisers."

We users can't fight against this stultifying environment on our own. Switching between apps and toggling settings can accomplish only so much. To break down Filterworld, change has to happen on the industrial level, at the scale of the tech companies themselves. Decentralization tends to give users the most agency, though it also places a higher burden of labor and responsibility on the individual. It's also the best way to resist Filterworld and cultivate new possibilities for digital life. But companies are unlikely to embrace decentralization on their own, because it's usually less profitable. The only path for change may be to force them.

For such a vast and powerful industry, affecting billions of people, the business of social networks doesn't face much government regulation. It seems to fall into a gulf between the hardware industry, where devices and manufacturing supply chains face scrutiny, and the traditional media industry, where what kinds of content businesses can broadcast has been a legal issue since the US Constitution enshrined free speech. Should social networks be treated like newspapers and television channels, responsible for everything hosted within their domains? They have long escaped that responsibility. Or should they be classified more like telephone lines, theoretically neutral transmitters of information? But they are decidedly not neutral, given their algorithmic judgments. Or perhaps social media belongs in the category of vice industries, with tightly regulated limits meant for the safety of individuals who might otherwise abuse it. After all, so many users are addicted.

No matter how we classify the digital platforms that make up Filterworld, it's clear that they need some form of regulation. As users, we only feel the consequences of their structures and adapt our behavior to them. New kinds of behavior, and thus new forms of culture, require new structures, which won't exist until the tech companies' monopolies and duopolies are disrupted.

## SEEKING TRANSPARENCY

The quickest way to change how digital platforms work may be to mandate transparency: forcing the companies to explain how and when their algorithmic recommendations are working. Transparency would at least give users more information about the decisions constantly being made about what to show us. And if we know how algorithms work, perhaps we'll be better able to resist their influence and make our own decisions.

After the 2016 election of Donald Trump, the American public became slightly more aware of how we were being manipulated by algorithmic feeds. Democrats couldn't understand how anyone had voted for Trump, given that their Facebook and Twitter feeds didn't promote as many posts from the other side of the political spectrum, creating one of Eli Pariser's filter bubbles, a digital echo chamber. Online, they lived in an illusion of total agreement that Trump was ridiculous. At the same time, his supporters were surrounded by content that reinforced their own views—another form of homogeneity. Recommender systems had sorted the audiences into two neat categories that didn't need to overlap, whereas in a human-edited newspaper or television news program, some mutual exposure might have been more likely. More likely but not guaranteed: traditional media can be biased into homogeneity just as well, as in *The New York Times*'s unwillingness to cover the possibility of a Trump win.

I recounted the criticism of filter bubbles earlier in this book; the phenomenon may have done more to cause the *surprise* of Trump's win than the fact that it happened. Liberals were simply caught unaware of his popularity in part due to social media, failed to take him seriously enough as a threat, and thus made it easier for him to win.

Trump did take advantage of algorithmic technology. His campaign used Facebook's targeted advertising program to great effect, pushing messages to voters whose online actions showed that they might be convinced by his politics. His campaign bought space for 5.9 million Facebook ads, spending $44 million in the five months before November, many times more than Hillary Clinton's campaign, which bought 66,000 ads. Trump's team worked closely with Facebook itself, using the targeted advertising software to test which messages had the most effect. Facebook ads are often bought based on outcomes rather than how many times they are displayed; the client pays for click-throughs and conversions to actions like political donations. The Trump campaign was all but guaranteed that the algorithmic feed would work in their favor.

On the users' side, it had also become more difficult to tell which Facebook content was promoted as a paid advertising and which was more organic, based on who or what you follow. The feed had become more chaotic, and thus more confusing and more manipulative. The combination led to a then-rare public backlash against Facebook.

An engineer named Krishna Gade, who had previously held management positions at Pinterest and Twitter, was hired in the midst of this drama, in November 2016. He became Facebook's engineering manager for the news feed, working on its content ranking system. It was a vital job at that moment. "There were a lot more inner questions being asked around how the news feed works," Gade told me. He recognized the homogenizing force of the feed: "With recommendation algorithms, you get the same kind of things over time. How do we break those patterns?"

First, Gade developed an internal debugging tool to understand how exactly the recommendation algorithm worked. It could tell why a piece of content was being promoted at a given time. Pieces of content came appended with a small link that displayed a few reasons for its appearance in the feed, the variables that made the algorithm register it. Screenshots from the early product show explanations like the user being friends with the poster, the user tending to comment more often on posts with photos, or a post being popular within a particular group that the user is a member of. The logic was basic, mostly revolving around that dominant metric of engagement—what is already popular gets even more exposure. But the feature at least made the feed seem more coherent. That is, if you bothered to hit the button and investigate.

For Gade, the feature was fundamental to how a digital platform should work. "Users should be given the right to ask for what's going on," he told me. This principle goes by the label of "algorithmic transparency," which argues that the variables and weights that go into the algorithms we interact with should be made accessible and public, like peering at the gears driving a clock face. In its ideal form, transparency is "a method to see, understand and govern complex systems in timely fashions," as Mike Ananny and Kate Crawford wrote in a 2016 paper in the journal *New Media & Society*. Knowing how and why something has been recommended might help to dispel the air of algorithmic anxiety that surrounds our online experiences, since we could identify which of our actions the recommendations are considering. Still, it leaves users responsible for themselves: Knowing how the algorithm works isn't the same as being able to control it. "Transparency alone cannot create accountable systems," Ananny and Crawford wrote.

In 2015, the FTC established the Office of Technology Research and Investigation, whose mandate included looking into the possibilities of algorithmic transparency. Even at that point, it was clear that algorithms were playing an increasing role in people's lives: "Consumers interact with algorithms on a daily basis, whether they know it or not. To date, we have very little insight as to how these algorithms operate, what incentives are behind them, what data is used and how it's structured," Ashkan Soltani, then the FTC's chief technologist, told *PC World* in 2015. But little progress has been made in that direction, particularly in the context of social media. The FTC office's actions have focused more often on regulating digital advertising, cryptocurrency, and privacy than on how feeds work.

After implementing the explanation feature years ago, Facebook has not gone far in embracing transparency. As I've experimented with it over months of my own Facebook feed, the most common reasoning it gave me was that a post is "popular compared to other posts you've seen." One could make that assumption about pretty much any algorithmically recommended piece of content found on any platform.

As recently as 2021, Nick Clegg, the president of global affairs at Facebook's parent company Meta (he was previously the deputy prime minister of the United Kingdom), was still projecting a path toward more transparency. "You should be able to talk back to the algorithm and consciously adjust or ignore the predictions it makes," he wrote in a post on Medium titled "You and the Algorithm: It Takes Two to Tango." According to Clegg, it should be possible to "alter your personal algorithm in the cold light of day, through breathing spaces built into the design of the platform." It's an evocative description, the suggestion of space separated from recommendations, but his employer has put little of it into action. One of the few controls Facebook currently gives users over their feeds is selecting accounts and groups to prioritize as "Favorites," meaning that the algorithm will promote them more often, or deprioritize with "Snooze" (seeing less of a particular account, though only temporarily). Soon enough, the algorithm reasserts itself. The user can't balance a range of topics, choose to see more of her friends than news stories, or dial down the political outrage in favor of positivity. Though each person's feed looks different, adapted to our interests and habits, they all work in the same fundamental way, dictated by the corporation.

Gade left Facebook in October of 2018. He decided to work on the problem of algorithmic transparency on his own, with a new company that he cofounded called Fiddler. Fiddler helps its clients break down machine-learning models and see inside of them. That could mean evaluating why an algorithmic banking process automatically offers a loan to one customer while denying another, or why a voice-controlled app like Amazon's Alexa consistently misinterprets a particular word. It could also give a much deeper view of exactly why the Facebook recommendation algorithm promotes a certain piece of content within the feed—that is, if Facebook allowed Fiddler to access its data and models.

Fiddler creates a dashboard of variables and outcomes, allowing its clients to experimentally tweak them and then update their internal models with the results. Its software can also look inside these algorithmic systems that are so often described as black boxes. The term *black box* "is a bit of an exaggeration," Gade told me. While machine learning develops abstract patterns that can be incomprehensible to a human being, other machines can perceive and represent them. "Fiddler gives you a lens into the structure," he said.

Gade gave me a demonstration of Fiddler's dashboards over video chat. After a company uploads its models and data, the software can "measure fairness," testing it using specific examples like different genders or races of user and ensuring the outcomes are consistent. Many recommendation algorithms are based on the interpretation of content, evaluating texts like posts, captions, or user reviews in order to gauge the relevance of a particular item. But algorithms can misinterpret language. Gade showed me a case in which a model was assigning the word *gay* a very negative connotation, meaning that content that included it wasn't getting prioritized. That could be a complete mistake if the word is meant positively—or perhaps it should be interpreted as neutral. If automated content moderation or recommender systems misinterpret a word or behavior, "You could potentially silence an entire demographic," Gade said. That's why being able to see what's happening around a given algorithmic decision is so important.

Twitter has provided an object lesson in the damage of nontransparency. When Elon Musk acquired the social network in 2022, the hope was that the entrepreneur would help the slow-moving service fulfill its potential. What ensued was a rash of random and half-baked changes that most often altered the user experience for the worse, particularly when it came to the feed. Each version of the Twitter feed—whether on mobile app, website, or the software

Tweetdeck—seemed to function differently. A user could toggle to the "Latest" feed, which suggested that the tweets would be in chronological order, only to find strange aberrations like clusters of tweets only from accounts that had paid for Twitter verification and constant interruption by recommended tweets. I began to feel that I couldn't trust how the algorithmic feed functioned day to day, let alone over years. Though I had relied on the service like a utility, it was a reminder that I never knew what was happening behind the scenes. There was no transparency, let alone stability, because Twitter had no real responsibility to its users.

## PUBLISHING VERSUS PROMOTING

Just as digital platforms aren't responsible for explaining their algorithmic feeds, they also don't take responsibility for what the feeds promote—they separate themselves from the outcomes of their recommender systems. They can do that because of the United States's 1996 Telecommunications Act, which included a Communications Decency Act with a piece called Section 230. Section 230 allowed the Internet to grow exponentially over the past decades. Our digital world wouldn't be the same without it. But in the social media era, it has also allowed the tech companies that have supplanted traditional media businesses to operate *without the safeguards of traditional media*. Section 230 makes a distinction between an open platform, like Facebook, and what users publish on it. "No provider or user of an interactive computer service shall be treated as the publisher or speaker of any information provided by another information content provider," the law states. This is an important distinction, because "publishers" are legally liable for the content they publish: if a magazine prints something defamatory about someone, for example, it can be sued by its subject. Facebook, in contrast, can wave off the risk because it is the user, not the platform, who is technically publishing the content.

The precedent for Section 230 came from two 1990s cases. In 1991, *Cubby v. CompuServe* began as a conflict between two digital media companies. Robert Blanchard's Cubby Inc., publisher of a news service called Skuttlebutt, sued Don Fitzpatrick's publication

*Rumorville* because it had published an article that defamed Skuttle-butt. *Rumorville* was available on an online forum hosted by Compu-Serve, an early provider of home Internet that was a major force in the 1990s. Blanchard sued CompuServe itself as well as Fitzpatrick. The US District Court concluded that CompuServe was only a distributor, not a publisher of the allegedly defamatory content. In other words, as a host, CompuServe acted more like a newsstand or bookstore. It didn't control the contents of what got published, just how the material reached consumers. A 1950s case already ruled that bookstores couldn't possibly legally vet every book that passed through their shelves and were thus freed from responsibility for what the books contained.

A second case on digital distribution had a different outcome. In 1995's *Stratton Oakmont v. Prodigy,* which was heard by the New York Supreme Court, Prodigy Services Company was the host of an online forum, including one space for discussions of finances. One of Prodigy's users published defamatory comments on the forum, targeting the brokerage firm Stratton Oakmont, Inc., and its president Daniel Porush. This case would seem similar to *Cubby v. Compu-Serve,* but Prodigy was more involved in the actual content that was published on its service. The forum had rules about what could be posted and imposed moderation systems, including automatic filtering and human moderators. The court determined that in this context, Prodigy was a publisher, not a distributor, and so was legally responsible for the material on its site. "Prodigy is clearly making decisions as to content . . . and such decisions constitute editorial control," the court decision read. Prodigy requested a dismissal of the case, based on the precedent of *Cubby v. CompuServe,* but to no avail.

The conflicting cases brought up a fundamental paradox: Internet services that did nothing to filter the content going to users were legally protected, while services that did try to filter the content, even just for basic quality or safety, were not protected. It was riskier for Internet companies to try to influence content at all. Two congressional representatives, Christopher Cox and Ron Wyden, decided that the issue needed to be resolved. "If that rule was going to take hold, then the internet would become the Wild West and nobody would have any incentive to keep the internet civil," Cox later told *Wired*. Cox and Wyden's Section 230 allowed digital platforms to mediate some content, particularly anything "obscene, lewd, lascivious, filthy, excessively violent, harassing, or otherwise objectionable," without being held liable for its publication. In other words, the online distributors could "in good faith" interfere with content as long as it seemed to be for the general good of the users. Section 230 was signed into law by President Bill Clinton in early 1996.

Yet mainstream social media in the 2010s bears a very different relationship to Section 230. In 1996, the Internet was still a relatively niche experience for its sixteen million or so users. It played a much smaller role in media distribution. Today, Twitter and Facebook have grown to encompass how hundreds of millions of people consume all forms of media, from entertainment to news.

Social networks displaced traditional publishers by absorbing advertising revenue; siloing content into algorithmic feeds; and mediating the relationship between publishers and their consumers. The consequence is that traditional media companies have been decimated, losing most of their revenue when compared to decades past, and publications are now forced to maintain themselves as responsible publishers with much smaller numbers of staff. Even with their restricted circumstances, traditional media companies continue to hold responsibility for every piece of content they publish. Meanwhile, digital platforms could claim they were not media companies at all with the excuse of Section 230.

The separations between roles blurred. In this new ecosystem, digital platforms took on some of the functions of publishers in deciding which content reached consumers. If CompuServe could claim neutrality in its court case, since it didn't influence what *Rumorville* published, Facebook has much less of a semblance of neutrality. The algorithm's curatorial actions are akin to a newspaper choosing which stories to put on the front page. Section 230 has served as a shield, distancing social networks from what individual users post on their platforms. That ranges from #MeToo investigations to racist comments or threats of violence. The law has become the target of growing skepticism, and lawsuits are attempting to hold social networks responsible for what they distribute.

In November 2015, a series of terrorist attacks, later claimed by ISIS, struck Paris. One hundred thirty people were killed, including a twenty-three-year-old American student named Nohemi Gonzalez. Gonzalez's family held Google, Twitter, and Facebook responsible for her death—particularly Google's YouTube—because the companies had promoted ISIS-related content to their users via algorithmic recommendations, and thus played a role in radicalizing the Paris attackers. In essence, they had to be responsible, to a degree, both for what was on their platforms and how it was pushed to viewers. The lawsuit was initially dismissed, on the grounds that Google was not materially supporting ISIS with its ad revenue and did not treat ISIS-related content any differently than other content, maintaining its theoretical neutrality as a distributor.

But in October 2022, the Supreme Court decided to take up the case alongside another lawsuit against digital platforms, perhaps identifying an important precedent to set in our era of omnipresent algorithms. "Whether Section 230 applies to these algorithm-generated recommendations is of enormous practical importance. Interactive computer services constantly direct such recommendations, in one form or another, at virtually every adult and child in the United States who uses social media," the Gonzalez family argued in the case's appeal. The Facebook whistleblower Frances Haugen, who leaked documents proving that the company was aware of the damage its algorithmic recommendations could cause, has also argued against the law. "If we reformed Section 230 to make Facebook responsible for the consequences of their intentional ranking decisions, I think they would get rid of engagement-based ranking," Haugen told a Senate panel in 2021.

Algorithmic feeds help automatically distribute misinformation and can speed ideological radicalization, feeding users ever more extreme content in a single category. The problem with Section 230 is that ultimately, and strangely, the law makes it so that no one is currently responsible for the effects of algorithmic recommendations. The tech companies themselves aren't liable, the systems are only regulated internally, and users are left to fend for themselves, short of basic content moderation. If algorithmic feeds mistreat us or contribute to an abusive or exploitative online environment, we, as users and citizens, have little recourse. One of our only possibilities is switching to another platform, and yet that, too, has already been limited by the problem of monopolization. Our relationship to algorithmic feeds feels like a trap: we can neither influence them nor escape them.

Repealing Section 230 would not be a panacea. In some ways, it protects users' free speech online and allows digital platforms as we know them to exist without being sued into oblivion for every stray tweeted insult or accusation. But there are proposals to modify it. In October 2021, following Haugen's Facebook whistleblowing, lawmakers in the House of Representatives introduced legislation called the Justice Against Malicious Algorithms Act, or JAMA. The bill would "lift the Section 230 liability shield when an online platform knowingly or recklessly uses an algorithm or other technology to recommend content that materially contributes to physical or severe emotional injury." It removes Section 230's protection in any instance of "personalized recommendations based on information specific to an individual." The bill does not cover results that come from a user's own search, like a Google query, or services like web hosting and data storage that undergird social networks, which are more neutral and fit better under Section 230's original purpose.

In February of 2023, the Supreme Court held hearings for the cases of *Gonzalez v. Google* and *Twitter v. Taamneh*, in which the family of a victim of another ISIS-linked terrorist attack sued Twitter, Google, and Facebook under the Anti-Terrorism Act, alleging that the companies had hosted and recommended ISIS content to users, thus providing meaningful support to the terrorist group.

Early on, Justice Elena Kagan all but joked about the court's ignorance of the issues around digital platforms. "These are not the nine greatest experts on the Internet," Kagan said, to a wave of laughter in the courtroom. But she also reflected on the dominant influence of algorithmic feeds: "Every time anybody looks at anything on the Internet, there is an algorithm involved," she said. The justices probed the uses and capabilities of algorithmic recommendations and debated if algorithms can be considered "neutral" (I would argue they cannot), but the general incomprehension was palpable. The plaintiff's lawyer, Eric Schnapper, stumbled painfully while describing Internet mainstays like YouTube video thumbnails. In May 2023, the Supreme Court ruled that the tech companies were not liable, and upheld the strongest interpretation of Section 230 once again.

Our feeds under a dramatically reformed Section 230 would look very different. Social networks would be forced to take responsibility for each piece of content on their sites that receives algorithmic promotion. Perhaps they would adapt by putting most content outside the reach of recommendations, meaning that users would have to intentionally follow or search for a given subject. The content that still receives algorithmic promotion would have to be vetted to ensure that it is wholly anodyne—clips of cute pet antics and feel-good news stories. The selection would be subject to a collective perception of what constituted acceptable, or neutral, news. (Such content would still be filtered, in a way, by having a singular filter imposed on it.) TikTok's wide range of niche recommendations, for example, would be impossible. One could imagine a TikTok feed made up of only clips that would fit in the anodyne TV show *America's Funniest Home Videos*. It would still be amusing, but hardly addictive or manipulative. Content moderation would have to be much stricter.

Changing the balance to emphasize linear, opt-in content over automated recommendations might be a good thing, if it can limit the possible exposure of harmful material online. But this would be a much more sanitized, and by necessity slower, Internet. The problem comes down to determining which kinds of content should be able to travel so quickly and frictionlessly across Filterworld, and which should be slowed down or stopped entirely.

If the 2000s saw the emergence of the mainstream Internet, and the 2010s saw the rise and domination of massive digital platforms, then the next decade seems likely to embrace decentralization once more. *Agency* might be the watchword: the ability of an individual user to dictate how they publish and view content. I have hope for an Internet that's more like Geocities, with expressions of individuality and customization everywhere, but with the multimedia innovations that have made the 2020s' Internet so compelling. It would be a messier, more fun place—more like a playground or a sandbox than the cubicle office floor that the Internet has come to resemble.

Open-source software like Mastodon, which allows its users to create and host their own Twitter-like social networks, provides one hint at what might be to come. But Mastodon also demonstrates some of the disadvantages of such different infrastructure. Audiences are smaller on self-hosted platforms, and interactions are more difficult. You might not be able to find any kind of content that you want. There isn't the possibility, or threat, of viral fame. But those are the trade-offs that we may have to make for a more sustainable overall digital culture.

## SLOWING DOWN AMPLIFICATION

As Molly Russell, the British teenager who died by suicide, experienced with the avalanche of depression content, recommendations accelerate negative material as much as positive material. While the system may treat all content the same, the consequences of promotion are not. The spread of misinformation online during the COVID-19 pandemic drove a viral craze for Ivermectin, a drug that is most often used for horses. The patients who took it were hurt much more than helped, sometimes even hospitalized *because* they ingested the medicine. The Ivermectin stories spread far because they attracted engagement, in part as a politicized issue fueled by the rhetoric coming from Trump and his administration. The misinformation turned out to be optimized for the algorithmic equation, creating the kind of instant interaction that prompts even more promotion.

The usual strategy to deal with this problem is moderation, or censorship for safety's sake: the problematic content is meant to be blocked out entirely, not allowed into users' feeds in the first place. Social networks filter both by means of machine-learning analysis—automatically censoring particular keywords, for example—as well as human moderators, who manually decide which content to let through. Facebook outsources much of its human moderation to a company called Accenture, which employs thousands of moderators around the world, including in countries like Portugal and Malaysia. These laborers face daily exposure to deaths on camera, recorded abuse, and child pornography. They keep the feeds clean for the rest of us, exposing themselves to psychic harm the way trash pickers digging through international electronic waste dumped in Ghana and elsewhere are exposed to poisonous chemicals. The toxic material doesn't just magically vanish because of the mediation of the algorithm. Once again, the human labor is obscured.

Some content always falls through the cracks, however, and once it's in the feed, nothing prevents it from being recommended. One way to combat algorithmic overreach is to regulate which kinds of content recommendations affect, as some reforms to Section 230 suggest. In the United Kingdom, a law called the Online Safety Bill is under consideration, designed to prevent cases like Russell's. "All services likely to be accessed by children will have duties to protect them from harmful content," the bill's Parliamentary statement dictates. Platforms that allow such harmful content will also have to be transparent about how it is treated in terms of moderation and recommendation. This could include removing or "deprioritizing" the harmful content—that is, recommending it less often or not at all.

Social networks must navigate a difficult set of priorities. We use them to communicate directly with each other, as messaging services or ways to follow updates from our friends. But they also play a broadcast role, reaching audiences of millions of users. Both of those kinds of content are subject to the same rules and forces, whether they are meant to be private or public. Tarleton Gillespie, a technology scholar at Cornell University who is now a principal researcher for Microsoft, explained what that gap means.

"Platforms have offered us up something that is meant for intimate, connected speech. Then they moderate it in a statistically broad, systematic way," Gillespie told me. There's little room for considering the specific nature of a given piece of content, since it lacks context and becomes atomized in the overall feed. That means we have also developed expectations about how the content we post travels online—namely, we most often expect it to travel as far as possible. "People have developed a notion not just that they get to speak, but there's some expectation of where it's supposed to go," Gillespie told me. In other words, we have come to expect algorithmic promotion almost as a right.

But perhaps this expectation needs to change, and we need to learn to exist in a digital world without so much automated acceleration. Reaching wide audiences of strangers isn't a right; it's a privilege that doesn't need to be possible for every individual user or post. The word *amplification* describes algorithmic recommendations' role in spreading content more widely than it would otherwise travel: like a megaphone, it turns regular speech into a shout. Amplification is at the core of Filterworld's problems; one format gets amplified above all. Using regulation to target amplification could create more balance in the ecosystem.

Daphne Keller is the director of the Program on Platform Regulation at Stanford's Cyber Policy Center. In 2021, Keller published an essay through Columbia University titled "Amplification and Its Discontents." "Amplification features can do both harm and good," she wrote. The trick in regulation is to "[harness] the benefits"—like helping users discover new voices or interests—while "reducing the attendant harms," like the acceleration of problematic content. "Most discussions in the U.S. of regulating algorithms are about content," Keller told me. But "there's no such thing as a baseline of what content should be surfaced to people." We can complain about hearing too much of the same music on Spotify or seeing too many of our family members' political opinions on Facebook, but there's no one perfect mixture of content, a selection of topics or tones, that fits for everyone.

The makeup of an algorithmic feed like Facebook's could be compared to the food pyramid for a healthy diet. The USDA recommends a minimum of fats, oils, and sweets, and a much larger number of fruits and vegetables. Regulating amplification could force feeds to incorporate specific proportions of different kinds of content, mingling a little bit of salacious material with a higher volume of informative, politically neutral, or geographically local material. Such rules would limit the infinite expanse that we now experience in our feeds.

A similar kind of law already exists for children's television.

The Children's Television Act was passed by Congress in 1990 and made stricter in 1997. It mandated that all major broadcast television stations had to feature at least three hours per week of material directed at kids. Aside from being "educational and informational," the television programs must meet other requirements, like limiting advertising and not displaying commercial website addresses. Pressure from the law prompted the production of shows like *Beakman's World* and *Bill Nye, The Science Guy*, according to a 1997 pamphlet from the Center for Media Education.

But the law became more difficult to apply as television splintered away from just a handful of basic channels into larger cable packages and then streaming services in the 2010s, which weren't subject to the same regulations. What kinds of shows qualify as properly educational is also somewhat ambiguous; some channels even began to use reality television shows marketed toward teenagers to fulfill their educational requirement. No matter if a show was informative, it could still become a commercial enterprise that encouraged consumerism: *Barney & Friends*, though it was produced for many years by public television, sold millions of branded toys.

Flawed as it is, the Children's Television Act has persisted for decades and has proven to have some teeth. In 2007, the American channel Univision faced a $24 million fine from the FCC for breaking the law. It had attempted to define its telenovela soap operas as proper educational content. The US government disagreed, the shows did not prove qualified, and Univision eventually relaunched its children's programming block under the title of Planeta U. The law creates a precedent for meaningfully influencing what kinds of content are broadcast to viewers. If we accept the fact that today's social networks make the same kind of editorial decisions as a media business like a TV channel, should they then be forced to feature certain kinds of content every so often, prioritizing information that might be good for us—or ultimately good for society?

Algorithmic recommendations take into account what we subconsciously gravitate toward: any piece of content that we mouse over for an extended period of time, let alone click. When we hesitate before swiping to skip a TikTok video, that data is considered. Like junk food or addictive substances, humans might simply need help with choosing the mixture of content they consume. As Keller told me: "We click with our monkey brains, the same ones that cause us to buy a candy bar in the checkout line at the grocery store." Algorithmic feeds accelerate these worst impulses, not just on an individual level but an aggregate one, across all the users of a social network. Titillating material—content that might be violent, provocative, or misleading—can be easier to discover than material that is more boring but also more valuable.

"That's not a great way to structure our information diet. It contributes to societal problems," Keller continued. She described the possible answer as "forcing platforms to put some veggies in with the all-candy diet that users are asking for." In essence, we would have to be okay with algorithmic recommendations not giving us precisely what we want or what we would be most likely to engage with—just like we accept that human news editors know best what's most important to broadcast to their audiences. (We don't expect the front page of *The New York Times* to conform to our personal preferences.) Such "veggies" in the feed could take the form of stories from a list of vetted publications or posts that are more like public service announcements—topics that we have collectively decided are worth bringing up, though such society-wide agreement seems scarcer these days than ever. Perhaps updates about Hollywood films are neutral enough, or digests of national news interspersed with feel-good local stories. Of course, that kind of mixture is exactly what traditional media used to provide, and it's the opposite of what we are accustomed to getting from social networks.

The rise of social media has created a new set of dynamics for culture and entertainment. Users have much more choice of what to consume at a given moment, and creators have a much easier time reaching audiences by simply uploading their content to the Internet. We don't have to just watch what a producer elects to put on cable television. We have come to expect individualization, whether driven by our own actions or an algorithm. But that seemingly more democratic and low-hierarchy dynamic has also given us a sense that the old laws and regulations don't apply, precisely because we can decide when to watch or listen to something and when to choose

another source. We might have more independence, but we ultimately have less protection as consumers.

Regulating algorithmic recommendations quickly becomes a free
speech issue. As Eric Goldman, a professor of law at Santa Clara
University who codirects the High Tech Law Institute, told me, "An
algorithm is just a way of codifying the service's speech choices."
Keller made a distinction between problematic content—marked
by threats of violence or hate speech—and "speech that's legal but
provocative." If a user constantly clicks on that kind of content,
expressing a desire for it, then should the law stand in the way? In
Molly Russell's case, she engaged with content about depression
and was recommended more of it. That could have been a positive
experience, helping her to find community and sympathy online.
But it also became negative, since such content was recommended
too often, another consequence of the vicious cycle of algorithmic
homogeneity.

If recommendations are to be regulated, certain decisions have
to be made based on content. "Which preferences are unaccept-
able and must be overridden by law?" Keller asked. "Say platforms
stop giving people what they want; you have to give them something else instead. What are the veggies, what information are we
forcing into the diet, and how do we decide what that is? I don't
know what the answer is," Keller said. She has suggested a system of
"circuit breakers" that are "content neutral." Rather than deciding
which content is positive or negative, any kind of content that goes
viral—accelerating quickly via recommendations—would be limited instead of promoted more, slowing down its spread and giving
moderators more time to judge if it's appropriate before it reaches
massive audiences. Circuit breakers could also bring us back to a less
globalized media ecosystem, when pieces of content stayed more
firmly within their original contexts. While this might limit innocu-
ous content like funny videos, it also means that Russell might not
have been exposed to many of the memes that harmed her. She
wouldn't have gotten that email of Pinterest "Depression Pins" urging her deeper down the rabbit hole.

Decisions about content ultimately have to be made by humans, both because machine-learning systems are not yet capable of making such subtle distinctions and because their consequences impact human lives. That human capacity is not scalable in the way that software is—one person can't safeguard millions of users or vet every post that gets algorithmic promotion. And the scope of what qualifies as dangerous, like a list of banned words, requires constant updating as it changes, since culture is never static. But there are other ways of deconstructing Filterworld that rely less on evaluating the content itself and more on targeting the basic structure of the 2010s' Internet. If we change how the platforms are able to work, then we can also change the end result of how we experience them.

## THE EUROPEAN UNION STRATEGY

Facebook, over the 2010s, was like a tiny detective tracing your steps around the Internet, noting down everything you looked at and clicked on, every term you searched, and every other person to whom you were connected. It didn't just track you on Facebook itself; without asking for particularly explicit permission, it followed you onto other websites too, with the help of tracking cookies and Like buttons. Its goal was to collect enough data so that it could serve you personalized recommendations and precisely targeted ads on its platform, selling your attention to advertisers who were seeking, say, anyone between the ages of forty and fifty who lived in Minnesota and had shown an interest in buying gardening equipment. Most apps functioned in the same way, creating an all-encompassing net of digital surveillance. Everywhere you went, your trail was picked up by some entity or another, slowly accreting into detailed profiles that the businesses could use to their benefit. The only way to escape the tracking was to hide from it, using an incognito web browser or faking your Identity with a virtual private network. Even then, digital platforms often offered fewer features if you weren't logged in to an account—which, of course, was continuously tracked.

In April 2016, the European Union adopted a law called the General Data Protection Regulation. It had been in development since 2012, with the aim of giving Internet users stronger rights to all of that personal data online and creating a unified regulatory structure across the EU's member states. GDPR, as it's usually abbreviated, uses the term "data subject" to describe all of us users. It means anyone who is identifiable from their data online, whether their name, location, or "one or more factors specific to the physical, physiological, genetic, mental, economic, cultural or social identity of that natural person." Data subject might be legalese, but it's an evocative phrase. In philosophy, a "subject" is any entity with agency and a unique personal experience. Data seems to stand in contrast to that; it's an immaterial, inanimate thing that documents experience—a record of something that has happened.

GDPR recognizes that these days, we *are* our data—data both documents what we have done and influences what we are able to do, or are most likely to do, in the future, oftentimes through algorithmic decisions. Thus, we should have some of the same kinds of control over it, and rights to it, that we have over our physical bodies. The law outlines a list of "data subject rights," like fundamental human rights, that digital platforms have to comply with. The first is the right to transparency, forcing companies to respond to users who request information about how and why their data is being used in "clear and plain language." The second ensures that users can make that request, giving them a "right of access" to information about which forms of data are collected, when tracking happens, and how long data is stored, as well as to request copies of the data itself.

In 2017, Judith Duportail, a journalist working for *The Guardian*, used GDPR to request all of the data that Tinder had on her— which amounted to eight hundred pages, including her Facebook likes; metadata about every match and conversation she had on the platform; and over seventeen hundred messages. (She was quite a data subject.) Duportail was "amazed by how much information I was voluntarily disclosing," she wrote. But she shouldn't have been: such data is the fuel for Tinder's product itself, and self-disclosure is the trade-off we make for automated efficiency. Romantic matchups— another kind of algorithmic recommendation—require intimate knowledge.

GDPR's third group of rights deals with modifying the data itself. The "right to rectification" means being able to edit or correct the data about yourself, while the "right to erasure" ensures that personal data will be deleted if they "are no longer necessary," if the user withdraws consent, or if they are unlawfully collected. It's also known more poetically as the "right to be forgotten," and it has existed in the European Union since 2014, though the United States has no equivalent. The fourth group is about opting out, giving users a "right to object," to choose to no longer be tracked. This is particularly applicable to advertising: "Where the data subject objects to processing for direct marketing purposes, the personal data shall no longer be processed for such purposes," the law dictates. If you don't want to be tracked for the sake of targeted advertising, you don't have to be—though ads can certainly reach you in other ways. It also includes "the right not to be subject to a decision based solely on automated processing." In other words, a user need not experience any algorithmic action unless they consent to it. You can prevent Facebook's tiny detective from following you around to figure out what to suggest next.

GDPR went into effect on May 25, 2018, impacting not just companies based in Europe but any company that offers goods or services to EU citizens, which includes almost every major digital platform. On the surface, the changes didn't look like much. Websites suddenly implemented pop-ups that, on your first visit, asked for permission to track you and offered the chance to peruse elaborate terms of service documents. "Cookies"—the term for the packets of data that websites use to track you, which derived their name from fortune cookies in 1990s computing—became common parlance. But it represented a sea change in terms of holding websites accountable for the wanton accumulation of personal data and enforcing actual consequences. After a slow start, EU countries have been actively applying the law to companies based in their jurisdictions, with a consistent growth in citations beginning in 2020. As of early 2023, there were over thirteen hundred fines under GDPR, totaling over 2.3 billion euros.

In November 2022, Facebook faced a $275 million fine for violating GDPR, after a data leak exposed the personal information of over five hundred million users, which was disseminated on a hacker forum. It wasn't the company's first fine. A September violation cost it $400 million after Instagram failed to protect the data of minors using its service, and in 2021, WhatsApp was fined 225 million euros for lacking clear privacy policies. The largest fine went to Amazon, which was charged 746 million euros for tracking users' data and not allowing them to opt out. Companies other than tech giants violate the law, too. In March 2020, the Dutch Data Protection Authority imposed a fine of 525,000 euros on the Royal Dutch Lawn Tennis Association, the national governing body for tennis in the Nether-lands, for "an illegal sale of personal data." The association had sold the data of its 350,000 members to its sponsors for marketing purposes without first asking for their consent—breaking GDPR's mandate that such a transaction has to be opt-in.

Though these penalties pale in comparison to tech companies' annual revenue, they do demonstrate how GDPR can provoke a certain amount of compliance. While a bill of data rights sounds like an ideal solution to Filterworld, the law has been disappoint-ing in other ways. All it takes is the click of an "accept all cookies" button for a user to be tracked just as much as they were before. As Nicole Gill, the cofounder of an American advocacy group called Accountable Tech, observed, it's in the companies' best interests to make choosing to be tracked as seamless and passive as possible. "Online services will find a way to follow the law that offers the least amount of friction to their users," Gill said. Frictionlessness is always the Filterworld ideal—as soon as you slow down, you might just reconsider what you're clicking on and giving your data away. "Friction allows people to think about their actions," she continued, a point that applies just as well to Spotify radio or the TikTok feed. If you think too much, you might stop.

I'm guilty of this passivity myself. When such GDPR notices began popping up on American websites, I most often just clicked to give away my data. If there was a website I liked to read—Eater, for example, the national food publication—I accepted the track-ing readily, because I figured, perhaps wrongly, that I could trust the site. When *The Guardian,* which I appreciated as a left-leaning British newspaper, asked me for my data I said yes, too. What could really go wrong? Having to opt out felt like a form of labor. If I was feeling righteous, I would angrily hit No. *Of course I don't want this surveillance!* But if I was feeling cynical, I would just accept, because maybe it would improve my algorithmic recommendations and result in some compelling personalization.

In part it was out of laziness and the tricks of interface design. The opt-in button is often darker and more prominent than the opt-out, so my brain took a beat too long to understand which was which. But it also felt like my personal choice wouldn't necessarily change how the website functioned, for me or anyone else. "Most people are just accepting anyway," said Paddy Leerssen, a scholar of digital platforms at the University of Amsterdam and a former fellow at the Stanford Center for Internet and Society. Ultimately, the law might place the burden more on the user than on the company. "This whole kind of individual responsibility type mechanism that the GDPR creates isn't really effective," Leerssen continued. Rather than targeting the data, newer EU laws take action against recommender systems more specifically. According to Leerssen, they are "command and control regulations, where the government is telling the industry what to do, rather than leaving it to a matter of user choice."

The Digital Services Act, which was approved in July 2022 and goes into effect in 2024, provides for some of the same kinds of transparency and communication around recommendations that GDPR does for data: Platforms "should clearly present the main parameters for such recommender systems in an easily comprehensible manner to ensure that the recipients understand how information is prioritized for them." But it also says that algorithmic feeds must be customizable, enabling users to change the balance of variables at will or choose a feed that doesn't leverage personal data at all: "options that are not based on profiling of the recipient."

Another EU law, the Digital Markets Act, was signed into law in September 2022 and addresses monopolization, encouraging competition. The tech giants are labeled "gatekeepers." The law bans combining data from different services operated by one company, such as Meta's Facebook and WhatsApp, without the user's consent. It also prohibits "self-preferencing," the way that Google and Amazon at times promote their own products under the guise of neutral automated recommendations, as in search results—one of the tricks that reinforces the homogeneity of the current Internet. DMA penalties can run up to 10 percent of a company's annual revenue, and 20 percent for repeat offenders, making compliance even more vital.

As they go into effect, these laws are likely to overhaul our algorithmic landscape, giving users much more agency when it comes to recommendations and the configuration of a content feed. The passive relationship would become a more active one as we begin to figure out our own preferences and shape our digital lives to follow our own tastes. Algorithmic feeds will appear less monolithic and impenetrable, as they do now, and more like the functional tools they are. There's no reason your feed needs to work exactly like my feed. The resulting profusion could lead to more diversity of culture online, as well.

Tech companies are responding to the new legal landscape. In August 2023, the parent company Meta announced that both Facebook and Instagram would add options for users to opt out of algorithmic recommendations entirely, removing the possibility of automated personalization. But that option would only be available for users in the EU—because the US has been much slower to adopt such legislation. When I saw the headlines, I was jealous. It was suddenly as if only EU residents could breathe pollution-free air.

## AMERICAN REGULATION

EU digital platform regulation has already heralded a major disruption in American social networks. Even though the laws don't necessarily apply in the United States, they have created a rare pressure to change. In April 2021, Apple announced an update to its iPhone operating system called App Tracking Transparency. Every app that wanted to track its users' data for advertising purposes would have to ask permission first, in a pop-up that allows users to opt out of being tracked. Apple also added a tracking menu with an option to turn off tracking from every downloaded app. It may not have looked like a significant change, but its consequences were immediate: early statistics showed that only 16 percent of users opted in to tracking, though that rate increased to around 25 percent a year later. Because my phone felt more personal and intimate than a web browser, I usually opted out. At least on mobile, the feature kneecapped the kind of targeted advertising that makes up the majority of tech companies' revenue. In early 2022, Facebook predicted that it would lose as much as $10 billion from the feature, which caused its stock price to drop more than 26 percent—a loss of more than $230 billion.

Apple's App Tracking Transparency presented a real-world experiment in how American users would react to enforced data privacy like the kind provided by GDPR. It turns out that we don't particularly want to be tracked unless we see the benefits of doing so. (Some video-game apps had much higher rates of opt-in tracking, for example.) Apple differentiated itself by offering simple privacy features and hurt its competitor in the process, demonstrating that perhaps the largest companies aren't so invulnerable as they seem. Data access is their Achilles' heel; cutting off their ability to collect it breaks the grip of Filterworld.

EU legislation arrives in a different form than US lawmaking usually does, according to Nathaniel Persily, a professor of law at Stanford University and the codirector of the Stanford Cyber Policy Center, among other groups. He told me that EU laws, including GDPR and DSA, tend to be broader and more ambiguous, demanding actions that might not be immediately possible. They are laws "to be fleshed out over decades." But such regulations will provide a functional model and path forward for other countries. "Europe will be the tail that wags the American dog here," Persily said. The persistence of GDPR has also proved another important argument: Having more personal data protection won't break the Internet. We can consume content more or less as we did before, just with a stronger sense of security and agency.

Persily has witnessed the changing relationships of digital platforms to their users and governments. In 2018, he helped to create Social Science One, a groundbreaking partnership between Facebook and academics that eventually allowed researchers to study the social network's internal data. In 2020, they released a URL Shares dataset totaling over an exabyte (a billion gigabytes), containing thirty-eight million links that were shared and clicked by Facebook users. To hear Persily tell it, regulation often follows controversy. Social Science One was incited by the Cambridge Analytica scandal, in which the British consulting firm gathered the data of millions of

Facebook users without their consent and leveraged it in political campaigns, including Donald Trump's. The mounting dissatisfaction with algorithmic platforms has created more openness toward regulation. "People desperately want something to get done," Persily said.

Out of the available strategies—ranging across enforcing algorithmic transparency, reforming Section 230, regulating the amplification of particular kinds of content, and protecting data rights—transparency remains the north star of platform regulation for Persily. It's the most important in part because in most cases, we simply don't know what's really going on in our feeds when companies only self-report. Transparent data, which would be accessible at least for researchers to study in secured, anonymized environments, is key to planning the best forms of future regulation, but it may also have the added benefit of putting real day-to-day pressure on tech giants without having to craft more explicit policy. "It will affect the behavior of firms. Once they know they are being watched, then their decisions will be different," Persily said.

It was always a struggle to get Facebook to cooperate with Social Science One—the company's lawyers hid behind the argument that they were violating user privacy by sharing any data with outside analysts. The conflict led Persily to start working on his own concept for federal legislation addressing social media. There needed to be a legal penalty for failing to share data that was in the public interest. "It is absolutely critical that we get some window into platforms to understand human behavior today, because most human behavior is occurring online," he said. Persily began drafting legislative language, getting feedback from social scientists and policy lawyers. Frances Haugen's Facebook whistleblowing lit a fire under him, and he released the draft the day she testified in front of the Senate.

Chris Coons, a Delaware senator, quickly reached out to Persily and adopted his text as the basis of a transparency bill, which a larger group began pushing forward. His concept became the Platform Accountability and Transparency Act, which was announced in December 2021 with bipartisan support. The academic ideas had moved toward becoming law. PATA forces social media companies to supply data to researchers, via requests that are vetted by the

National Science Foundation. Companies that don't comply would then lose the protections of Section 230 and be liable for everything on their platforms.

PATA joins other possible legislation like the NUDGE Act, a 2022 bipartisan proposal by Senator Amy Klobuchar and Cynthia Lummis. (The elaborate acronym stands for "Nudging Users to Drive Good Experiences on Social Media Act.") In the United States, these efforts are more of a beginning than an end: we may have realized that algorithmic feeds are harming us, as individuals as well as collectively, but we're far from understanding how best to mitigate their effects at a governmental level.

Regulation offers political solutions for what is often observed as a political problem. It's true that some of the most visible problems of algorithmic feeds broach the political, with issues of free speech, harassment, technologically encoded bias, and industrial capitalism. But in Filterworld, the feeds impact more mundane aspects of life, too. Any attempt at regulating online hate speech will also end up influencing the way we choose which television show to watch or which album to listen to. Algorithms' monopoly on our attention can be broken down, too.

Yet regulation cannot be the only answer when it comes to culture. (Governmental policy rarely succeeds in that arena.) A law can force a platform to ban problematic content, but it can't make Spotify recommend you a more challenging or creatively interesting playlist of music. Unfortunately, we do not have a constitutional right to personal taste. Therefore, we also must change our own habits, becoming more aware of how we consume culture and how we can resist the passive pathways of algorithmic feeds. The same way we might choose to buy organic-labeled food in a grocery store, we have to seek out the digital spaces that support nonhomogenized culture and that allow artists to express themselves without the crushing pressure toward sameness.

We have to be careful about which feeds we follow as well as understand precisely how our attention is transformed into economic support for creators. Targeted advertising might be one of the worst possibilities. The digital landscape is like a forest; Facebook and TikTok might be towering trees, blocking out much of the sunlight, but there are other possibilities growing in their shadows if you look for them.

There are already ways to pay artists directly for what they create online. Bandcamp serves as the digital equivalent of an indie record store for independent musicians; users can buy digital files and streaming access directly instead of Spotify mediating the exchange. Patreon enables creators to paywall anything they choose to, whether writing, images, or audio. It offers a linear feed of posts that the user subscribes to monetarily, a much more powerful relationship than a Twitter follow. Substack does the same for email newsletter subscriptions.

In 2008, the *Wired* editor Kevin Kelly famously wrote that a creator needs to find only "1,000 true fans" to fund their work and allow them to make a living—one thousand people who might pay them $100 a year. It's an entirely different model from the larger digital platforms, where audiences have to be as big as possible. "A thousand customers is a whole lot more feasible to aim for than a million fans," Kelly wrote. Yet all of these smaller platforms face the temptation of becoming more algorithmic as they try to grow and serve the maximum number of users, creators and consumers alike. They are also constantly threatened by giant tech companies that could acquire them or stamp them out. There is no guarantee their non-algorithmic functionality will stay the same.

The most powerful choice might be the simplest one: Stop lending your attention to platforms that exploit it. There is a way to do that while continuing to use digital technology, sticking to websites and companies that treat users better. We can return to a more DIY Internet. But the more dramatic option is to log out entirely and figure out how to sustain culture offline once more. The digital identity crisis of the past decade has made change seem impossible. Facebook slowly choked the open Internet like bright-blue digital kudzu. As the platform became inescapable, I felt myself losing interest in it as well, because it's impossible to serve every purpose at once and remain successful at all of them. If Facebook was everything, it was also nothing, an undifferentiated mass of content. Other platforms decayed in the same way: Instagram under Mark Zuckerberg, Spotify under Daniel Ek, Twitter under Elon Musk. By 2023, social media seems to have entered a new phase in which its downsides are more obvious than its advantages.

I feel somewhat stifled online these days, in part because I can't express myself as much as I once could, in the days of personal blogs and slowly developed conversation with other people. The templates are too restrictive, and the pace is too fast. Even though the technology was much worse two decades ago, the experience, or the ecosystem, had its advantages. I think there's a way of recapturing some of that creative energy, the atmosphere of lo-fi possibility and freedom. While regulations can provide for some minimum of control over algorithmic feeds, the reconstruction of culture is a different process, more like planting and cultivating a garden. It takes time. First, we need to seek out the appropriate digital structures, and then we need to carry out the daily labor of determining a new way of living online.

# CHAPTER 6

# In Search of Human Curation

## MY ALGORITHM CLEANSE

By the summer of 2022, I had become wholly trapped in Filterworld. Two years of the pandemic had made me dependent on digital feeds to conduct much of my life: interacting with friends; watching television and movies through streaming services; and getting real-time news about the world around me through Twitter (and there was *never* not news). All the media and text that reached me was mediated through digital platforms in processes I had little control over. My phone was glued to my hand as a tool to soak up any spare second of nonstimulation. The feeds ensured that I would always have something new to look at, twenty-four hours a day, no matter whether the people I followed had posted anything recently or not. TikTok was the ultimate fulfillment of the forever-feed. It didn't matter whether I was awake and restless at three a.m., walking our dog in the middle of the afternoon, or in a restaurant bathroom during dinner, I could always access new content streams that were always refreshing.

It's hard to overstate just how smoothly the feeds infiltrated my life. Following them all was like chain-smoking throughout the day, one information binge at a time, from the wake-up Twitter scroll to find out about overnight news to the nighttime crawl of the Netflix home page to determine what to watch. My dissatisfaction with this situation was a long time coming, exacerbated by the pandemic; as a writer and a consumer of all kinds of culture, these platforms were the place where I connected with the people who exposed me to new and interesting things. I appreciated the years that I had invested in being on Twitter and Instagram, the personal and professional relationships I had developed in those spaces. But I began to think that as much as the feeds brought me things I never would have seen or heard otherwise, my overdependence on them was also cutting me off from a different realm of experiences that I had forgotten about over the course of the decade: the encounter with scarcity rather than infinity, the process of judging and choosing for myself what I wanted to see in a given moment, without the option to scroll away.

If one form of algorithmic anxiety is about feeling misunderstood by algorithmic recommendations, another is feeling hijacked by them, feeling like you couldn't escape them if you tried. Perhaps too much now depends on these feeds, and their influence is too pervasive. Regulation, so far, has been less than effective, and the experience so compelling and convenient that most Internet users struggle to give it up. Algorithmic recommendations are addictive because they are always subtly confirming your own cultural, political, and social biases, warping your surroundings into a mirror image of yourself while doing the same for everyone else. This had made me anxious, the possibility that my view of my own life—lived through the Internet—was a fiction formed by the feeds. So much of my perception of what my friends were up to on a given day, what was going on in various cities, which news stories mattered, even the weather, was dictated by what I saw on automated apps. What's more, those feeds were all increasingly fractured and flawed, presenting posts from days ago as if they had just happened. Ultimately, my sense of self was beholden to the responses I got from my invisible audiences, whose attention was algorithmically mediated, too. I wasn't sure who I would be without algorithmic recommendations; I don't know that anyone else who has spent years of their life on digital platforms can be totally sure. A fear took hold: In passively consuming what I was interested in, had I given up my agency to figure out what was truly meaningful to me?

To combat that looming futility, I did the only thing I could do. I decided to see if I could live my life without these feeds, go without them for a while the way some people might give up sugar for Lent or alcohol in January. I would say no to their attractive offer of thinking for me and try to do it myself.

It sounded like an easy enough thing to accomplish. All I had to do was delete some apps from my phone and sign out of some accounts on sites that I drifted toward far too easily on my laptop. But at the same time, it felt impossible. My work life was on Twitter, my social life was on Instagram, my music was on Spotify. I worried I would miss out on something vital, like observing a friend's life event from afar, reading a new favorite essay, or grabbing a work opportunity that would have come to me only online. FOMO was too light of a phrase—I feared, against all evidence to the contrary, that not to be on social media in the constant way I had been, always participating in the communal feed, would be not to exist. If the algorithm wasn't registering me, then was I even participating in this vast communal conversation? Posting online is like the artist On Kawara's series "I Am Still Alive," begun in 1969, in which he sent out hundreds of telegrams with the titular phrase, as if to constantly prove it.

Yet when I thought twice about my anxieties, I realized they were relatively inconsequential. What would I really miss if I didn't see a dozen photos of a friend's vacation, or the latest reviews of hyped-up novels, or which viral arguments were dominating Twitter at a particular moment? In the context of my day-to-day, physical life, these bits of content had almost no impact. I feared the loss of some connection, but that connection is, after all, more ambient and less direct than chatting with neighbors when I walk my dog. I figured that there must be a happier medium between the state of constant hyperawareness I entered while being online all the time, chasing algorithmic feed updates, and a state of total ignorance. How much digital input did I really need? The fear of disengaging might turn out to be worse than the reality.

I began thinking of my experiment as an algorithm cleanse, an information diet that would ideally leave me healthier than before. I also wanted to find out what it would take to follow contemporary culture without the assistance of so many recommendations. But I kept putting off the commitment. Finally, one weekend in

August 2022, the prospect of keeping up with the feeds became *more* exhausting than exiting from them. At the time, the boisterous nerd king Elon Musk, one of the wealthiest men in the world thanks to his takeover of an electric car company, was threatening to buy Twitter outright and turn it into his private playground (he finally succeeded that October). The mood on the platform had soured, turning even more negative than usual. Instagram had become increasingly unusable, too, as its feed began promoting video clips above all—provoking mass complaint from its users—in a race to catch up with TikTok.

TikTok itself was a kind of numbing, since its responsiveness to user input felt like a form of mind-reading, removing my need to think at all. I could take five-minute (or more likely fifteen-minute) breaks from immediate reality with minimal disruption, like a salvia trip that takes you utterly and briefly out of the world, albeit more pleasant. The TikTok "For You" feed was a fulfillment of "the Entertainment" in David Foster Wallace's novel *Infinite Jest*: a piece of content so compelling that no one could stop watching. As addictive as it was, Wallace described his fictional Entertainment as "oddly hollow, empty, no sense of dramatic towardness—no narrative movement toward a real story"—which is an apt description, too, of TikTok's drift toward formless vibes and feelings, away from coherent information. Surely bingeing on these technologies wasn't making me any smarter or able to generate more complex thoughts, which was presumably my job as a writer.

When I left social media, I didn't say goodbye or make an announcement on my various feeds. To publicly acknowledge the cleanse was to jinx it, not to mention an example of the kind of self-aggrandizement that social media encourages. No one cares when you stop tweeting; the algorithm will simply slot in the content of some more willing participant, because, in Filterworld, everyone is replaceable. The majority of your followers are unlikely to even notice your absence because, at least to the algorithm, your sleepy account is deemed no longer worthy of prioritization.

So, on a Friday evening in August, I simply cut myself off at the end of the workday. Of course, I had logged out plenty of times before. But knowing that I wasn't going to get back on for a while—

I planned for a few months of cleanse—the silence was deafening. While social media had been a 24/7 portal to infinite real-time information, my phone suddenly became a static brick.

The first weekend wasn't so bad. Weekends are when we're supposed to be logged out anyway, though when I had to do a few hours of work I missed the ambient camaraderie of Twitter chatter, like a classroom of kids all stuck inside at recess. The following Monday, however, was torture. My thumb itched for swiping, and my brain went through withdrawals from not having the constant onslaught of information. The symptoms were akin to the physical manifestations of anxiety: nervous twitching, short temper, general discomfort. Far from being relaxed by the change, I was perturbed by the absence. Perhaps I was being dramatic, but the difference was dramatic, too. I had gone from seeing hundreds, or even thousands, of individual bits of information and multimedia a day to just a handful. By cutting out algorithmic feeds, I had stomped on the brake pedal of my digital consumption habits.

For pure stimulation, I downloaded a few "fidget apps" onto my phone—games that allow you to stack blocks or flip light switches, a digital iteration of worry beads. One called Antistress offered options like vacuuming a dirty floor into satisfying cleanness. They assuaged my restlessness but were just as pointless as tweeting into the void—action without meaning. Instead, I started a file on my laptop titled "Tweets, Not Tweeted," where I wrote down every observation I would have otherwise posted. Looking back at the document, the drafts are not inspiring: "Marxist Nora Ephron: 'Everything is capital.'" "I miss the days when you could tweet by texting 244244 on your flip phone." These were jokes that might net a handful of likes, but they made no sense outside of Twitter itself. After all, that was the venue my sensibility had evolved to fit.

As with any kind of withdrawal, the cleanse made me cranky. No longer getting constant feedback from an invisible audience applauding with faves and retweets, I lobbed too many mundane observations at Jess in real life and got annoyed when she (deservedly) ignored most of them. My constant fidgeting and casting about for stimulation became so distracting that Jess often fled the apartment for unusually late-night, unusually *long* dog walks.

In the following weeks, I discovered that the Internet wasn't really designed to function without algorithmic feeds anymore. These feeds worked like vital shipping lanes, ensuring various forms of content reached their intended targets without either the creator or the consumer having to work very hard. The creator, whether a person, brand, or publication, could post something and trust that it would reach people who were following them, though not with 100 percent efficiency. The consumer could open their feed and see content that was compelling to them, at least most of the time. Blogs and other websites whose function was to aggregate headlines and highlight trends, like the original Gawker.com, had vanished in the onslaught of feeds. Because this system was so entrenched, publication websites had dismantled their home pages to the point that they often featured only a few stories on the screen at a time, with a maximum of images and a minimum of text. When I browsed them, I felt like an unexpected visitor, someone who wasn't supposed to be there. The sites all but shouted: *Don't you know you're supposed to be on Facebook or Twitter!?*

During my cleanse, I also discovered that recommender systems pop up in unexpected places. I eventually turned to the *New York Times* app as my primary way of checking in on news, but that app features a "For You" tab, much like TikTok's, that uses your previous actions to suggest a slew of articles you are deemed likely to click on. It immediately pigeonholed me into arts and culture pieces, with the odd item of real-estate porn, which I appreciated. But that kind of limited horizon was exactly what I was trying to avoid. I stopped using that tab, yet found it difficult to get a broad view of the news elsewhere on the app. The screen was still limited to a handful of items that the editors deemed important but that didn't always line up with my interests. I had to confront my own expectation of personalization.

The day Queen Elizabeth II died in September 2022, I hadn't checked on the news in a while, and Jess only informed me hours later. When I ended up, out of boredom, using the NYT app to read an op-ed by David Brooks, a form of writing—and a writer—I'd had no previous interest in, she considered staging an intervention. I suddenly understood those old sitcom scenes when someone folds a newspaper at the breakfast table and cites a banal headline. Bereft of niche Twitter drama, this was the main source of novelty.

Escaping algorithms entirely is nearly impossible. Google Search is still driven by an algorithm, after all, and every email client automatically sorts messages to some degree—I couldn't very well turn off my spam filter. Since I almost entirely lack a sense of geographical direction, I'd be lost without the Google Maps recommended routes. But I could still go without those primary feeds that I had relied on for cultural consumption. In the absence of recommendations, I was left with things that I intentionally chose to consume, like email newsletters. The digital equivalent of hand-printed pamphlets, these missives offered a way to connect directly with publications or writers who I wanted to hear from—voices that I trusted. The newsletter format had become popular once more precisely to avoid the dominant influence of the algorithmic feed. I appreciated them because, like a print magazine, they were composed and finite—the opposite of a feed.

As I had hoped, I began reading long articles in a single sitting more often and left fewer tabs open in my browser, since I wasn't faced with a cascade of alternative options. The graphomanic desire to tweet subsided after a month, or at least turned toward longer diaristic writing, not limited to 280 characters and pithy jokes. In my list of untweeted tweets I instead observed how little the kind of thoughts that get posted on Twitter resemble normal, coherent thoughts, as they are shorn of context and forced to exist as atomized bits of ambient consciousness. (As the saying goes, "Twitter is not real life.") But it was the shift in my relationship to photography that was the most striking. Nothing had changed about my iPhone camera, which I still had in my pocket at all times, but without the public venue of Instagram I had much less desire to take photos. The few photos I did take were different, too: they were images that I wanted to capture for myself, more often weirder or uglier than the established aesthetic of Instagram. I took fewer photos at parties and dinners and more of city streetscapes and my neighborhood dog park lit up in the dark, images that wouldn't have read well in the app's frame. (Snapshots of my dog did not decrease, however.)

Outwardly, my life may not have been dramatically altered by the algorithm cleanse, but I did gain a sense of clarity and a less crowded mental landscape. I realized that intentionality was part of what gave things significance: I could appreciate each story, photo, or album more because I had chosen to seek it out. That also meant I had to work harder to find what I wanted, forgoing the help of those automated content highways. By the second month of my experiment, when I had adjusted my habits, I began to feel a sense of nostalgia. It reminded me of how I interacted with the Internet as a teenager, back before mainstream social media existed.

## DIGITAL CULTURE BEFORE ALGORITHMS

In 1998, the Japanese artist and writer Yoshitoshi ABe released an anime television show called *Serial Experiments Lain.* When I discovered it a few years later as a teenager in the United States, thanks to the early Internet, it became a formative part of my aesthetic sensibility as well as a way to question what it meant to be online in the first place. ABe's work isn't very well known in the United States, particularly when compared to a phenomenon like Studio Ghibli films, but it combines the literary darkness of a Kafka story with the visual impact of a van Gogh painting. *Lain,* as it's usually shortened, is a fable of life in the Internet era. In the show, a teenage girl named Lain discovers a virtual realm called "the Wired." The show's color palette is dark but soft, sunk into the mood of a lit bedroom late at night, which is where Lain spends much of her time. It reminded me of the basement where the computer desktop was stationed in my own home, where I often found myself physically alone but immersed in the abstracted togetherness of the Internet.

The show was mind altering, as great art should be. In Lain's world, the Wired is an interconnection of all communication on Earth: television, telephone, and the Internet. Together, they form a total synthetic reality that exists across physical and virtual space— recognizing that whatever happens online influences the real world, too. Through her experiences in the Wired, Lain discovers her own identity beyond that of a shy junior high schooler. It becomes a space of total independence for her, through which she can define herself.

Despite my hesitancy around algorithmic feeds, I could never give up the Internet entirely, because it has brought me too much over my lifetime. Its positives still outweigh its negatives. As it did for Lain, the Internet has defined my life. The question I'm pursuing is not whether we should abandon our digital lives, but how we can improve them, make them even more valuable. (A globalized world seems unlikely to ever forgo digital networks again.) From the time my parents connected dial-up to an aging desktop computer in the basement of my childhood home, the Internet has offered escape, a space to discover new bodies of culture, to meet new people, and to construct a worldview that went beyond what I had immediate access to, like a Library of Alexandria—open twenty-four hours a day, always staffed with helpful people. My family encouraged all of my interests, but couldn't have introduced me to the kinds of novels, music, video games, and television that I found online. When I was feeling marooned in the Connecticut suburbs, without any thriving street life or cultural institutions to turn to save a few grungy music venues, the Internet was the most culturally radical space within my reach.

I imagine much of the American millennial generation feels the same way; like getting your own car, the open Internet provided an immediate freedom for self-determination. We all take different paths in developing our sense of personal taste, figuring out what we like and what we don't. But the modes that we discover ourselves through are similar, dictated by our era and the technology that surrounds us. While previous generations might have had dance halls or independent radio stations to help them discover new music during their formative teenage years, and young people in the twenty-first century have TikTok feeds and Spotify playlists, millennials in the late 1990s and early 2000s had online forums and MP3 piracy. These required much more labor to find what you like and consume it than the frictionless avenues of algorithmic feeds. While avoiding that labor may be convenient, it also makes our personal tastes flimsier, less hard-won.

Prior to streaming and social media, culture often felt relatively scarce and finite. Either you had access to something or you didn't. One of my earliest memories of multimedia is this: As kids, my younger brother and I would turn on the television early every weekday morning to try to catch a Super Mario cartoon. We'd make sure to have a VHS tape loaded in the VCR, because we wanted to witness and capture a specific episode, like taping a song from the radio onto a cassette. One special episode, I recall, had something to do with Mario rescuing Yoshi from a fiery dungeon. After we saw it the first time, it acquired mythical status in our minds, but we could access it only by chance through cable programming. There was no way to Google it or stream the vintage show online. Our luck had to be twofold: the episode had to be on that day, and it had to record successfully onto the waiting tape. (The tape was not always reliable.) Only then would we fully possess it and be able to watch Super Mario at will.

The experience was slow and full of friction. Yet the challenge of holding on to the episode was why it acquired such a compelling aura for me. I invested so much time and emotional energy into it that I still remember it some twenty years later, although now it remains on a VHS tape lost in the bowels of that house. I can't say the same for any piece of generic digital content delivered through a feed. We might discover things in our feeds, but we must grab on and dig deeper into them for ourselves before they disappear once more into the ether. We must consciously fight against the speed and the frictionlessness of Filterworld.

Digging deeper was once the default task of finding culture, particularly on the early Internet. My first introduction to anime was *Dragonball-Z* on American cable in the late nineties, but when I wanted to find more complex storytelling than its endless adolescent battles, I had to go online. I found forums where much more experienced anime fans debated their favorites, not in order to gain followers or monetize their expertise as on today's platforms, but out of personal passion. Those forums were "communities of consumption," a term that academics have used to describe the diverse groups of people that congregate online around a particular shared pursuit, whether swapping product tips or discussing avant-garde literature. One paper described communities of consumption as a form of "mutual learning"—we collectively figure out what it is that we're looking for and how to find it. The likes of Twitter and Facebook, with their unstable interfaces and manipulative algorithms, are less conducive to mutual learning.

There are various ways to go down a cultural rabbit hole. Algorithmic recommendations do it almost instantly. You shortcut from not knowing that ASMR sponge-squeezing videos exist to being immersed in dozens of them thanks to TikTok's feed. I felt that sense of acceleration one morning when, while I was still in bed, the app began delivering me a slew of video diaries from American expats in Denmark, showing off the country's parental leave policies and cozy coffee shops. It stood to reason that these people would exist, but I had no idea they were making digestible minute-long documentaries of their lives. I followed some of the accounts, but as soon as they flooded in, they also subsided, and I couldn't find my way back to that specific genre. There was no hashtag explicitly linking them; the algorithmic feed had curated them together based on the content's pattern of engagement, matching it to my own. The same happens for a particular genre of music on Spotify or an argument happening on Twitter. In the moment, the content feels all-encompassing, and yet it's totally insignificant once you wander away.

The slower and more careful approach is to seek out these seams of culture yourself and chart your path, bookmarking accounts, connecting with other people interested in the same things, and comparing notes, the way I did on anime forums or the early days of Twitter, before it became too vast to maintain a grasp on. This is a more conscious and intentional form of consumption—a form that was mandatory before feeds made it so easy to outsource our choices about what to consume online. It recalls the term *connoisseur*. In an art history context, the descriptor dates as far back as the eighteenth century, when connoisseurship referred to amateur collectors who could tell which artist painted a work based solely on looking at it. They sought out the artist's signature gestures in a given work, which they had studied and cataloged. Connoisseurs developed expert knowledge, largely through the act of consumption. The German Johann Joachim Winckelmann was one such connoisseur; though he was not born into nobility and began his career as a schoolteacher, he became one of the foremost collectors and scholars of ancient Greek and Roman art. His efforts helped form the basis for the discipline of art history.

On TikTok, it's harder to become a connoisseur because you have little chance to develop expertise or assemble the context of what you're looking at. You must work at it, get off the slick routes of the feed, and gradually refine the thing that you seek. The benefit of the slower, self-managed approach to culture is that it might lead to a greater appreciation of the content at hand, and you might be able to lead another person down the same path that you followed, showing them how to appreciate the same things. It's more sustainable and more respectful of culture, treating it as something important rather than ephemeral, merely fodder for brief attention spans. A lot of human effort is required to create something original, no matter the intended outcome. As my art-critic friend Orit Gat once told me, partly joking but also serious, you should look at a painting for as long as it took the artist to paint it. Flipping through so much incoherently assembled content in our feeds, we don't have the opportunity to assimilate it, to learn and understand, much less pass on that understanding to others. That encouraged shallowness of consumption contributes to the overall flatness of culture in Filterworld.

As a young teenager, I tried to become a connoisseur of anime. From the clichés of *Dragonball* I progressed, thanks to forum recommendations, to still-cringey romantic-comedy anime titles like *Love Hina* and *Chobits*. These were overindulgent of the male gaze (another term for the genre was "harem anime") but felt novel to me at the time, with their interpersonal dramas and sci-fi tropes. I had no one around me to talk to about these discoveries, only the nascent online community. I found out how much further there was to go in my own connoisseurship when I discovered Yoshitoshi ABe's series, like *Lain*. After *Lain*'s introverted cyberpunk narrative, ABe created an anime called *Haibane Renmei*, which translates to "Charcoal Feather Federation." It was even stranger. In it, a girl named Rakka is reborn from an insectoid cocoon as a kind of purgatorial angel, complete with vestigial wings growing out of her back. She emerges in that form, as if from a bad dream, into a bucolic, ancient-seeming walled town surrounded by fields. Rakka has involuntarily joined a kind of cult. The angels, called Haibane, cannot own anything new, are not allowed to use money, must hold down jobs in the community, and are forbidden from leaving the town walls.

Despite the bleak scenario, the show is comforting. If it at first appears as a nightmare, it grows into a mythological fable. I didn't know the word *elegiac* when I first watched *Haibane Renmei* as a fourteen-year-old, but it's the one I would use now—sad and gently haunting, invested with a pleasurable melancholy. The atmosphere was enhanced by the scratchy line work of its animation and the dull, organic color palette. Years later I discovered that the show was inspired by Haruki Murakami's novel *Hard-Boiled Wonderland and the End of the World*, originally published in 1985. One piece of culture led to the other, and I followed that thread. The novel and the anime share a mood, a vocabulary, and a philosophy—they both feature walled towns, a certain lo-fi steampunk aesthetic, and the narrative of comprehending your life in a new way by traveling through a different world, which may or may not be part of the real one. *Haibane Renmei* was one of my first cultural discoveries that truly felt like my own—something new that I encountered in silence. I intuited that most of the people around me wouldn't necessarily like or understand the show, but it nevertheless spoke deeply to me. It was personal.

I would not have had access to such art at the time without the Internet—not only because that's where I discovered it, but because that was the only place it was to be found. When *Haibane Renmei* debuted in Japan in 2002, it was not immediately translated into English. Anime aficionados congregated online and produced "fansubs"—DIY translations from Japanese that were turned into captions for digital files of the show. Fansubs were products of passion. Though far from perfect (many had terrible spelling and textual glitches), they nevertheless offered first glimpses of shows we Internet denizens couldn't have consumed otherwise, short of learning Japanese ourselves. It was another benefit of the online community of consumption.

The fansubs, in turn, wouldn't have been available to download without that source and scourge of so much of early Internet culture, file piracy. There were no streaming services, but there were tools like Kazaa and BitTorrent, which allowed users to collectively upload and download any kind of media they wanted—MP3s, movies, PDFs. If at least one other person devoted their Internet connection to uploading a particular file, you could search for and download it, with varying degrees of quality and speed. The more users uploading a single file, the faster it could be downloaded, leading to a loose form of quality ranking, without feeds or algorithmic recommendations. The more "seeders," as BitTorrent called uploading users, the better the file at hand was likely to be. Sometimes that quality was literal, in terms of resolution or subtitles. But it was also abstract, a measure of artistic achievement or cultural significance: more people felt that this particular thing was worth the cost and risk of sharing it.

I remember waiting days and even weeks for albums or anime seasons to fully download, the green progress bar slowly filling. This was before the era of always-on computers; I had to make sure the desktop stayed awake to keep BitTorrent chugging along. Sometimes, after all that work, the files would be mislabeled, whether by mistake or malice, and I would have to start over again. But the sharing network made me feel connected to these other fans. It was something I was missing in the rest of my life, the chance to delve into this obsessive interest with other people and without judgment—in fact, with approval. (Of course, there was also an element of intentional rebellion, a seeking of difference by not just casting myself in with, say, the high school track team, though I couldn't have done that if I tried.) It's almost a cliché to note that my generation grew up on the Internet, but I can say that I first became aware of myself as an adult person on the Internet, a being separate from my immediate context. It was a space in which I could construct myself out of the disparate inspirations I found there. Engaging so intimately with culture, almost ingesting it into the self, is an activity that we are perhaps most capable of as teenagers.

In his 1983 book *The Gift*, Lewis Hyde defines artwork as something freely given by the artist through her creative act, no matter where it ends up: "a work of art contains the spirit of the artist's gift." But in a way, taste can be a gift, too. It costs nothing to introduce someone to a new piece of culture that you think they might like, and the act might benefit all parties involved. Culture, after all, is not a one-to-many broadcast system but a peer-to-peer network, like BitTorrent, where we collectively determine what means the most to us by intentionally sharing it. As Hyde wrote, "The spirit of a gift is kept alive by its constant donation."

I had a similar rabbit-hole experience with music. I inherited from my mother an appreciation for Dave Matthews Band, the pinnacle of shambolic nineties acoustic jam bands, that I can't totally excuse but also can't erase. I bought CDs at the monolithic Borders outlet an hour's drive from my house, the same place I found a newly available crop of translated Japanese manga. But online I traveled a more circuitous route to find my taste in music.

My first real home was a forum for a massive multiplayer online role-playing game (MMORPG)—a video-game world that you inhabit with thousands of other players at the same time over the Internet—that had an ancillary music section. Then I moved to a devoted Dave Matthews Band forum called AntsMarching.org (again, cringe). Finally, over the course of the early 2000s, I landed at a slightly broader indie music forum called UFCK.org, which gathered DMB fans who had become somewhat disaffected with the band—grown out of it, perhaps.

Like an archaeologist brushing away centuries of dirt, I can find only bare traces of UFCK online now, mostly remembrances or "refugee" threads on other forums after it shut down in 2006. But at the time, it was the center of my online life, and it was where I found the recommendations of other bands and musicians that became central to my taste: Andrew Bird, the Decemberists, Sufjan Stevens. This selection was far from unique; it became a kind of generic musical taste for North American teenagers who were too online or too hipster, an early symbol of online homogeneity cutting across geography. But in my real-life surroundings, it was unusual. I didn't know anyone else who was listening to these bands. The forums also functioned as archives for concert recordings, particularly for DMB. Tapers would bring recording equipment—microphones, booms, and tape decks—to concerts, then share the result online. Members of the forums debated which DMB concert or single live performance of a song was best, stretching back through to the band's formation in 1991. The collective discussion formed a DIY canon in this small subset of music appreciation—following an ecosystem established earlier by the Grateful Dead and Phish.

Over time, I gathered my own digital archive of concert MP3s via file sharing, sorted by year, the way an oenophile keeps a wine cellar of aged bottles. I started to appreciate mid-nineties recordings the most, staking out an opinion that 1997 was the band's best year. It didn't matter that the recordings were staticky and incomplete, or the performances unorthodox. Having to consciously accrue a collection and think through what you enjoy most about a particular creator or body of culture means becoming a connoisseur. The term has a pretentious quality, but we can become connoisseurs of anything: reality TV shows, noise music, apple pie recipes. What we gain with algorithmic feeds in terms of availability—having instant access to a broad range of material to be scanned at will—we lose in connoisseurship, which requires depth and intention. It's ultimately a form of deep appreciation, for what the artist has done as well as the capacities of our own tastes.

Economically, the kind of piracy I was practicing as a teenager was unethical, not to mention most often illegal. I knew that I was stealing these albums and television shows, the ones that had been commercially licensed in the United States. The artists weren't benefiting financially from my fandom. (This problem was nothing new; novelists in the nineteenth century faced pirated editions of their books from foreign publishers just as musicians in the 2000s confronted piracy from Napster, as the historian Orlando Figes memorably described in his book *The Europeans*.) But as a model for cultural distribution, as it existed in the 2000s, I can think of nothing better than the ecosystem of forums and file sharing. It was my Library of Alexandria. The earlier era of the Internet was a much less mediated environment of word of mouth, with specialized knowledge filtering from one person to another, slowly building up to groups and communities, cohering into a holistic culture that was nevertheless graspable.

I must admit that my admiration for this period is driven in part by nostalgia. We all dream of that period of youth when the self is relatively unformed and encounters with art have a staggering power. Teenagers are more open to new experiences, regardless of what technology they use to consume them, and have the tendency and time to indulge obsessions, to become connoisseurs. But I've realized that what I appreciated so much about those online interactions is that they were built on person-to-person recommendations, not automated ones. Someone had to care enough to tell me what they liked, and I had to care enough to trust them and give it a fair try. Such cultural recommendations—communicating approval—are social and moral acts. We tell each other that we like things the same way that bees perform dances to pass on the location of a particularly fruitful flower. The very act brings us together.

Recommender systems, then, are a much more abstracted version of this exchange. Within them, our net behaviors are aggregated by an algorithm, then crunched and averaged and spit back out to create templates of consumption that are imposed on other people. In the guise of speeding it up, it actually impedes that organic development of culture and instead prioritizes flatness and sameness, the aesthetics that are the most transmissible across the networks of digital platforms. In a way, this book is an attempt to recapture recommendations from recommender systems. We should talk even more about the things we like, experience them together, and build up our own careful collections of likes and dislikes. Not for the sake of fine-tuning an algorithm, but for our collective satisfaction.

Recommending things is a professional human job, after all. There are people who work to figure out what culture we should be exposed to and what we might appreciate, adapting their approaches to the moment and expanding the boundaries of what is considered tasteful. You might find them in a boutique, at an art museum, on a radio station, or behind the scenes at a movie theater. These professional recommenders are called curators. They make sure that exposure goes to what merits it. They perform the labor of contextualization and introduce us to what's new, challenging us enough that we avoid homogeneity. They guide our consumption. Though the word might get overused on the Internet, what we really need is more curation—the cultivation and deployment of personal taste.

## THE POWER OF CURATION

Curation begins with responsibility. The etymological ancestor of the word *curatore* was a term for ancient Roman "public officers," according to an 1875 dictionary, positions that predated the emperor Augustus, whose reign began in 27 BCE. They managed various aspects of the city's upkeep: there were curatores of the Tiber River, the purchase of foodstuffs, the aqueducts that carried water into the city, and the hosting of public games. In Latin, *curare* meant to take care of, and *curatio* indicated attention and management. Over the centuries, the word's meaning became less mundane and more spiritual, but still related to caretaking. By the fourteenth century, the noun *curate* referred to a person working as a religious guide. In the 1662 English-language *Book of Common Prayer*, a curate was the deputy priest of a parish, guiding his parishioners and looking after the "cure"—care—of their souls. Since at least the mid-nineteenth century, *curator* has specifically described the manager of a museum and its collections, whether artworks or historical artifacts—a steward of objects instead of people.

The word's etymology hints at the importance of curating, not just as an act of consumption, taste displaying, or even self-definition, but as the caretaking of culture, a rigorous and ongoing process. The second half of the twentieth century saw the rise of celebrity curators, powerful tastemakers whose choices influenced the collective tastes of their eras. Beginning in 1932, Philip Johnson, the Museum of Modern Art's first curator of architecture (a department that his family wealth also funded), was one of the figures responsible for popularizing the aesthetic of modernist design. By showing off the stark industrial furniture of Ludwig Mies van der Rohe and others, which appeared shocking at first, in the space of a museum, Johnson gradually made it palatable. In the 1960s, the Belgian-born Henry Geldzahler worked as a curator of American art at the Metropolitan Museum, gradually focusing on living artists, which was rare at that time for such an institution. Geldzahler used his position to support the early Pop era of artists, including Andy Warhol and David Hockney (his close friends), as well as artists like Robert Rauschenberg and Jasper Johns. (A curator's work is always somewhat personal, but Geldzahler took it further than most.) The garish and banal qualities of Pop art initially shocked viewers, but the curator helped to contextualize it, arguing for its importance until the movement became widely accepted as part of the art-historical canon by the time Geldzahler left the Met in 1977.

Those decades saw "the rise of the curator as creator," as the museum-studies scholar Bruce Altshuler put it in his 1994 book *The Avant-Garde in Exhibition.* In the late twentieth century and the early twenty-first, we have seen a set of celebrity curators emerge, including Hans Ulrich Obrist and Carolyn Christov-Bakargiev. They operate on an international scale, like diplomats without port-folio, and work across different institutions, alighting at a museum or gallery to organize exhibitions that reflect both their personal sensibilities and the current moment. Curatorial practice became a strategy for asserting and restoring visibility on an international scale. The Nigerian curator Okwui Enwezor organized major exhi-bitions like the 1989 *Magicians de la Terre* and 2002 Documenta, a German survey of contemporary art that happens every five years. In those exhibitions, Enwezor placed artists from overlooked coun-tries and backgrounds alongside already famous names from the Western art world, making a powerful argument for contemporary art as a global exchange of ideas—the German Anselm Kiefer next to the Chinese Huang Yong Ping and the Australian indigenous artist John Mawurndjul.

In a sense, the individual star curators are the opposite of recom-mendation algorithms: they utilize all of their knowledge, expertise, and experience in order to determine what to show us and how to do it, with utmost sensitivity and humanity. Given the scope of their careers—truly one of the world's coolest jobs—it is no wonder that the figure of the curator has become a glamorous archetype and a label that others want to latch on to. Even machines are trying to become curators.

Beginning in the early 2010s and extending over the course of the decade, with no sign of stopping today, the word *curated* became ubiquitous. Once an arcane term used only by specialists and aca-demics, it is now applied wantonly to grids of Instagram posts, cosmetics color palettes, and fashion brand accessories. Here are only a few of the excessive usages of curation that I've observed: An influencer "curates" the companies she creates sponsored content for, or curates the guest list of an event. A restaurateur curates a bar menu, or a food market curates the vendors occupying its stalls. A hotel curates its selection of rooms, as if each one were its own unique experience. A streaming service curates the content it offers. A musician even "curates an unconventional career," according to NPR. In the social network era, we've all had to curate our identities, in the sense of selecting which pieces of content best represent us on a profile page. In a 2012 lecture, the Internet artist Jonathan Harris summarized the shift: "Curation is replacing creation as a mode of self-expression." Rather than a form of committed caretaking, it more appears as an act of narcissism.

The aura of the word is aspirational, meant to impart a sense of significance and quality, like a "Very Special" designation on a bottle of cognac. Wouldn't you want something that is curated over something that is not? Lately, the word simply indicates a choice between a group of options, a decision that was made by a human with some semblance of expertise and intention. Yet algorithmic recommendations are also often described as "curating" a feed, even though there is no consciousness behind them. As I write this, my phone offers an automatically "curated" library of the photos I've taken, sorting them into theoretically meaningful and attractive highlights. (By what metric, it doesn't say.) The semantic satiation of the word has happened because the prevalence of algorithms has turned choices between things into a novelty. When we don't have to make a selection, doing so, or knowing that someone else did, becomes a kind of luxury, albeit a pathetic one. If we extrapolate from that contemporary definition, before the era of feeds, everything must have been curated, from the television shows on cable to the songs on the radio.

What is lost in the overuse of the word is the figure of the curator herself, a person whose responsibility it is to make informed choices, to care for the material under her purview. If you had asked me in high school what I wanted to do with my life, I would have said that I wanted to be just such a curator. My desire was inspired by books on the history of modern art and visits to the Museum of Modern Art in Manhattan, which I would take the commuter train to from

Connecticut a few times a year. I attended an after-school program at the Aldrich Contemporary Art Museum, where the staff curators would talk to students about the artists with whom they were working to organize shows and complete commissions.

In high school, I had envisioned, on some level, that a curator's role was principally to decide where things went on white gallery walls, like an extreme version of interior decorating. I figured they chose precisely where to place each painting and its neighboring works of art, designing the order in which the works in the show should be experienced. I was right, in a way—arranging artwork is a big part of the job. But this is only its most public aspect. When, in college, I did a summer internship at the contemporary department of Boston's Museum of Fine Arts, I realized that the labor went much deeper. It was also a scholarly, almost ascetic job, like that of the priestly curates. Behind those placement decisions were hundreds of hours of research, writing, thinking, and maintenance. It wasn't necessarily glamorous: I spent most of my internship time updating a card catalog of where physical artworks resided in storage. But my proudest moment came years later, when I realized that a few sentences of label text I had written for a massive Philip Guston painting had been installed in the museum, and I saw curious visitors going up to the label and reading my words. I had participated, in a small way, in that public curatorial process and was responsible for telling them what they needed to know about Guston and the painting.

The Internet might have an overflow of curation, but it also doesn't have enough of it, in the sense of long-term stewardship, organization, and contextualization of content—all processes that have been outsourced to algorithms. To determine the role of curators in the algorithmic gridlock of Filterworld, I met up with Paola Antonelli, a curator who joined the Museum of Modern Art in 1994 and is now the senior curator of its Department of Architecture and Design as well as a director of research and development. Antonelli is one of the most innovative curators of our time, and I'm lucky to have known her for more than a decade, carrying on a meandering conversation about art, design, technology, and the future of culture.

Antonelli was born in Sardinia, Italy, and studied architecture in

Milan. After landing at MoMA, she led the expansion of its design collection, which began back in Philip Johnson's day, and collected a series of unorthodox objects that may not initially seem to belong in a museum. In 2010, under Antonelli's charge, the museum acquired the @ symbol (which was free, since it was in the public domain) and in 2012 it acquired a batch of fourteen video games that were representative of the medium's history, including *Tetris, Myst,* and *The Sims.*

Antonelli makes the argument that the world is full of design, from a fire hydrant on the street to the keyboard you type with. Her curatorial practice recontextualizes these everyday objects and highlights the genius of their creation. In her exhibition "Talk to Me" from 2011, she gathered pieces that addressed "the communication between people and things." "Things talk to us," she wrote. The show ranged from physical blocks that could be used to write code to a device that simulated menstrual pain for those who can't experience it and an actual New York City MetroCard vending machine from 1999. The show was installed not in the usual spartan mode of modern art exhibitions, but almost as an exciting retail store, with pieces displayed on bright orange shelf modules in the middle of the floor.

I remember being shocked by the energy of the layout when I encountered it. Antonelli's three-dimensional collage of objects evoked a world of interactive technology, in which devices both digital and physical are constantly mediating our interpersonal relationships. An entire philosophy was encoded in the unpretentious and yet rigorous way that Antonelli ordered her selections. Algorithmic feeds, in fact, could fit in as objects in that exhibition.

On the appointed day, I took the Amtrak train from D.C. to New York City and walked through Midtown, the same blocks I had traversed going to MoMA as a teenager, past familiar public sculptures and sidewalk halal carts where I had often eaten lunch before arriving at the museum. The journey is always a pilgrimage to me: I feel like a medieval peasant traveling to a cathedral. It was where I learned about so much art I love and where I could see the artworks I read about in books, like Picasso's radically abstracted *Les Demoiselles d'Avignon,* casually hanging in a gallery. MoMA's overall collection includes around two hundred thousand objects, and however large the physical institution becomes, it could never display them all. So its dozens of curators are constantly making choices about what to show and where to put it.

I met Antonelli outside of the museum's staff wing. Curators are often fashionable (adept at choosing things), but Antonelli had exchanged the typical black ensemble for a red blouse with white stripes on the lapels and a matching skirt. Many years ago, she had concluded that curators at their best are "trusted guides." "They are specialized in something," she said, whether that's olive oil in a supermarket or American paintings from the 1960s. What's more, curation is a two-way street: one always must be aware of the viewers, their perceptions, reactions, and even emotional states. "It's a performance art of sorts," Antonelli told me. "You earn your stars, your trust, and your credibility, and once you've earned it, you have to keep it." The performance doesn't end once the exhibition opens.

Curators must also respect their audience's capacity to think for themselves. Antonelli tries to leave her exhibition theses open-ended, "90 percent baked." The remaining 10 percent gives space to the audience to bring their own experience to the work, completing the idea or argument on their own. When things are too predetermined or set in a template, audiences are alienated, because they feel no agency. "I believe that my job is not to tell people what's good and what's bad, but rather, it's to stimulate their own critical sense," she continued. Just as a chef's amuse-bouche wakes up the appetite so one can better appreciate the meal that follows, the curator's selection stimulates our senses to consider what's in front of us. This kind of holistic sensitivity is something an algorithmic feed is incapable of replicating.

To explain her approach, Antonelli walked me into gallery 216, which mingles design and architecture with some visual art, featuring many pieces that Antonelli had acquired for the MoMA collection herself. She chose a piece by the artists and researchers Kate Crawford and Vladan Joler to anchor the room. Called *Anatomy of an AI System*, it's an infographic on black background expanded to the size of a wall that documents the various forms of human labor, infrastructure, and data that go into Amazon's Echo device. From it, Antonelli took up the theme of "extraction." In the first corner of the gallery, a trio of pieces collide: alongside *Anatomy of an AI System* are installed a leather form that resembles a prone cow but is a functional bench, and a location icon instantly familiar from Google Maps, printed some six feet tall.

The cow was Julia Lohmann's *"Waltraud" Cow-Bench*. Its headless form was creepy but cute, the gleaming brown leather that it was made from taken off a once-living cow and molded into a cow shape once again. "This cow exists as a reminder. It's almost like a grounding element," Antonelli explained. It represents the extraction of resources, animal and environmental, to create rarefied objects. It's still an object, however; children sometimes climb on it, and the guards must rush in. The Google Maps pin icon was designed by Jens Eilstrup Rasmussen in 2005 and was gifted by Google to MoMA at Antonelli's request. She decided to print it much larger than it appears on screens, its rounded red teardrop shape almost becoming an abstract painting, as a way of defamiliarizing it.

Those three pieces together form a tableau in the gallery, both visually and conceptually striking. Each one is unique in terms of medium and subject, and yet they share a certain tone that Antonelli has drawn out by putting them in proximity. Perhaps it's a shared approach of turning our environment inside out from its surface, reversing the familiar viewpoint to the point of discomfort. Rather than complementing each other or flowing smoothly together like a Spotify radio playlist, they contrast and clash, bringing out new facets of each work. That corner of the gallery, with its striking juxtaposition, brought to mind the iconic surrealist line by the poet Isidore Lucien Ducasse: "Beautiful as the chance meeting on a dissecting table of a sewing machine and an umbrella." The collision of different objects always brings out a new kind of beauty. "There's a non-algorithmic quality to what's included in the permanent collection and the curation of the galleries," Antonelli said.

As she swept authoritatively through the galleries, Antonelli noticed slight flaws in various displays. In one room, the wall labels looked too worn and dog-eared. In another, a projector wasn't beaming as it should on an exhibition title to complete its lettering. Then she observed that a gallery was missing guards—who were particularly important, given that the pieces were interactive video games. She dictated text messages to her staff on her phone, and an assistant rushed down to address the problems. In order to earn the audience's trust, every detail must be right.

The slow process of curation works against the contextlessness, speed, and ephemerality that characterizes the Internet. "When you think of social media, it's this white noise, it's dead space," Antonelli said. (An apt description of Filterworld as a whole, where nothing stands out.) "That's where the algorithm becomes your antagonist," she continued. Algorithmic feeds disrupt curated juxtapositions and make it that much harder to interpret the broad swath of culture, to figure out which themes join things together and which aspects set them apart. Instead of a productive progression through experiences, we have an increasingly indistinguishable morass. As anyone who has been on the Internet knows, it is difficult to learn via feeds. Learning, in the sense of the accretion of understanding, always happens off the platform, when you have time to put things together for yourself. Even then, organizing material on the Internet, as my artist friend Hallie Bateman said, is like building sandcastles on the beach as the tide comes in—your careful collections are almost inevitably going to be destroyed, just as Spotify's interface changes once messed around with mine.

A collection like MoMA's is vital because it becomes a lasting document of our moment. There are so many objects, pieces of content, and artifacts out there that some choices inevitably have to be made about what to consume and what to preserve. Every curator brings in her own viewpoint. Collectively, humanity builds up a record of what matters in our culture, which is often called a canon. The canon can expand and change, widening to encompass new ideas, but its existence is inevitable. It's not just based on popularity. "Some curators say, I don't want a canon anymore," Antonelli said. "But you know what? We can't escape it, so we might as well embrace it." With curators' help, the canon incorporates things that are strange, disturbing, discomfiting, or shocking as much as the straightforwardly beautiful or appealing. They are constantly urging us to reconsider what a specific object or aesthetic experience means.

Antonelli returned to her office, and I wandered around MoMA until I came to a retrospective of the French surrealist artist Meret Oppenheim, who lived from 1913 to 1985. I didn't know much about Oppenheim save her famous sculpture of a teacup, saucer, and spoon covered in gazelle fur, from 1936, titled *Object* and sometimes appended with *Breakfast in Fur*. It's an icon of surrealism, the fur turning the familiar item into something both bizarre and compelling. But her other work, arrayed in rigorous chronology through half a dozen gallery spaces, was a surprise, from the cartoonish, angsty-yet-funny paintings of her youth to freestanding sculptures of paganesque nature gods. Walking through the exhibition felt like a breath of fresh air, because it captured the entire lifelong creative practice of an individual artist in all its complexity. Though Oppenheim lived in a different time, her presence and perspective were immediately present in the galleries, through the laborious act of curation.

On Instagram, I might have found Oppenheim's teacup and perhaps a glamorous black-and-white portrait of the artist on my recommended page. Her art is exactly the kind that succeeds on the platform—visually surprising and pleasing at first glance. The images would be inspiring as they flashed through the feed, but I wouldn't learn much else about Oppenheim, about her collaborations with fashion houses or her rare public visibility as a woman artist in the mid-twentieth century, much less see her early doodles. ("Nobody will give you freedom; you have to take it," she said in a 1974 speech.) My point is not that we must gather an understanding of art only through museum exhibitions; rather, it's that the view we have of culture through algorithmic feeds is often so blinkered as to be useless. We're not encouraged or informed enough to get beyond it, because that would not provide fodder for the app's advertising revenue. Human curation is the expanded and deepened view, and ultimately the more satisfying one.

However much we rely on or ascribe to them, the core function of algorithmic feeds is to put one piece of content next to another one, whether on Netflix, Spotify, Facebook, or TikTok. The recommendations decide what belongs together and dictate what path you will follow, which forms an inevitable narrative in your mind. My argument for the kind of curation that Antonelli and others practice is that the act of putting one thing next to another is an incredibly important one and should be left to people with deep knowledge about or passion for the subject at hand—people who care about the significance of proximity. They are our "trusted guides," as Antonelli put it. That practice of ordering can even become an art form in itself.

## DJ AS CURATOR

Though curation is an important act, a decision made on both feeling and intellect, that doesn't mean it's a rarefied one. We can find it from many different sources, and it's easy to overlook it or take for granted the labor that goes into it. I was reminded of the importance of curation, as a contrast to the automated feed, on a particularly arduous road trip.

The weekend after Thanksgiving in 2022, when most of America gets back on the road to return home, Jess and I were driving to our apartment in Washington, D.C., returning from a visit to Connecticut. It wasn't ideal timing; the roads surrounding New York City were packed. The saving grace amidst the congestion was a radio show that we stumbled upon by chance. It was on 90.7 FM, a station called WFUV, which began in 1947 and is based at Fordham University in the Bronx. A DJ named Paul Cavalconte was doing his weekly *Cavalcade* show from eight to eleven p.m. that night.

I knew nothing about Cavalconte at that point. But what we heard in the car was his smooth, sweetly monotone voice, like the green felt on a pool table, opening a tunnel for us, somewhere beyond the windshield, into his own musical universe. That week, he structured his show around "Leftovers," reflecting the Thanksgiving context. He had created a playlist of covers and B sides, the kinds of recordings that might not reflect a musician's entire body of work but were more interesting for it, a compilation of deep cuts. But as we drove and the DJ kept up his patter, we began noticing a deeper structure. Cavalconte made a kind of daisy chain as one artist covered another:

the band Death Cab for Cutie covered Cat Power's "Metal Heart," then Cat Power covered Bob Dylan's "Stuck Inside of Mobile with the Memphis Blues Again," then Bob Dylan covered Joni Mitchell's "Big Yellow Taxi." The juxtaposition of covers unveiled links of influence within a realm of singer-songwriters. Each artist was an admirer of the other and brought out specific qualities of their songs that hinted at the artist's own original musical sensibility as well, like Cat Power highlighting the underrated melody and propulsion of Dylan's singing with her own smoky, wry voice. Particularly since I was starved for recommendations in the midst of my algorithm cleanse, it made a powerful impression.

Just like Paola Antonelli arranging artworks in a MoMA gallery, the way that Cavalconte lined up the songs communicated something about them, building to a broader picture of culture. DJs are curators, too—behind the playlist we could sense the deep expertise and sensitivity that it took to put it together. I get frustrated when Spotify toggles into its automated radio mode because nothing links the tracks that it puts together except genre or a sameness of sound. Listening to Cavalconte's show, by contrast, I could always feel the human intelligence behind it, which made it infinitely more compelling. Like the labels on each object in an exhibition, Cavalconte also periodically paused to offer some musical history or his personal perspective on a particular set of tracks. While the role might not be as high-profile these days (due in part to the intrusion of algorithms), DJs also help their listeners in that vital process of discovering new culture.

As I've written this book, independent radio DJs have stuck out in my mind as an ideal form of non-algorithmic cultural distribution. Even pre-Internet, radio stations beamed out a round-the-clock stream of music and information, all selected by hand. When accessed by actual radio waves, they are also specific to their geographic area (the waves can't travel forever) and exist in real time, responding to a context that's shared with the listener—whether that's the weather, time of day, or a regional dialect. Described this way, it sounds almost utopian, but it's also mundane: The miracle of people speaking to us through our speakers has become familiar, though it was once as unusual as a digital feed of machine-sorted content. But when a DJ on a trusted radio station plays something, we still tend to listen more closely, pay attention for longer than if we could instantly skip to the next recommendation.

Like an art exhibition, the radio station can challenge our sense of what's possible. That happened to me one night when I was a senior in high school. My sense of direction is terrible, and I often got lost on the unlit roads that twisted through the hills of my hometown. On late drives back from my friends' houses, I would listen to the local radio station WPKN, a noncommercial station with a staff of volunteer DJs that originated at the University of Bridgeport. *The New Yorker* once labeled it, only semi-ironically, "the greatest radio station in the world"; I was lucky to grow up in its range. On Saturday nights around 2005 a woman hosted a jazz and blues show; I didn't know her name, but I became familiar with her voice, which was thin and raspy and often trailed off into silence, with the characteristic haphazard interruptions of indie radio. I wasn't a particular fan of jazz or blues, and wouldn't be for many years afterward, but WPKN always came in clear and played music much more interesting than what was on the commercial stations.

That night, a jazz track started with a series of pounding piano chords and a drum backbeat alongside percussive thunks from an upright bass. Then a single horn melody traced over the background like a shooting star or a bird whirling against a clear sky. Though structurally it was a standard jazz quartet, it was unlike anything I had ever heard before. The track kept unspooling as I drove, charging along every time I thought it might stop, moving through periods of rhythmic calm and then into discordant horn solos that only dipped occasionally into recognizable melody. It lasted more than thirteen minutes, bringing me all the way back into the driveway. When the song finally subsided, the woman's voice on the radio explained that it was John Coltrane's recording of "My Favorite Things" from 1961, the full version rather than the much shorter radio edit that became a hit as a single. (I wasn't even aware of the original song by Rodgers and Hammerstein from 1959.) On the track, Coltrane played a soprano saxophone that Miles Davis had bought for him the year before, an uncommon instrument for jazz at the time. And with that brief but informative note, the DJ went off into her next set of songs. I sat in the driver's seat gently stunned.

Ever since, that recording has remained one of my favorite pieces of music. Everyone has a similar story of how a piece of art—painting, music, film—took them by surprise, left them ineffably changed in an instant. But without the help of curators and the context of established cultural channels like radio stations, we're less likely to have these encounters.

If the same Coltrane track had autoplayed on Spotify, I might have heard it, in a literal sense, but I wouldn't have listened to it in the way that I did when it was on the radio. Spotify's recommender system has never suggested such a long song for me, perhaps because that kind of time commitment too often leads to skipping the track, a negative indicator by the algorithm's standards. (Recall the streaming era's shortening song lengths.) Nor would I have learned anything about Coltrane or his influences. Spotify publishes lengthy biographies of artists and develops its own handmade playlists, but its interface makes it difficult to find any information about a particular album without leaving the app to just google it, even the original recording date of a rerelease, much less which musician plays which instrument. Unlike in a CD jewel case or a vinyl gatefold, there are no liner notes that reflect the aesthetic sensibility of the artist.

The algorithm is a bad substitute for a human DJ. Perhaps Spotify is aware; in 2023, it launched an AI DJ that could intermittently tell listeners the names of songs in the algorithmic playlist, but using it felt more insulting than innovative. Creativity is required. As Jess and I drove home from Thanksgiving, we listened to all three hours of Paul Cavalconte's WFUV show. When we lost the radio signal heading south somewhere in New Jersey, we streamed it from the station's website over our phones. In the weeks that followed, I struck up a conversation with Cavalconte, wanting to figure out how that ordinary miracle of a playlist had come together, and how he saw his role evolving in the age of algorithmic feeds.

Cavalconte has worked as a DJ for more than thirty years and looks like you'd imagine one: a little nerdy, a halo of hair cresting a high forehead, wide eyes and a wide grin, communicating infectious enthusiasm. He lives only a ten-minute drive away from WFUV's studio, in the family home he grew up in, where he eventually transformed the basement apartment into his own sound studio, surrounded by shelves of thousands of records. He was an only child, and his parents were on the older side, so his earliest exposure to music came in the form of their classical and jazz record collection, a mixture that was leavened by rock when he went to school. He attended Fordham University during the early 1980s, volunteering at the radio station, which was entirely run by student volunteers at the time. While he was growing up, during the period of peak FM, radio DJs "were a kind of cultural arbiter," he told me in the same buttery voice, tinged with New York accent, that I heard on the radio.

Cavalconte got his first part-time job on the radio at WLIR, an influential progressive rock station based on Long Island. The station was known for allowing DJs to have a more casual tone on the air and play more obscure album tracks, not just radio singles. WLIR was early to embrace new music genres that became popular in the eighties, including post-punk, the slightly more melodic successor to mid-seventies punk, with bands like the B-52s, and No Wave, a noisier, atonal movement emanating from the New York City art scene. The music that the station played still challenges mainstream taste today. Its purpose was to stay on the edge of culture and provide a curatorial channel to listeners; the station even set up its own supply chain for getting same-day deliveries of the newest records from the United Kingdom. After WLIR, Cavalconte's career crisscrossed New York radio stations: WNEW-AM, WNCN, Q104.3, CD101.9, WRXP, all names that had their own formats, personalities, and what we would now call brands attached.

Cavalconte DJed classical and jazz shows, too, taking on whatever format the gig required. He returned to WFUV in 2013 and started Cavalcade in 2015. In 2017, he also took over the Saturday night and Sunday afternoon slots on WNYC, which the DJ Jonathan Schwartz had occupied with meandering shows drawing on the twentieth-century Great American Songbook, before he left the station in a harassment scandal. It's an iconic time slot, broadcasting a real-time atmosphere over New York City as its residents get ready to go out or relax before a new week begins—a hefty curatorial responsibility.

DJs' selection of specific songs linked by the banter interspersed between, plus their individual voices—the best sounded like "cool teachers," Cavalconte said—"drew you in just a little, a few toes into the deeper water" of the counterculture. "It was an indoctrination of sorts; it was very subversive," he said. As he spoke, Cavalconte's voice slid into full radio mode, slowing down and enunciating each word. The hair stood up on the back of my neck. "When I was growing up," he said, "the DJs all had these sonorous voices; they were really sexy sounding. I want to go where he or she is taking me— the world of the dimmed light and the smoldering cigarette in the ashtray. You imagine this after-hours ambience of the radio studio, and just the tone of someone's voice takes you there." He continued, "The DJ was part of the original community of influencers, these people we were so envious of who got paid to do this—dress like a slob and drink free beers and listen to free music."

Like the museum curator, the DJ cultivates an atmosphere of trust in which the consumer can take in new culture. "If the man with the nice voice has lured you into the circle, maybe something magical will happen. There's a need for that kind of companionship," Cavalconte said. "Curation is now companionship." That statement made me think about how algorithmic feeds are absent as companions: they just surface a piece of content and leave you alone with it until you lose patience and decide to skip to the next song or video.

A DJ set on an indie radio station is a holistic immersion that has been planned out for you by another person, an experience informed by the curator's taste and knowledge. The music choices form a "larger storytelling concept," according to Cavalconte. More commercial stations have to follow the dictates of corporate music lists and rigid song quotas, of course, but for his weekly WFUV show, Cavalconte simply explores his own music taste across eras and genres—American standards, folk, jazz, rock, pop, hip-hop— built up over decades of research and practice. "Taste is a larger frame of reference; it's an intricate series of value judgments that you consciously or unconsciously made all along," he said. The recommendation algorithm is a kind of opponent for the curator, like the steam-powered machine that John Henry raced in the folktale to build a railroad tunnel. The fact that this "thing"—the algorithm—"has now become your friend, your arbiter of taste, it's gross. I don't want any part of that; I want a real person, someone to invest in," Cavalconte said.

Still, there's a certain metaphor in the digital filtering machine. "The way I do it is algorithmically, but it's generated from within my own mind and frame of my experience," Cavalconte explained. "I try to be as free association as possible, to put myself on the shrink's couch and play that game. If it's something silly, go with it." During his Thanksgiving set, that took the form of adding in a few Taylor Swift songs. The choice of the contemporary pop star was an "ironic brushstroke" amidst the more classic musicians and cover songs, Cavalconte said. (Try asking the Spotify algorithm for irony or humor.)

Recommendations between people are a two-way exchange: the curator must consider the value of what they are passing on, and the consumer must remain open-minded, giving up the option of skipping the track if it's not immediately appealing. "You must get somebody to come on board with the idea that they don't have control. In fact, the whole point is that you acquiesce to the loss of that control," Cavalconte said.

While personalized algorithmic recommendations emphasize the familiar and recognizable, tailoring the content toward the least objectionable options, DJs work to highlight the unfamiliar and unusual. There's no guarantee that you'll like what they play, but the hope is that you'll at least be interested in it. That differentiation is important in culture at large, too. It's very possible to be interested in something but not like it, in the case of a difficult piece of music or an abstract painting. A piece of art can provoke you and leave you confused or perturbed but still drawn in. Perhaps more commonly in Filterworld, you can also like something but not find it interesting, as in the case of Netflix's *Emily in Paris:* it's pleasant enough to watch, but when it's over, the experience immediately leaves your mind like the bubbles effervescing in seltzer. (Actual interest requires the presence of some texture, rather than total ignorable ambience.)

Curation progresses forward instead of in endless reiterative circles. "It's a question of making something available to someone who otherwise wouldn't have known about it," Cavalconte said. "You don't know what you want until you've got it."

Without the added friction of curation, culture tends to become more and more generic. Cavalconte has observed this effect with music in the era of algorithmic feeds—which he pays attention to both professionally and personally. "Technology has allowed people to have much more instant access to music and to be able to taste-test music in a rapid-fire kind of way, rather than the discipline of sitting and listening to an album and experiencing the prosaic, novelistic way that the message of the album unfolds song by song," he said. Individual tracks have superseded albums in importance, and albums have become baggy collections of excess material, sprawling more into mood background than concise statements. Unlike a vinyl album or cassette tape, the format of streaming doesn't impose any time limits; the more tracks there are, the wider the spread of fodder for algorithmic recommendations and royalties based on streams.

Take Taylor Swift's output. She released three new albums from 2020 to 2022 and released two re-recorded versions of her earlier albums as well, fulfilling the Spotify CEO Daniel Ek's dictate that contemporary musicians must constantly release new music. (In 2020, Ek said that it wasn't enough for artists to release an album every few years; they have to create a "continuous engagement with their fans.") Even though, in 2014, Swift had removed her music from Spotify because she felt it devalued her work, she eventually embraced the endless stream of content. Two of those original albums, *Folklore* and *Evermore,* are a pair of downbeat folk records that are nearly indistinguishable. *Midnights* from 2022 was an album of chilled-out, reflective, synth-heavy tracks that came with its own immediate batch of seven similar B sides. Listeners got more music, but it was more of the same. (Drake, another of the world's biggest pop stars, released a stream of mixtapes over those years as well, including 2022's *Honestly, Nevermind,* which saw the rapper's graphomania reduced into scant, repeating lines of narcissistic angst over ambient synth washes.)

Just like the generic Instagram design aesthetic of minimalist interiors, music has settled into a generic style under the pressure of algorithmic feeds. "Everything sounds like a loop, with one-dimensional sounds. Rhythm is a more dominant characteristic than melody," Cavalconte said, citing the "bedroom pop" of Billie Eilish, one of the stars who emerged wholly in the era of Filterworld. The brevity and instant skipability of TikTok videos has condensed musical artistry into seconds-long self-contained segments, which is all the time a "sound" has to capture a user's attention. Unfolding over many minutes is not an option.

"The key change is almost nonexistent in contemporary music, because it's a hook that doesn't work anymore," Cavalconte said. He hummed a few lines of Whitney Houston's "I Wanna Dance with Somebody," with its climactic key change. The technique requires a musical narrative that sets up the melodic contrast, with a clear before and after. It's not reducible to a sound bite. "That building of suspense—now there's no building of anything. It all has to happen in the first thirty seconds," he said.

That observation is not just the DJ's hunch. One researcher found that a quarter of the songs from the Billboard Hot 100 from the 1960s to 1990s featured a key change, but only one song in the 2010s did. Where the nineties had rambling narrative songs like Biggie's "Juicy" and Tim McGraw's "Something Like That," or the Streets's 2004 concept album *A Grand Don't Come for Free*, storytelling in general in pop music also seems to have lately fallen off in favor of overall vibes and moods. Lyrics avoid requiring too much attention from the listener.

Streaming-era songs are often brief, too—Grimes, for the deluxe version of her 2020 album *Miss Anthropocene*, released a few "Algorithm Mix" iterations of songs, cutting down their run time, making them denser and more immediately compelling, better for algorithmic feeds. (It's not dissimilar to the "radio mixes" of the past.) On average, hit songs have gotten shorter in the past two decades, decreasing a total of thirty seconds from 4:30 in 1995 to 3:42 in 2019. Data scientists at UCLA calculated that the average length of a song released in 2020 on Spotify was just 3:17, and that length is trending even shorter. The musicologist Nate Sloan has argued that the collective shortening is caused by the incentives of streaming services—Spotify, for example, counts thirty seconds of listening as a "play" and pays out royalties based on that metric. There's no financial benefit to going any longer.

It's not that music today is worse than in decades past, or that artists aren't trying hard enough. (As a committed fan of ambient music, I personally appreciate the embrace of atmospheric qualities.) But it's clear that the default forms of culture are determined as much by the demands of platforms as the artists' sense of personal creativity. Seeking out human curators, rather than following the current of the feed, can help us break that self-reinforcing cycle. It's the curators' job not only to expose us to new things but to help us experience culture in a different, perhaps more authentic way.

"That's my thing—to make it radical, to make it interesting," Cavalconte said. He used the example of Sandro Botticelli, the fifteenth-century Florentine painter. Botticelli painted his *The Birth of Venus* with the goddess emerging from the ocean, in the 1480s. Today it's one of art history's most famous paintings, but at the time it was shocking and strange, an image you wouldn't "like" on Instagram. Taste is an imaginative exercise meant to be uncomfortable.

## REVIVING CURATION ONLINE

Curation is an analog process that can't be fully automated or scaled up the way that social network feeds have been. It ultimately comes down to humans approving, selecting, and arranging things. But that's not to say curation can't exist online just the way it does in a museum exhibition or on a radio show. Now that we've seen the flattening effects of the dominance of algorithmic feeds in culture during the latter half of the 2010s, entrepreneurs and designers are building new digital platforms that put curation first and deemphasize automated recommendations. They are much smaller than the likes of Facebook and Spotify, both intentionally and by necessity.

The Criterion Collection is a company that began in 1984 with the goal of grouping together a canon of important contemporary films from around the world and then licensing and publishing them in various formats: videocassettes, CD-ROMs, and DVDs. Criterion became one of the best-known and most important brands for film curation, a kind of Michelin Guide to cinema but available for consumption at home. It built up a library of over a thousand productions, collecting indie hits and art films, with a century's worth of material by directors ranging from Jean Cocteau to Akira Kurosawa, Spike Lee, and Alfonso Cuarón. Over the decades, it has moved from one media format to the next, preserving a group of art pieces that otherwise might have been washed away by technological change.

In 2008, Criterion began moving its offerings online, first through a streaming service called Mubi and then through Hulu and later FilmStruck, another subscription streaming service that was created by Turner Classic Movies. It was also available on Kanopy, a service users could access through libraries and other institutions. But in 2018, FilmStruck was shut down by its owners under Warner Media. *The New York Times* described the news as "devastating," and lists popped up of the best titles to watch on the service before it disappeared. It prompted Criterion to launch its own digital streaming service, called the Criterion Channel. Today, Criterion is available anywhere with Internet access, a hypercurated version of Netflix. The library comes with a rich set of viewing guides, historical interviews with directors, video essays from critics, and timely selections of films. Those bespoke recommendations and contextual material set it apart from Netflix's algorithmic home page.

I spoke with Penelope Bartlett, who was the Criterion Channel's director of programming until 2022. Bartlett started as a Criterion programmer—people who choose which films to feature, another kind of curator—in 2016, after working at film festivals and as a producer. The job is "really akin to what a programmer does at an art-house theater: selecting thematic programming, putting films together in interesting, appealing packages," she said. That could take the form of retrospectives of specific directors or specific actors, progressing through their careers, or setting up particularly good double features.

"It's truly thoughtfully curated by the staff of the Criterion Collection versus some kind of algorithm," Bartlett said. Even with the assistance of algorithmic recommendations, the breadth of content available online can induce a kind of decision paralysis. "People are often overwhelmed by the multitude of options in the streaming space. We spend hours figuring out what to watch," Bartlett continued. Criterion's programming is "just trying to help people enjoy and discover movies in exciting ways that also feel manageable, something that you can get through in an evening."

Bartlett described her role as an attempt to "hold people's hands." "Sometimes people are a little bit intimidated by these filmmakers who have made thirty movies. You don't really know where to start; you end up not watching any of them because you're not sure what the entry point is," she said. An algorithmic recommendation based on which movie was watched the most times might not be the best choice. The purpose of Criterion goes beyond superficial recommendation: "It's not just what should I watch, but why should I watch it, what else could I watch with it." Criterion acts as a kind of content seal of approval, not dictated by audience numbers or sales but by sheer artistic quality, as determined by its staff curators.

Criterion helped me discover my own film sensibility. The Hong Kong director Wong Kar-wai has become one of my favorite filmmakers, for his lambent visual aesthetics and the slow, nostalgic, romantic quality of his storytelling. I first encountered his 2000 film *In the Mood for Love* as a teenager in a local Blockbuster, on the foreign-film shelf, in a DVD case with the Criterion logo on the cover. The film's aching portrait of dual marriages in mid-century Hong Kong and the missed connections of love (not to mention the characters' diets of takeout noodle soup) have stuck with me ever since. It was thanks to the company, and an anonymous but much appreciated Blockbuster employee, that I was introduced to Wong's work at all. From *In the Mood for Love,* I made my way to his earlier film *Chungking Express,* a comedic noir about a bummed policeman, and *2046,* a more obscure, science-fiction-inflected sequel to *In the Mood for Love.*

Without the serendipitous Blockbuster discovery, I might have totally missed Wong's work in that formative period of my life, since I lacked access to film festivals or repertory art-house theaters— but all these films are now available online. The streaming Criterion Channel combines the instant, nongeographic accessibility of the Internet with the deep, responsible curation of a library or museum—the best of both worlds, without the relentless distraction of unbounded feeds. It's a vision of how the Internet *could* work if we decided it should.

## PAYING FOR CULTURE ONLINE

Another step toward a more curated Internet is to think more carefully about the business models that drive the platforms we use. There's an axiom about the Internet that might have originated in a comment on the forum MetaFilter in 2010: "If you are not paying for it, you're not the customer; you're the product being sold." When digital platforms are free to use and make money through advertising, content is reduced to a way of attracting attention. When you are paying directly for the content itself, however, the content is more economically sustainable and tends to have more resources invested into it, which is better for both creators and consumers. On streaming services like Netflix and Spotify, users are paying subscription fees for access to content, but that funding is spread across all the content on the platform—and both businesses are increasingly turning to advertising for revenue as their growth in new subscriptions has slowed.

Smaller-scale streaming services are providing an alternative ecosystem, where you can subscribe to a specific set of curated content and better support its creators. Criterion is one option for streaming video, but others exist that focus on British television, thriller movies, or anime. Idagio, a streaming service solely for classical music, launched in 2015 as a form of "fair-trade streaming," as its founder, Till Janczukowicz, told me—like coffee companies that promise a nonexploitative deal for the coffee farmers. While Spotify pays out to artists and labels based on number of listens that last over thirty seconds, Idagio, which hosts much longer recordings than the usual pop song, pays out based on the percentage of their time a user listens to a particular label, down to the second. If a user spends 30 percent of their time listening to recordings from Deutsche Grammophon, for example, then the century-old German classical music label receives 30 percent of that user's su royalties. As a rule of thumb, the more directly and pro content creators get paid by a platform, the more sustai

The past decades of the Internet were largely premised on content being as free to access as possible. In the 1990s and early 2000s, websites seemed like an insignificant side expense for businesses, not mainstream products. Then, with the rise of Google Search and AdSense, advertising became the primary business model of the Internet. Since more traffic meant more money, it didn't make sense to restrict access. As social networks emerged, companies like Facebook, Twitter, and YouTube absorbed more of the advertising revenue by capturing users' attention with algorithmic feeds and selling their own ads, forcing creators and publishers to game the system. Only in recent years have we begun to realize that selling attention can be harder and less sustainable than selling the content itself and avoiding the mediation of feeds. Up until March 2011, anyone could read *The New York Times* online. Its decision to implement a strict paywall and charge readers for its digital content was seen as risky and unorthodox. But it is now one of the most successful journalism companies on the planet, with more than nine million digital subscribers, because it embraced the paywall so early. While it may seem as though culture online is more commodified when it is paid for directly, in reality, culture *should* be the product, as classical music is on Idagio, not your attention.

Janczukowicz moved from the traditional classical music world into digital technology because he saw the culture that he loved falling behind in the Internet era. A German impresario, Janczukowicz began playing piano at the age of five but gradually moved into writing about classical music, organizing workshops, producing recordings, and managing famous musicians and conductors. He worked with the likes of the Chinese pianist Lang Lang, the Japanese conductor Seiji Ozawa, and the Finnish conductor Jukka-Pekka Saraste. As he shepherded their careers, he noticed that their work wasn't as available as it could be. "If they aren't retrievable in digital space, they are losing relevance," Janczukowicz told me. He summarized the goal of Idagio: "We are not here to build a streaming service. The main driver, the mission behind it, is how can we use technology to maintain a culture?" ("Maintaining culture" is precisely what Filterworld fails to do, in its accelerated race to the lowest common denominator.)

While Spotify's algorithm inevitably shepherds the user toward popular pop music, Janczukowicz argued, Idagio is built to support more niche artistic creations. The service is "content complete," meaning that Idagio has arranged licensing deals for more than two million tracks, getting as close as possible to hosting every recording of classical music ever produced, including twenty-five hundred orchestras and six thousand conductors. For ten dollars a month, the service provides something like a perfect digital library—a listenable Wikipedia. You can find any classical recording you're looking for there, and then explore further based on any detail of the album. Of course, this is easier to accomplish for a limited genre like classical than a wider one. But unlike many tech companies, Idagio doesn't pursue scale at all costs; it doesn't need to expand infinitely and address every genre. As Bartlett from Criterion told me, "We don't need to be at the level of those huge streaming services. If we have a loyal, dedicated audience, we should be able to sustain ourselves at the level that we need to be able to continue." Beyond the technology, the capitalist growth-at-all-costs mindset is also fundamentally to blame for the flattening of culture in Filterworld.

Catering to every kind of user at once is an intentional decision that often comes at the cost of usability. In the same way that Facebook expanded to encompass every form of content online, streaming services have often attempted to provide all things for all consumers. The path of chasing something that will appeal to, or at least avoid offending, the highest number of people leads to homogeneity. And that homogeneity is inevitably cast in the mold of dominant groups: white, cisgender, heterosexual. It's hard to develop an individualized identity through an algorithmic mold meant to apply to billions of people at once. By contrast, building smaller communities of consumption devoted to more specific subjects can lead to a much deeper sense of engagement, both with the content and among the users. Sustainability at a small scale still counts as success. That is something we've missed as the Internet has prioritized frictionless convenience and broadcasting to as many people as possible at once.

"I don't believe in this isolated convenience of pushing a button and you get music immediately," Janczukowicz said, evoking the interface of Spotify. While you can still stream anything you want at any time on Idagio, "I'm also interested in context." A listener might leave a Tchaikovsky concert and want to find more symphonies by the Russian composer or look for the same orchestra playing a Beethoven symphony, for example. Spotify makes that level of granularity next to impossible. But Idagio's interface, which has the crisp geometry of a Dieter Rams design and an emphasis on text rather than images, makes it effortless. You can browse by composer, performer, composition, or chronology, with every performer identified and live recordings labeled differently from studio sessions. PDFs of the printed CD booklets are available at the click of a button. It's a revelation, the solution to Paola Antonelli's critique of digital platforms as undifferentiated "dead space." You don't realize how much information and navigation is missing from most platforms, gone in favor of algorithmic recommendations, until it's restored.

When I subscribed to Idagio, I was delighted to find my favorite composition by the French composer Erik Satie, *Gymnopédie No. 1* from 1888. Its gentle, meandering, sparse solo piano melody, like taking an aimless walk on a rainy day, has become very popular on TikTok, where it provides the soundtrack to more than 150,000 videos that range from footage of jellyfish to personal stories about falling in love. I immediately pulled up a list of dozens of different performances of the piece on Idagio, played by musicians across the world and over the course of the last half century. They included a particularly slow and sonorous version from Jeroen van Veen, a Noriko Ogawa performance on a piano from 1890, and a more upbeat performance by Francis Poulenc from 1951, when the piece wasn't nearly as well known as it is today. Satie originally noted only that it should be played "slow and sorrowful"; each recording gave me a different view of the music and how it had been reinterpreted over time. On Idagio, the structure of the platform is adapted to its specific content, improving the cultural experience. On TikTok, by contrast, Satie isn't even named on the *Gymnopédie* recording that is used most often, and on Spotify, variations in album cataloging make keeping track of performers and dates a mess.

As I used Idagio more, I found myself wandering through the corridors of classical music in an organic way that I never could have without the service, following a particular pianist like Jae-hyuck Cho or delving into Chopin's nocturnes, listening to many different performers and pieces. I have very little knowledge of classical music, yet the product made the experience enjoyable and less intimidating even than listening to a classical radio station. It is very much possible to host enormous bodies of culture online without the help of algorithmic feeds; after all, culture itself offers a kind of algorithm to follow, as each artist influences and inspires others, referencing and building on history. Those are the kind of connections from which Paul Cavalconte built his radio playlists. I thought about Janczukowicz's description of the need to "maintain a culture." It's not just that the music needs to be available to be listened to online; it's that it must be presented in a coherent fashion, in a way that allows for education beyond passive consumption. The same applies to any other cultural form. If you enjoy something, why not learn more about it and dive deeper?

In my conversations with curators, I found a tone of caring and caretaking that is missing entirely from massive digital platforms, which treat all culture like content to be funneled indiscriminately at high volume and which encourage consumers to stay constantly on the surface. For YouTube, one video is the same as the next; all that matters is whether you're likely to click on it so that you're exposed to more advertising. But that beautiful sense of care, both for the viewer and for the culture at hand—being sure to present an artwork, album, or film in the right way—makes the encounter with culture so much better. It is better for the artist just as much in terms of being understood and appreciated for what they tried to accomplish, which is so often the goal of art.

We turn to art to seek connection, yet algorithmic feeds give us pure consumption. Truly connecting requires slowing down too much, to the point of falling out of the feed's grip. You can't stay in an algorithmic flow state while reading a CD booklet.

## RETURNING TO THE FEEDS

The initial weeks of my algorithm cleanse were difficult, but then I adapted and time passed quickly. I had no burning desire to return to that corner of the digital realm. But after three months of abstinence, I decided to go back, in large part due to the news cycle. As a journalist covering technology, I *had* to know what was going on online, and the primary subject of the moment in late 2022 had become social media itself, with Elon Musk's fraught acquisition of Twitter.

I also missed my ambient awareness of friends' lives. While I appreciated not being bombarded with Instagram photos of their vacations on Lake Como, I did not get to see their book recommendations, the nice meals they cooked, or their cute pet snapshots, all of which my algorithm made sure to deliver. I grudgingly logged back in and restored the apps to my phone. My thumbs quickly relearned their old patterns.

But I was surprised to find that something had changed in my brain chemistry, even during my relatively short absence from social media. Escaping algorithmic feeds was like becoming a vegetarian and then seeing a juicy steak—what once might have been appealing was now off-putting. My pace of consumption had slowed, and I was much more deliberate in selecting what to read, listen to, or watch. When I returned, the feeds felt too fast and chaotic, too far from chronological.

Gradually I got used to them again as my tolerance ramped up once more. But the feeling of aversion stayed with me. The time off had made me understand in a more visceral way that the drama of the Twitter feed had very little to do with day-to-day life offline. (That I needed to learn the lesson in the first place speaks to how immersed I was.) The gamified pursuit of likes on my posts lost meaning when I wasn't spending so much time on platforms where the likes and followers were meaningful. I asked Jess if my behavior or attitude had been any different while on the cleanse; she said that my initial crankiness gave way to being calmer overall and "less insecure about what was happening online." (She did complain that I wasn't able to post any good photos of her on Instagram, however.) I found myself noticing more when friends looked at their phones while hanging out, precisely because there wasn't as much to interest me on mine.

Like tobacco companies manufacturing low-tar cigarettes, the algorithmic feeds create the problems they are marketed as solving. We don't need to be exposed to thousands of digital updates a day arranged by what we might find most compelling. Even if we don't log off entirely, chronological feeds and incentives to post less instead of more might be better for us, and better for culture.

Rather than floating on the surface of things, I had used my algorithm-free time to investigate what I found interesting and figure out what I was looking for in my aimless time online. I was more satisfied by concentrating on just a few cultural creators. When I got my Spotify Wrapped recap of 2022, that summary of my taste for the year, it informed me that I was in the top 0.01 percent of listeners to Bill Evans, the innovative jazz pianist whose career peaked in the 1960s. Though the number seemed extreme, almost embarrassing, I understood why I had gotten it. My constant writing soundtrack had been the Bill Evans Trio's 1961 concert at the Village Vanguard, a complete recording that stretched over three discs. I got to know every second of the album, from the unavoidable tape glitch on the first take of "Gloria's Step" to the two back-to-back takes of "Jade Visions" that end the concert. "Jade Visions," an elegiac, meditatively simple track buoyed by rhythmic bass chords, was composed by the trio's bassist, Scott LaFaro, who died in a car accident later in 1961, at the age of twenty-five. I got more from the album the more I listened to it, as if it were the only CD in my collection. I kept listening long after any algorithmic recommendation would have swept me away to other musicians or albums.

I found that the way to fight the generic is to seek the specific, whatever you are drawn toward. You don't need to be a credentialed or professionalized expert to be a connoisseur. You don't need to monetize your opinion as an influencer for it to be legitimate. The algorithm promises to supplant your taste and outsource it for you, like a robotic limb, but all it takes to form your own taste is thought, intention, and care. Curation is a natural facet of human behavior: Just as we select which food to eat or which colors go together in an outfit, we organically form opinions about which pieces of culture appeal to us and which don't.

There's a time and a place for the kind of lean-back consumption that technology like Spotify radio or the TikTok "For You" feed encourages, but I worry that its fundamental passivity is devaluing cultural innovation as a whole, as well as degrading our enjoyment of art. Culture is built on personal recommendations, not automated ones, as we share, interpret, and respond to the things that we love. That human process of recommendation could be as easy as sending a friend a link to something they might like, along with a few words about why they might like it—starting a conversation about what culture means to both of you.

## MY RECOMMENDATION

It seems fitting to end this chapter with a personal recommendation, something that I initially discovered through algorithmic feeds but has come to feel like a fundamental part of my taste and of myself. It's an album from 1982 called *Awakening,* by the Japanese musician Hiroshi Sato, and beyond being—in my opinion—one of the best albums ever made, it's a perfect demonstration of the various forces of Filterworld that this book has documented. My first exposure to Sato came from YouTube's recommendation algorithm. I stumbled upon a track from the album called "Say Goodbye," but on YouTube it was a reissued version titled "This Boy," uploaded by a channel called Boogie80. It came with little other information, but the evocative cover image of a tanned man swimming in the ocean and the airy opening arpeggio played on a modular synthesizer immediately grabbed me.

I pulled up the YouTube link dozens of times and marveled at the song's perfect pop concision and plangent English-language lyrics, mourning a breakup—"hope you won't be lonely"—before I bothered to explore Sato's work any further. The song seemed to exist in a vacuum, even though it had over two million views. When I started listening to the full *Awakening,* "Say Goodbye" was still the only song that stuck out to me for a while. Something about the musical palette kept me intrigued, however. It wasn't quite soft rock, nor was it the over-the-top sound I associated with American eighties music. On a handful of the album's tracks like "Only a Love Affair," the Canadian Australian torch singer Wendy Matthews guest starred with a soaring voice that sounds like the epitome of a neon-lit nightclub.

Sato's album became the kind of music that I put on when I cook dinner—it got a daily play in full during the pandemic—and Jess and I reliably danced to it in the kitchen, indulging in a brief moment of art's ability to transport you somewhere else entirely. *Awakening* includes two versions of a song called "Blue and Moody Music," whose lyrics sketch a scene of practicing the piano late at night into the morning and taking solace in the instrument. The first recording is Sato alone, at a downbeat pace with keyboard flourishes. It's easy to imagine the musician at a grand piano overlooking some illuminated city skyline. But the second version takes the song to a transcendental level, with driving synth trills that are almost tropical, constant riffing electric guitar in the background, and Matthews in full operatic mode like a star shooting across that night sky, with Sato's rougher voice singing backup in a complementary contrast. The recording only accelerates toward its ending; rather than stopping, it fades out in full bloom, as if to continue forever. It's genius, a singular piece of music that's both completely of its time and completely timeless. Yet Spotify's play count tells me that "Blue and Moody Music (Wendy's Version)" is one of the less popular tracks on the album, with 280,000 listens to more than three million for "Say Goodbye," the YouTube hit.

How had such a masterpiece made its way to me? I began to research its origins as a way of sating my own obsession. Sato was a famous pianist, producer, and songwriter in Japan for decades, until his death in 2012. But his exposure to American listeners was algorithmic in origin. In the mid-2010s, YouTube's recommendations began fixating on a Japanese genre called "City Pop," a nebulous musical movement that emerged in the late 1970s and early '80s. It began with bands like Happy End, an influential outfit in Tokyo that was the first to make rock and psychedelic-folk music with Japanese lyrics. Happy End didn't last long, but its members included Haruomi Hosono, who collaborated with many other musicians like Sato and experimented with synthesizers in the more avant-garde band Yellow Magic Orchestra. (Hosono later created an ambient electronic-music soundtrack for the first Muji store, aesthetics that fit very much within Filterworld.)

Sato, Hosono, and others began merging the surf-rock and yacht-rock sounds coming out of the United States from bands like the Beach Boys with their own tech-forward sensibility. In 1977, the critic Tōno Kiyokazu (quoted in an authoritative 2020 paper by the scholar Moritz Sommet) described "City Music" as music with an "urban feeling." The critic also noted, though, that the term "doesn't hold any particularly deep meaning." It is "something that looks like you understand it, but you don't." In other words, a certain ambiguity might be part of its nature. It is evasive, reflecting back whatever you project at it. Tatsuro Yamashita's 1978 album *Pacific*, which Hosono worked on, is an indicative example: It has blatant Hawaiian influences, with slack-key guitar and atmospheric sound samples of ocean waves. It's almost kitschy. But the final track on the otherwise immaculately tropical album is a fully synthesized, discordant, robotic soundscape, as if the island was actually a mechanized sci-fi dystopia. Slick surfaces can be deceiving.

City Pop was also influenced by another technological innovation: the invention, in 1979, of the Sony Walkman. The device was created because Masaru Ibuka, a former executive of Sony, wanted to be able to listen to long classical music recordings on international flights. So he asked the company to make him a portable music-listening device, which the engineers accomplished by modifying a portable tape recorder. Ibuka liked it so much that he passed it on to the company's chairman, Akio Morita, who decided to manufacture it. (It was a gut decision, not based on market predictions, because the device itself was wholly unprecedented.) Sony sold hundreds of thousands of them. Suddenly, music could envelop the listener wherever they went, whichever music they chose. Like algorithmic feeds, the Walkman was a dramatic form of personalization. In a 1984 article for the journal *Popular Music* titled "The Walkman Effect," the Japanese musicology scholar Shuhei Hosokawa wrote that the "listener seems to cut the auditory contact with the outer world where he really lives: seeking the perfection of his 'individual' zone of listening." With the Walkman, physical reality conformed to the listener's mood, the same way recommendations bend digital spaces toward users' desires.

The device created a need for music as a mobile, semi-ignorable soundtrack to life. Cars, another perk of the boom economy, which the growing population of middle-class Japanese salarymen used to take weekend drives out of Tokyo to beaches to surf, provided another opportunity for ambient listening. City Pop was music for walking and wandering around, going shopping, sitting on a train. Some City Pop musicians sold or wrote songs as commercial soundtracks, participating in the explosion of capitalist consumerism, lending it their sunny, romantic air with jangly guitar and orchestral horns.

The original eighties fad for City Pop faded within a few years, but the genre stuck around in physical form as dusty vinyl records. Then, in the 2000s, Japanese DJs digging through crates of old albums in record stores rediscovered the genre and began bringing it back into rotation. (Such a revival might be much more difficult in the future, given the relative ephemerality of digital files and the platforms that host them.) The revival spread abroad, through niche forums and blogs, inspiring Western DJs to plan trips to Tokyo to buy their own records. Then City Pop hit YouTube and went mainstream around the world.

For some reason, music like Sato's provided an ideal solution for the recommendation algorithm. One track took off in particular: Mariya Takeuchi's bouncy 1984 "Plastic Love," an earworm with a shuffling R&B backbeat and soft synth keyboards. It's a pure pop confection. Takeuchi's clear voice rises above the rhythm section, singing about recovering from heartbreak—"Love is just a game / All I need is to have fun with it"—interspersed with lyrics in English: "I know that's plastic love." A version uploaded on YouTube in 2017 by an account named Plastic Lover netted over sixty-three million views, an amount only possible for such an obscure track through the algorithmic feed's promotions. In fact, the anonymous uploader was first exposed to it by the feed as well. As they told the *Pitchfork* writer Cat Zhang in a 2021 interview, "People tell me they get the song in their recommendations all the time. That happened to me too—I wasn't the first uploader of the song. At first I wasn't really interested in it, but it kept haunting me in my recommendations." The algorithm itself was responsible for its popularity.

Various explanations have been proposed for City Pop's runaway success online. Some writers have connected it to the popularity of lo-fi chill music streams on YouTube, the relaxed electronica that provides ambient music for studying or working. Those streams attract millions of listeners, who might then be pushed to another source of synthy, unobtrusive, mid-tempo music. "The algorithm will simply route listeners from 'lo-fi beats' videos to 'Plastic Love,'" Zhang found in another 2021 *Pitchfork* investigation. In the last few years, the City Pop genre became synonymous with the platform itself. On the website Rate Your Music, one user even identified it as "Japanese YouTube Recommendations Core," collecting City Pop YouTube videos with over one hundred thousand views. In the case of "Plastic Love," the track may have been helped along by the beatific black-and-white photo of its singer that covered the YouTube video—an evocative image of total freedom and carefree happiness, Takeuchi grinning, eyes wide, blurred slightly by motion. "There's a perfect kismet between the song and the photo," the photographer, Alan Levenson, told Zhang. Like a brightly colored ceramic vase against a white backdrop on Instagram, the image was optimized to transmit itself as a YouTube recommendation thumbnail.

Alongside any algorithmic promotion, it's also true that these are simply good songs, written by talented musicians at a peak of their creativity, though they were not necessarily hits when they came out. (Contrary to the 2000s hipster credo, just because something is popular doesn't mean it's bad, and obscurity doesn't make something de facto good.) The songs are not good by accident; they were written to reach an audience, though the scale of the audience they ultimately ended up reaching could not have been predicted.

Perhaps like Damon Krukowski's Galaxie 500 track "Strange," which went viral on Spotify separate from the rest of the band's work, City Pop possessed the most normal, agreeable, average sound of pop that no one could click away from. The genre was obscure, and yet it was an average of musical styles that could be found accessible by users across an international platform. City Pop's aural aesthetic was part Eastern, in its Japanese creators; part Western, in its inspirations; part nostalgic, in its eighties sensibility as seen from the 2010s; part futuristic, in its embrace of music technology that was new at the time, like synths and electronic drum machines. City Pop possesses a kind of junk-food density of appealing ingredients.

The combination of soaring vocals, heavy synthesizer washes, R&B instruments, and drumbeat inertia is irresistible, and its underexamined Japanese origin story made it exotic enough to be unfamiliar to Western audiences online.

The name itself likely helped: "City Pop" is vague, identifiable with any city, anywhere, like the AirSpace aesthetic I noticed through Airbnb, but for music. Writing in *Spin*, Andy Cush observed of similar Japanese ambient recordings that became popular on YouTube, "If the music weren't so good, it might feel like a trap." Of course, this is the trap of Filterworld. Algorithmic feeds mold a form of culture that is compelling enough and yet decontextualized so fully and spread so widely that it becomes empty and meaningless, offering so many aesthetics without content.

In some ways, that emptying process has already happened for City Pop. A 2015 article in the *Japan Times* observed that the genre was "a simplified indie buzzword used to induce feelings of sophistication, fashionableness and nostalgia." And as City Pop saturates its potential audiences, gradually boring them in turn, algorithmic recommendations will have to find new grist for the mill of digital consumption. I recently came across references to "Indonesian City Pop," which was music from the same era elsewhere in Asia. A YouTube video uploaded in December 2020 collecting a few dozen tracks of sweetly melodic synth-driven soft rock has almost two million views. Its title is "Jakarta Night Drive—80s Indonesian Pop Kreatif/City Pop/Jazz Megamix"—a search-algorithm-optimized hash of words. The video that plays underneath the music is a set of infinitely looping nighttime anime cityscapes that have more to do with Japan than Indonesia.

In the "Jakarta Night Drive" video, a specific culture has been reduced to a vaporous mood, to be adopted, replicated, and distributed online as fast and as far as possible, attracting shallow engagement that in turn drives advertising revenue for the creator and the platform. One comment on the video sums it up: "Algorithm brought me here from Korea." Guided along by the feed's recommendations, a global population of users collectively converge on a particular set of cultural themes like so many monarch butterflies instinctively migrating to a particular grove of fir trees in Mexico.

These themes may be the fundamental commonalities of human culture, the things we can't help but love: short songs, consistent backbeats, dramatic visual clarity, bright colors, punch-line humor, and controversial arguments. But more likely, the fixations of Filterworld are dictated by the structures of the digital platforms culture now flows through, and the boring ubiquity of a few aesthetic modes is the consequence of the platforms' globalization and monopolization. Filterworld consists of one fundamental, unavoidable reality: never in human history have so many people experienced the same things, the same pieces of content disseminated instantly through the feeds, to our individual screens. Every consequence flows from that fact.

It is neither good nor bad to encounter that "Jakarta Night Drive" video on YouTube. In fact, it's quite a cool artifact, a glimpse into a corner of the international heritage of culture that I never would have seen without the platform. But what matters more is what you as a user do after you see the video, after the music sticks in your head. You could let it drift by and trust that the recommendation algorithm might bring it back someday, and you'll enjoy it once more whenever it does. Or you could identify the DJ of the compilation and pay them a tip for their cultural curation. Or you could buy a digital copy of one of the songs or albums that are included. Or you could research the history of Indonesian pop music and chart for yourself how it followed the growing influence of international capitalism in the country under the dictator Suharto. Any one of these latter choices would be better for the continued survival and strength of culture, and your satisfaction as a consumer, than allowing the feed to wash over you with the aura of the aesthetic alone.

To resist Filterworld, we must become our own curators once more and take responsibility for what we're consuming. Regaining that control isn't so hard. You make a personal choice and begin to intentionally seek out your own cultural rabbit hole, which leads you in new directions, to yet more independent decisions. They compound over time into a sense of taste, and ultimately into a sense of self.

# Conclusion

In 1939, Walter Benjamin completed a revised version of his essay "The Work of Art in the Age of Mechanical Reproduction." The technology that he considered in the essay, photography, had already existed for over a century when he wrote it. The first photograph to include human figures had been made in 1838 by Louis Daguerre, who documented a Parisian boulevard as seen from the window of his studio—an utterly normal scene and yet an unprecedented achievement to freeze it as an image. Photography became more commonplace over time, and by Benjamin's era, it was a mainstream product. Anyone could have their portrait taken or buy a postcard of a picturesque scene and send it to someone else so that they could see it, too. In his essay, the critic came to grips with how photography had changed culture, disrupting our sense of the uniqueness of a singular work of art. The technology of reproduction, like photographs or gramophone records, "enables the original to meet the recipient halfway," Benjamin wrote. "The cathedral leaves its site to be received in the studio of an art lover." While a certain kind of authenticity was lost in the age of photography—the reproduction was not the same as the original; a postcard was just a shadow of the actual cathedral—accessibility had been gained. The kind of rarefied high culture that Benjamin prized became a mass experience: "mass art," as he referred to it elsewhere.

"Just as the entire mode of existence of human collectives changes over long historical periods, so too does their mode of perception," Benjamin wrote. Technology changes both the forms of culture that we produce and our perception of that culture, the way we take in the man-made world around us. (Both changes happen at the same time.) The proliferation of photography as a new form of perception caused a crisis in visual art, Benjamin argued, ultimately liberating it from the need to document reality—a task better left to photos—and inspiring the idea of "pure" art. That is, art not concerned with representation or any social function, "art for art's sake," as the nineteenth-century aesthetic credo went.

Photography also commodified the world, in a way, "by flooding the market with countless images of figures, landscapes, and events which had previously been available either not at all or only as pictures for individual customers," Benjamin observed in a 1935 essay, "Paris, the Capital of the Nineteenth Century." Photography exerted a pressure on culture to be photographable, to circulate as photographs, and culture inevitably adapted in turn. "The work reproduced becomes the reproduction of a work designed for reproducibility," he wrote.

I bring up Benjamin once more to point out that the force of technology shaping culture has been happening forever, and that force is neutral, not inherently negative. No matter how photography disrupted the aura of a singular artwork, no one today would call for giving up the reproduction of images, nor suggest that we should forsake recorded music and listen only to live musicians. (Benjamin's essay was more of a celebration than a castigation of photography.) What's more, it takes decades, if not centuries, to determine just how a technology has influenced cultural forms. Artists integrate it into their creative processes, and consumers slowly begin to see it as normal; only when a new tool has become unremarkable can its effects be judged. We see the same process happening in our own time with the globalization of digital platforms and algorithmic feeds, an inextricable pair of technologies that change our perceptions just as the invention of photography did.

Culture has to follow the dominant modes of perception of a given era. While a twentieth-century building might have been designed to be photographed, the twenty-first-century work of art is "designed for reproducibility" through algorithmic feeds, like Patrick Janelle's cortado glamour shots on Instagram or Nigel Kabvina's cooking videos on TikTok. They each contribute and conform to a generic, flattened, reproducible aesthetic. Hence the general state of ennui and exhaustion, the sense that nothing new is forthcoming.

Even in the short time of their rise, algorithmic recommendations have warped everything from visual art to product design, songwriting, choreography, urbanism, food, and fashion. All kinds of cultural experiences have been reduced to the homogenous category of digital content and made to obey the law of engagement, the algorithms' primary variable. Any piece of content, whether image, video, sound, or text, must compel an immediate, albeit often superficial, response from the viewer. It must make them tap the Like or Share button, or prevent them from hitting Stop or Skip, anything that would interrupt the feed.

The twin pressures for creators to inspire engagement and avoid alienation have meant that so many cultural forms have become both more immediately enticing and more evanescent, leaving behind nothing but an atmosphere. This enforced ephemerality of feeling and impermanence of context has hollowed out contemporary culture, leaving it less experimental and powerful than it might have been otherwise, without these pressures.

Algorithmic recommendations have become so influential as the new cultural arbiters because of their ubiquity and their sudden intimacy in our daily routines as consumers. Smartphone screens allowed us to always carry the Internet around with us, and digital platforms' feeds are what deliver the Internet to us. In the process, they compress everything into content that fuels them. Like water flowing into a pot, the creative impulse changes to fit the shape of the containers that we have for it, and the most common containers now are the feeds of Facebook, Instagram, Twitter, Spotify, YouTube, and TikTok.

In terms of how culture reaches us, algorithmic recommendations have supplanted the human news editor, the retail boutique buyer, the gallery curator, the radio DJ—people whose individual taste we relied on to highlight the unusual and the innovative. Instead, we have tech companies dictating the priorities of the recommendations, which are subjugated to generating profit through advertising. In Filterworld, the most popular culture is also the most desiccated. It is streamlined and averaged until, like a vitamin pill, it may contain the necessary ingredients but lacks any sense of brilliance or vitality. This process happens not by force, in the way of a mold stamping metal, but by compliance, as creators voluntarily shape their work to pursue the motivation of algorithmic exposure and access to audiences. This is not to say the creators are cynical; they have few other options, because garnering attention on digital platforms is the most reliable method of earning a living in the culture industries of the early twenty-first-century Internet. What we gain in acceleration—ever more content, ever faster—we lose in individuality and texture, the quality that makes great works of art compelling.

We are left with the widely acceptable and yet rootless and meaningless symbols of a digitally globalized civilization: generic minimalist interiors with subway tiles on the walls; espresso topped with a flat cloud of steamed milk in a ceramic mug; the artificially puffy lips and high cheekbones of surgery-augmented Instagram face; hushed singing voices set to programmed drumbeats and soothing waves of synthesizer in endless loops; abstracted blobs of pastel color ready to be captured by a smartphone camera and reproduced on a small screen. Like continents settling, these symbols will shift over time on the tides of fashion and personal taste, insofar as taste is still exercised. But their homogeneity will remain entrenched until this platform ecosystem is broken up, whether by law or by user decision, with enough people deciding to abstain. In the meantime, by the dictates of capitalism, Filterworld is required to grow constantly. To plateau or shrink is to fail.

Algorithmic feeds are different from other iterations of technological innovation because they do not just present us with an unusual new format to consider, like camera film or the television screen. They also try to anticipate our individual cultural desires for us in personalized recommendations using the newfound tools of data surveillance and machine learning. Algorithmic feeds stand between the human creators and the human consumers, making an infinite series of decisions about culture. The technology has never been applied so widely and experienced by users so constantly, and in such personal aspects of life, no less. If photography reproduced the work of art, then perhaps algorithmic recommendations reproduce the desire for art itself, cheapening and deadening that feeling of creative curiosity, making it more easily satisfied by less. The changes the feeds induce are not just aesthetic but insidiously psychic, mediating the choice to consume as much as the content being consumed.

If there is a simple answer to breaking down Filterworld, then it might be something like a version of the slow food movement, as it was popularized in the 1990s, but for culture. Slow food was a reaction to the domination of industrial farming; it argued for a deep consideration of where food comes from and how it is made, considering not just the end product but the entire process of how it arrives at the consumer. The movement rewarded farmers who pursued small scale, businesses that grew sustainably over the long term, and chefs who knew and prized the provenance of their ingredients. Customers learned to prize these qualities, too. (Though the qualities of provenance and obscurity sometimes became extremist fetishes of their own.) We need to bring that same understanding of sustainability and specificity to the way that we consume and support culture online, too.

Resistance to algorithmic frictionlessness requires an act of willpower, a choice to move through the world in a different way. It doesn't have to be a dramatic one.

After I got a haircut one afternoon in D.C., I noticed once again a café I had walked past hundreds of times in my years living there. It was called Jolt n' Bolt, a kitschy vintage name from a time when coffee was fetishized more for its caffeine than for its taste or single-origin sourcing. It opened in 1994, not long after the first Starbucks opened in D.C., which was the chain's first location on the East Coast. I had never been inside; the name, clip art–style logo, and dark interior were turnoffs. It wasn't Instagrammable. But that day, I decided to go in. Its interior was indeed drawn straight from the 1990s, with dark matte paint and signboards mounted above the counter for menus. The small tables were fake-wood laminate with padded metal chairs. Salon-style hanging of canvases by local artists crowded the walls. The drip coffee was dark roast to the point of burnt. This, too, was an identifiable style, the somewhat grungy local coffee shop, still surviving in smaller, slower cities like Portland, Boston, and D.C.

I felt both bemused and sad that this was a rare experience, something like visiting a museum. Our phones and feeds absorb so much of our attention and dominate so many of our preferences that stepping out of their conveniently predetermined paths and choosing an experience not immediately engaging feels somewhat radical. This applies to fashion choices as well as food, which television shows we watch, which books we read, which furniture we buy, where we travel. If we shift our priorities away from the space of algorithmic digital platforms and once more to the physical world, in which everything is not instantly evaluated in terms of engagement, we might find ourselves building not only better culture but better communities, relationships, and politics as well. The anthropologist David Graeber once wrote: "The ultimate, hidden truth of the world is that it is something that we make, and could just as easily make differently." The same is true of the Internet.

There is no pure form of culture that happens outside of technological influence, nor is there a singular best way to consume culture. We cannot just rid ourselves of algorithmic influence, even if we wanted to, since the technology has already inexorably shaped our era. But the first step of escaping the algorithms' grip is recognizing it. By moving away from the mindset of passive consumption and thinking about a post-algorithmic digital ecosystem, we begin to construct that alternative, demonstrating that the influence of algorithms is neither inevitable nor permanent. Eventually Filterworld itself, with its set of entrenched styles, will prove to be a finite phase of culture, precisely because it will run out of fuel and run aground on its own self-referentiality. Something new is on the horizon; whether it is a flood of even more artificial content generated by artificial intelligence machines or a renaissance for human self-expression depends on our choices. As Benjamin wrote: "Every epoch, in fact, not only dreams the one to follow but, in dreaming, precipitates its awakening. It bears its end within itself."

# Acknowledgments

*Filterworld* would not exist without my incredible editor at Doubleday, Thomas Gebremedhin, who saw the importance of the book's conversation immediately. No author could hope for a better sounding board or partner in wading through text. Anyone in doubt of the necessity of cultural curation online should view his Instagram stories. Johanna Zwirner, Nora Reichard, Elena Hershey, Anne Jaconette, and the entire staff of Doubleday, under Bill Thomas's leadership of the imprint, made the entire process, from acquisition to rollout, a sincere joy. I'm so thankful to Oliver Munday for his tireless work on the cover design and the total clarity of the result. My agent and friend Caroline Eisenmann, as always, coaxed these seeds of thoughts into coherence in her inimitable, indefatigable way.

So much life happens in the course of thinking about and writing a book, so much that doesn't make it into the book itself but persists like its shadow. While I was working on *Filterworld,* I got married to Jess Bidgood, whom I can only describe as the love of my life. Before that, we got a dog named Rhubarb, my other great love. I want to remember the people who passed away during this time, especially my beloved grandparents, Alfonse and Mary DeSalvio, who showed me so much about pursuing a personal vision.

Thank you to friends, including Delia Cai, for constant commiseration on book writing and wandering the ruins of the 2010s Internet; Nick Quah, for sharing the struggle of the media business; Tatiana Berg, Gregory Gentert, and Erik Hyman, for their hospitality at Monroe Street; and the members of our group chats and a very timely trip to Provence. I'm grateful for many conversations with Katy Waldman and Nate Gallant.

My research assistant Ena Alvarado's help was invaluable. Thanks also to the publication editors whose input and advocacy over the years fed this book, including Michael Zelenko, William Staley, and Julia Rubin. Rachel Arons, my editor at *The New Yorker,* has been a source of stability, inspiration, and no small amount of laughter as we attempt to cover the absurdities of the Internet. Thank you to Michael Luo and David Remnick for supporting and encouraging my work at the magazine.

I wrote the vast majority of this book in the lobby café of the Line Hotel (a converted basilica with lofty ceilings) around the block from our apartment in Washington, D.C., where I was kept company by the kind baristas DJ and Myesha. It takes a good vibe to write a good book.

## ABOUT THE AUTHOR

KYLE CHAYKA is a staff writer at *The New Yorker,* where he writes a column on digital technology and the impact of the Internet and social media on culture. His debut nonfiction book, *The Longing for Less,* an exploration of minimalism in life and art, was published in 2020. As a journalist and critic, he has contributed to many publications, including *The New York Times Magazine, Harper's Magazine, The New Republic,* and Vox. He was the first staff writer of the art publication Hyperallergic. Chayka is also the cofounder of Study Hall, an online community for journalists, and Dirt, a newsletter about digital culture. He lives in Washington, D.C.